Mad Minutes and
Vietnam Months

ALSO BY MICHEAL CLODFELTER
AND FROM MCFARLAND

*Warfare and Armed Conflicts: A Statistical Encyclopedia
of Casualty and Other Figures, 1494–2007, 3d ed.* (2008)

*The Lost Battalion and the Meuse-Argonne, 1918:
America's Deadliest Battle* (2007)

*The Dakota War: The United States Army
Versus the Sioux, 1862–1865* (1998; paperback 2006)

*Vietnam in Military Statistics: A History of the
Indochina Wars, 1772–1991* (1995)

Mad Minutes and Vietnam Months

A Soldier's Memoir

MICHEAL CLODFELTER

McFarland & Company, Inc., Publishers

Jefferson, North Carolina, and London

The present work is a reprint (with corrections) of the softcover edition of Mad Minutes and Vietnam Months: A Soldier's Memoir, *first published in 1988 by McFarland.*

LIBRARY OF CONGRESS CATALOGUING-IN-PUBLICATION DATA

Clodfelter, Micheal, 1946-
   Mad minutes and Vietnam months : a soldier's memoir / Micheal Clodfelter.
      p.   cm.
   Includes index.

   ISBN 978-0-7864-6725-9
   softcover : 50# alkaline paper ∞

   1. Clodfelter, Micheal, 1946–   2. Vietnamese Conflict, 1961–1975 — Personal narratives, American.   3. Soldiers — United States — Biography.   4. United States. Army — Biography.   I. Title.
   DS559.5.C56   2011
   959.704'38   87-43170

BRITISH LIBRARY CATALOGUING DATA ARE AVAILABLE

On the cover: *upper left* author Clodfelter, *upper right* Wendell Rose (Tuy Hoa, September 1966, photograph by Michael Siede)

Manufactured in the United States of America

McFarland & Company, Inc., Publishers
  Box 611, Jefferson, North Carolina 28640
   www.mcfarlandpub.com

To Wendell Rose, the "Hard Core Pointer,"
and the grunts of Charlie Company,
2/502nd Airborne Infantry, 1966–67

Acknowledgments

This book is as true and accurate a reflection of my Vietnam experiences and the experiences of the units with which I served as memory and research can provide. The only fictitious element is the changing of many, but not all, of the names of individuals involved in this memoir to protect their privacy. In all but one case I have used the actual names of my comrades killed in action, as a way to honor their sacrifice. Other than my own memory, the two sources I most depended on were the recollections of Wendell Rose of Campton, Kentucky, to whom I am greatly indebted and whose real name is used in the pages to follow, and the brigade and battalion unit histories compiled by the 1st Brigade, 101st Airborne Division and the 2nd Battalion of the 502nd Airborne Infantry. I was also assisted by information provided by John Yeager, Jr., of Weirton, West Virginia, a former sergeant with the 101st from December 1966 to September 1967, by my stalwart comrade from the 1st Platoon, James Henk, by my taping partner from Survey Platoon, Max Patterson, and by several other men with whom I served in Vietnam. Finally, I want to recognize the contributions of Donny, my boyhood friend, with whom I shared the dream and the nightmare.

Table of Contents

Preface

The *Mad Minutes* of the book's title comes from the bush language of grunts and describes the general discharge of all weapons along a defense perimeter at a predesignated time to break up or discourage any potential enemy attack. But in a broader sense, the term describes the essence of the Vietnam combat experience for me and my comrades in Charlie Company, 2/502nd Airborne Infantry, in 1966. Vietnam was a few mad minutes of unnerving and unexpected violence in the midst of days or even weeks of monotonous, exhausting search for an enemy who was as elusive as the end of each grunt's tour in 'Nam.

This book is an attempt to describe the intensity of the mad minutes and the agonizing search for the release that those moments of blind violence provided. For those who, like myself, started the search with the light of glory in our eyes and ended it dimmed by a dark jungle and our darker deeds, mad minutes became part of a mad experience in a mad war that carried us beyond glory into a territory from which none of us ever really returned.

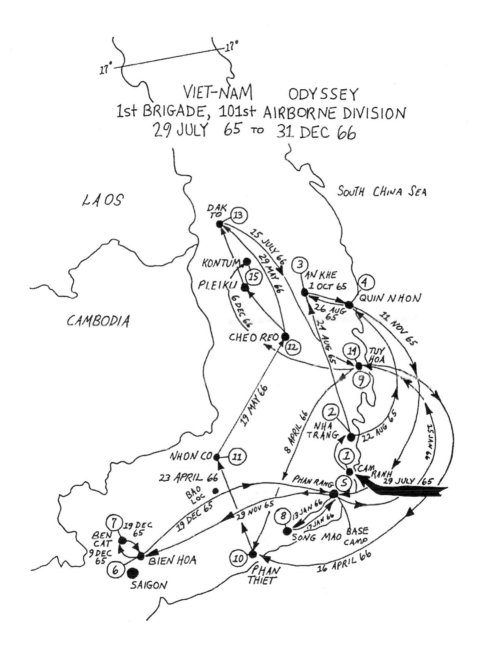

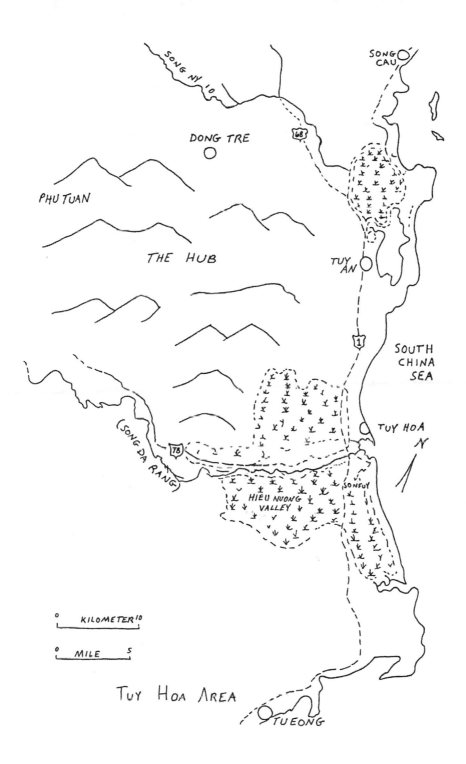

SONG
CAU

SONG NY 10

DONG TRE

68

PHU TUAN

THE HUB

TUY
AN

1

SOUTH
CHINA
SEA

TUY HOA

N

(SONG DA RANG)

78

SON FUY

HIEU NUONG
VALLEY

0   KILOMETER 10

0   MILE   5

TUY HOA AREA

TU EONG

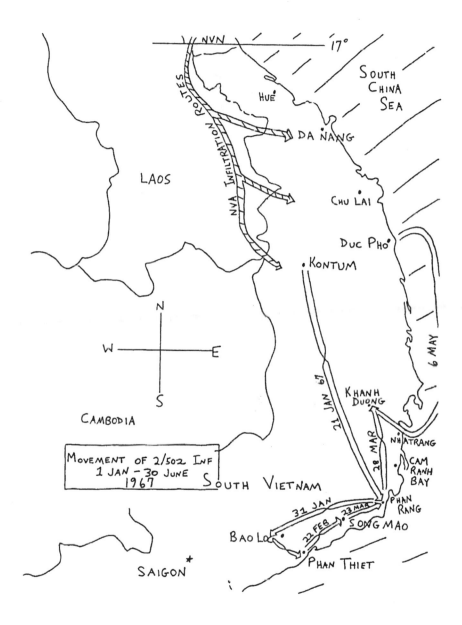

Prologue

The names go on and on, all of them etched in black granite and some of them burned into my brain. The toll, 58,261, is just a number — except for the tiny fraction of that toll who fought and died beside you — until you stand at the apex of that long low wall, its inscribed black wings spreading out on either side to carry the burden of all those names. Then you begin to grasp the enormity of the sacrifice that Vietnam demanded of us as individuals and as a nation. You hope our leaders have learned and that our government never again commits us to a conflict without first carefully weighing the possible costs and consequences against whatever can be achieved.

It was easy, standing there in that hot August sunshine of Washington, D.C., in 1983, to spot the Vietnam veterans in the crowd of visitors. They were the men, once nineteen-year-olds who had fought America's first teenage war, but now solemn-eyed and graying into their late thirties and early forties, who went back time and again to the guide books sited at either end of the monument to help visitors locate the names of their dead buddies or relatives on the wall. Some had five, ten, or twenty or more names to look up, instead of the one or two searched for by the families or friends of the fallen. The Vietnam veterans were not just tourists gazing at another monument in a city of monuments, but pilgrims taking a symbolic journey back to their youth and innocence, back to a time and place where they irretrievably lost both. They stood longest before the monument, seeing not just names and touching more than just black granite. They looked back at a long march and a longer year, touching emotions and moments that had long been buried for some, or, for many others, had never left them for a second even after the passage of a dozen years or more.

I had twenty-six names from my division, the 101st Airborne, to look up in that directory of the dead and then locate on the wall. Rena, my wife, had one; a boy she had grown up with and went steady with in high school before he was drafted and sent to 'Nam in 1969, where a booby trap mine ended his life two weeks after arriving in country and two weeks before his twenty-first birthday.

They were all up there, staggered and clustered in the order they had fallen in 1965, '66, and the first days of '67. Lieutenant Earls, Sergeant Blanco, Specialist 4 "Rocky" Goddard, Pfc. Tommy Morales, and all the rest—nine gun apes from the 2/320th Artillery with whom I served for a year in Vietnam, and seventeen grunts from Charlie Company, 2/502nd Airborne Infantry with whom I humped the bush for five more months.

If all those Screaming Eagle paratroopers, ages eighteen to twenty-two when they died (except for one "old-timer" who was twenty-eight), had died for anything, it was for their buddies or for their own sense of self. As I stood there sweating under a hot sun, carrying a burden that in many ways was heavier than the sixty-pound rucksack I had staggered under in 'Nam more than sixteen years ago, that black wall made all those young men who could never accompany me into middle age live again for just a moment. They are preserved forever in my memory, as well as on this monument—a memorial to all those who paid so dearly that we might profit from our mistake and learn by it.

I was the son of a hard working Kansas couple who defined decency by the good examples they set, but I was also the child of Gary Cooper as Sergeant York and John Wayne as Sergeant Stryker. Throughout my boyhood, war worked the pump that fueled my fantasies. With my best friend Donny, who would later also go off to Vietnam and return with a worn out soul and a new name, Max, short for Maximum Casualty, I waged backyard battles with armies of toy soldiers complete with networks of trenches, earthworks and bunkers; fought Midway, Jutland and Leyte Gulf over again in a green sea of neighborhood grass with fleets of cut-out cardboard battleships, cruisers and destroyers; and recorded after-action reports of these miniature campaigns, taking immense pride in the statistical glow of generaling the most victorious army of plastic toy soldiers on my block.

Donny and I also mobilized the neighborhood to fight. At first it was afternoon-long battles of stick rifles and shouted bullets, but we graduated to clashing regiments of rock hurling juveniles armed with BB guns, and numerous casualties sobbing home to Mommy.

My reading material started with G.I. Joe comic books and ended with military histories, as I filled my mind with a martial heritage I was determined to make my own. Great generals and Medal of Honor winners were my heroes, not quarterbacks or home run sluggers; tanks turned my head about the time my peers were drawn to sports cars.

War promised me everything noble and manly: courage, sacrifice, glory, adventure and excitement. My teenage imagination often transported me from the frosty milo fields of Rooks County, Kansas, in which, shotgun in hand, I stalked prism-colored pheasants, to a shrapnel shrouded battlefield somewhere on the Siegfried Line or along the Thirty-eighth Parallel, my twenty-gauge transformed into an M-1 Garand, my hunting buddies turned into camouflage-helmeted comrades-in-arms, and my feathered quarry becoming Wehrmacht soldiers or Red Chinese infantrymen. My teenage mischief making — shooting out street lights with BB guns, hurling eggs at cop cars, erecting flaming barricades at intersections — was reinterpreted in my mind as daring commando raids behind enemy lines.

I regretted that I had been born too late for the carnage of Tarawa, the grandeur of D-Day, or the Marine retreat from the Chosin Reservoir. I envied the veterans I met who had been granted the honor of passing through hell. I longed for the day that high school graduation would liberate me from an unexciting small town life and enable me to earn my first real prestige as a U.S. Army paratrooper.

In the fall of 1964, not yet eighteen, I endured the ravings of jump school gorillas for three weeks — Ground Week, Tower Week and Jump Week — and hurled myself five times from the open door of a C-119 Flying Boxcar, 1,250 feet above the ground. But the pulse of pride in bearing the winged badge of the paratrooper on my chest quickly faded and the prestige paled under the banal realities of garrison duty. Peacetime military service, with its inspections and work details, was a drag.

Then, with the initiation of the American air war against North Vietnam in February 1965 and the landing of the 9th Marine Expeditionary Brigade at Da Nang on March 8, my spirits revived. History finally seemed to be cooperating in my search for glory.

Destiny seemed certain to include me in its design when Lyndon Johnson decided to intervene in the civil war that had broken out in the Dominican Republic in late April 1965. My barracks buddies must have thought I had executed a PLF (parachute landing fall) on my head during my last blast (parachute jump) when I yelled in exaltation upon the receipt of Immediate Ready Force alert orders for the 101st Airborne Division to which I was assigned at Fort Campbell, Kentucky. At last, it seemed, in the streets of the western hemisphere's oldest city, Santo Domingo, I would experience my baptism of fire. We packed our combat gear, rigged our howitzers, trucks and other big equipment for a heavy (parachute) drop and waited in our barracks for the word.

My excitement quickly became disappointment when the 82nd Airborne Division was granted the distinction of being the first ground combat unit of the U.S. Army to be dispatched into combat since 1953. My envy mounted as I followed the involvement of the All American Division in the Dominican Civil War, and I brooded over the treacherous workings of fate.

My spirits once again skyrocketed in May with the revelation that the cancellation of our Dominican concert had been due to a previous booking for a symphony of arms in Vietnam. Yet glory and the magic agony of battle would still elude me there. As an artilleryman, Vietnam provided me with sweating toil, insect bites, diarrhea, drudgerous guard duty in mud-lush OPs (observation posts), and wearying hours of depositing the soil of Vietnam into sandbags, but with very little combat.

My romantic notions of war began to dull as the exhausting, frustrating months passed with nothing but a few snipers' bullets and the shells of mortarmen to break the tedium. In many ways the despair which often overcame me on lonely, eventless nights of staring into the jungle gloom from the parapet of a sandbag bunker was even greater than the oppression of the garrison. So close to battle but yet still so distant, I had crossed 6,000 miles of ocean to seek my destiny but had only deepened my sense of loss.

Determined to go where the action was if it would not come to me, I extended my tour of duty in 'Nam by six months and transferred to one of the brigade's infantry battalions. As a grunt (infantryman) my ambitions were realized in part. It was like a dream taking substance and structure but with ragged and cutting edges. Though I won medals for valor, they seemed more like compensation for duty done and pain endured than the shining emblems of honor I had envisioned. I clashed with the enemy but those clashes were mere firefights, deadly enough on the small scale of the individual foot soldier and fraught with terror, but never of a size and intensity to be called a battle or to be imprinted later in the pages of history. I earned the Purple Heart, not as a result of a wound received in the heat of battle but rather from clumsily stumbling over and impaling my leg on a shit-smeared punji stake. I took part in half a dozen battalion-size or bigger operations, yet most were only fruitless and deathly wearying humps through the never ending bush. I was given meager morsels of a tainted glory instead of the great banquet I had sought.

The twenty or so men of my platoon and the limitless jungle became my world. We measured our body counts in ones and twos, the duration of our battles in minutes. Malaria and booby traps claimed more casualties than did firefights. The Viet Cong were a far less encountered enemy than the mountains, mosquitoes and mud. The enemy became confused with the people because so often they were the people, and thus murder also became confused with the kind of killing that is excused by combat.

I began to suspect that my pursuit of glory was a hopeless task; that history flowed in too great a river to alter its course so that an insignificant human rivulet such as myself could be swept into its current. Glory seemed hollow, glittering and seductive on the surface, but really only mud and monotony and horror.

This book is the story of my quest for glory and my search for history and of the disillusionment I felt when my flirtatious quarry at last turned in its flight to confront me with tragedy and truth. It is also a story of a romance with war not entirely ended with Vietnam. Though I have witnessed the atrocities committed on the human body and soul by war, though many of my naively romantic illusions of war were forever destroyed along with the lives of friends and foes alike, though I feel that the Vietnam War was the greatest of tragedies for both Vietnam and America, still my attraction to war remains.

War is a clinging mistress once you have succumbed to its passions. It is not so easily rejected, much like an old lover from whom you wish to part but who somehow draws you irresistibly back. For all its disappointments and raw realities, I find it difficult not to look upon my months in Vietnam as the most meaningful of my life. Such feelings remain in part because of the maturing effect the war had on me, forcing me to think instead of merely fantasize, to begin to question rather than blindly accept, to develop new perspectives and a broader compassion. But those months seem the most meaningful also because Vietnam provided me my only experience with war, a saddening, sobering experience and one that would begin to undermine my confidence in my government and nation, yet one I still cling to like the memories of a lost love affair.

Part I
Redleg

Chapter I

The *General Leroy Eltinge*

We rose before dawn on July 7, 1965, and tumbled into cattle trucks for our last ride through Fort Campbell. Arriving at the airfield, we climbed down with our heavy loads of duffle bags and combat gear to board civilian airliners that would fly us across country. Landing at San Francisco International Airport, we were crammed aboard buses for the ride to the dock at the Oakland Army Terminal. There to greet us were a few Red Cross "Doughnut Dollies" and the 510 feet of rusting gray steel called *General Leroy Eltinge*.

Max Patterson, a farm boy from the Missouri Ozarks and the other end of the tape team to which I was assigned in the artillery battalion's Survey Platoon, loudly complained, "Holy Christ, boys! I know no one figgers on us crossin' the ocean in that rust bucket."

The long line of uniformed men began the ascent up the gangplank, then the descent into the crowded hold of the ship. The gray hulk had been built a quarter of a century ago to carry 2,500 soldiers to our fathers' war. But today the Liberty Ship was forced to accommodate the 3,700 paratroopers of the 101st Airborne Division's 1st Brigade: three infantry battalions; 1/327th, 2/327th and 2/502nd, each with a strength of 792 men; the 2/320th Artillery Battalion; a company of the 326th Engineer Battalion; a troop of the 2nd Squadron, 17th Cavalry; and assorted support and administrative units. Ours was to be the third U.S. Army combat brigade committed to the Vietnam War, the 173rd Airborne Brigade from Okinawa and the 2nd Brigade of the 1st Infantry "Big Red One" Division from Fort Riley, Kansas, having preceded us.

The 460 men of the 2/320th were herded three decks down. We were stacked like cordwood, four bodies high, into our racks and then instructed to somehow shape space in which to stack our gear.

At 0600 the following day a tugboat lashed ahold of our ship and towed us out toward that blue expanse of sea with which we would become so familiar. From the dock, an Army band played a medley of martial melodies. That was the extent of our send-off. No admiring throngs to give us a hero's farewell. No flag waving veterans shouting out words of encouragement to a younger generation sailing off to distant battle as they had in 1918, 1942 and 1950.

We thousands lining the deck of that ship of another war and another era carried with us no battle cries. Vietnam 1965 had no catchy counterpart to such cries as "We're off to keep the world safe for democracy!" or "Remember Pearl Harbor!" unless it was something on the order of "Remember the Gulf of Tonkin!" Vietnam was not then the universally unpopular war it was to become in later years, but neither was it a popular crusade such as the world wars had been. For me this represented the first tarnishing of my dream. We were bound for war and, disappointingly, no one seemed to notice or care.

I leaned against the railing beside Pfc. Spencer Hartnett, a gun ape from Bravo Battery, from which I had just recently transferred to my new job as an artillery surveyor with Headquarters Battery.

"Well, Spence, we're finally on our way," I said. "I'm nervous as hell ... half scared to death and half itchin' for action!"

"I don't know about you," Spencer replied, "but pure undiluted terror is about all I'm feeling right now. When this boat started moving away from the dock I got this sick feeling in my gut that hadn't been there before. I must have kept it pretty well buried before, but you just can't fight it off when the boat starts moving and the dock starts sliding out of sight ... and you know you're going and there ain't shit you can do about it."

"Sure," I said. "Everybody's gonna go through that sinking feeling at first, but you know it's gonna be one hell of an experience, one that most people will never have. Shit, man, we're gonna be part of history. While Joe Blow back on the block will be leading his dull routine life, you and me will be making the headlines and making history."

Hartnett could tolerate my enthusiasm no longer. "Christ, you make it sound as if we're to experience a real honor by maybe getting our fuckin' heads blown off! " Nodding to the gray rock of Alcatraz which we were passing, he said, "I'd rather be locked up on that rock than be blown away in some half-assed war I don't even begin to understand. I don't think you quite grasp the fact that this shit is real, that real people are getting wasted over there. You can kick all the commie ass you want for the One O' Worst. I'm gonna hunker down and see if I can't come back in 365 days with the same number of balls I'm heading over there with."

I nodded, as if conceding the point, but his words had failed to penetrate. I, of course, was immortal and nothing but glory awaited me over there.

It was but a few nautical miles before the serene sea fumed into an angry ocean. At first the careening ride was fun, like thrill rides at an aquatic amusement park. Troopers howled with laughter at the misfortune of those near the bow of the ship as they were drenched and upended by the mountainous waves slapping huge fingers of sea water around the *Leroy Eltinge*. But the fun soon turned sour as men began lining the sides of the ship to heave-ho.

We arose the next morning to an ocean whose fury had abated but which was still inflicting casualties. The head was awash in bulkhead-to-bulkhead puke, which splashed from side to side as the ship heaved. Max Patterson spent so much time with his head in the commode that he seemed to have evolved into a new life form, half human and half porcelain.

Those men who were not seasick had to contend with the boredom. Some wrote letters; others gambled or gathered in groups around some guitar strumming trooper. A few of the more gung-ho line companies made an effort at the "Daily Dozen" rite of calisthenics, but their unsteady jogging, jumping jacks and push-ups on the rolling, crowded ship were pure folly. A staff sergeant of 2/327th Infantry squealed his bagpipes as he paraded up and down the deck like a Scottish piper exhorting the "Thin Red Line" of Britannia forward to battle against the regiments of Napoleon.

Six days out of port the barons at the head of the brigade finally decided to notify their knights and men-at-arms of our destination. Lt. Colonel Rogers, the brigade XO (executive officer) made it official. His speech was brief and to the point, Vietnam being the point, and it culminated with his chanting of the division's slogan, "We have a rendezvous with destiny! " I, at least, was determined to serve as honorably as did the men who took that same slogan and wore the same Screaming Eagle shoulder patch into Normandy and the snowy copses around Bastogne. The test was approaching and very soon we would know if we could measure up.

Such were my feelings on that gray morning in 1965. They seem, in some ways, so distant from me now. But attitudes were different then. America, and myself along with it, was just beginning to change, to lose its and my innocence, and Vietnam was to be the catalyst for much of that change. It is not that I have turned completely away from the essential error of seeking fame and proving courage in the flames of battle, although I now recognize that war is the most wasteful way to discover whatever truths lie in a man's soul and that in the end the price war demands for such discoveries is far too heavy to pay. Our generation was to earn no universal shame on the battlefield, and I feel that American soldiers in Vietnam demonstrated a courage equal to that shown by any generation. But, sadly, the glow from the stars of our sacrifices was to be extinguished by the darkness of political blunders and military misconceptions.

But the flood of regretful backward glances, the divisions and torments that this war would create within America and within myself were in the future. I did not then question my government's motives or the establishment's truths; I questioned only myself in relation to what I felt was the acid test of a man's courage and worth — the trial by combat. I would go on to take and pass the test of battle and answer those original questions to my satisfaction in Vietnam, but other questions have arisen in their place. Among them is whether by trying so hard to pass the personal test of my courage, I might have come perilously close to failing the greater test of my humanity.

By July 18 it hardly seemed as if we still sailed in the same sea. Now hardly a ripple disturbed the placid leagues of ocean. Far and away the greatest change was the departure of a bitterly cold wind and the arrival of a breezeless heat. The sleeping holds became unbearable. A mass exodus from this ship-borne Black Hole of Calcutta soon took place as hundreds sought refuge topside. G.I.s sprawled across and stuffed themselves into every fraction of space on the greasy, open decks of the ship.

On the 24th we steamed into the American naval base at Subic Bay in the Philippines. The brigade had been promised passes and a beer bust upon our arrival there for refueling, but we were granted a respite of only two hours.

Eleanor Roosevelt had once referred to paratroopers as "a bunch of under-worked, oversexed, overpaid, and drunken shoeshine boys." On this occasion, at least, we failed to measure up. This was due, not to any improvement in the moral character of the new generation of airborne soldiers over the men who had jumped on D-Day and at Arnhem, but to the briefness of the time allotted us to sack and pillage the base and to the fact that all bars and honky-tonks had been closed in apprehension of our arrival.

The following day we departed Subic Bay for the South China Sea. It was during this last leg of the voyage that the brigade suffered its first casualty. A rain squall suddenly descended upon the mob watching the nightly movie on an upper deck, and in the rush to flee from the downpour a soldier slipped. Before he could regain his feet, another trooper bounded off a nearby ladder directly onto the chest of the fallen G.I., crushing the life out of him. I didn't know the victim but his freakish death had its effect on me. After Vietnam, life would sometimes seem like a long vigil on death row, prolonged by stays of execution granted by medicine or fate. But before that moment in 1965 death was a complete stranger.

After twenty-one days and nearly 7,000 miles we at last sighted the mountains looming above the coast of Indochina. Before us was Cam Ranh Bay on the Annamese coast of central South Vietnam. It would soon be a great logistical base for U.S. forces, but on July 29, 1965, it was still only a giant's sandbox with a few hamlets ringing the blue arc of the bay. The only American military personnel there were a few hundred "straight leg" (non-airborne) engineers, breaking ground for the 12,000 that would soon join them. It was to be the 1st Brigade's primary mission to guard these support troops.

As we steamed toward the bay, a squadron of B-52 Stratofortresses soared high overhead flying eastward toward their Guam base, bomb bays empty and a patch of jungle somewhere pockmarked from 750-pound bombs. The sight of those steel condors stoked the fires of my admiration for the peasant army that would oppose us.

"How in hell can those gooks fight on against weapons like that? I've heard that some of them have nothing better to fight with than rusty old muskets and even crossbows. Helicopters have flown back from the bush with arrows stuck in their skin."

Squinting his face against the rippled, reflected glare of the sun upon the sea, Max Patterson replied, "You don't expect me to explain how those slope-head bastards think, do you? Maybe they've all been psyched out by that com-mie witch doctor with the funny lookin' goatee who hangs out up there in Hanoi."

"I just don't understand what keeps them going," I said. "Why do they fight for such a hopeless cause?"

"I wish to hell that Victor Charles thought it was as hopeless for 'em as you do. Hell, if them Cong want this asshole of Asia so bad, I say let 'em have it. It don't look from here like no paradise and sure as hell ain't worth even my ratty ass."

Patterson seemed right; what we could see of Indochina from the deck of the *Leroy Eltinge* seemed far removed from Eden. Before long it was to bear a closer resemblance to hell.

Chapter II
Cam Ranh Bay

An hour or so later our ship anchored alongside the dock. A long journey had at last ended; a longer one was just beginning. The 2/320th Artillery was the first unit to disembark, so we panted and puffed up the stairwell with bags and gear and weaved our way down the gangplank to set foot on the dusty soil of Vietnam. The welcoming committee consisted of only the truck drivers who were to carry us part of the way to our campsite. They had to suffer through the usual taunts and jeers hurled at straight leg (non-airborne) soldiers anytime they encountered the collective egos of a group of paratroopers. The truckers fired back with gleeful predictions of our impending doom at the hands of the Viet Cong, then paid back our scorn by smashing into every crater the pitted road had to offer. By the time the deuce-and-a-half-ton trucks had screeched to a stop alongside the waiting landing craft that were to glide across the bay, we were clamoring for a mass bayoneting of the drivers. "Mother fuckin' leg bastards ought to be court-martialed!" moaned Staff Sergeant Harold T. Tinker, my pot-bellied survey section chief. Then, upon sighting the boats, his moaning intensified, "Well, hell! Not another mother fuckin' boat ride!"

But this boat ride was of mercifully short duration. Once on the opposite shore, we hefted our bags and trudged along the twisting path towards our campsite under a savage sun. Gushing sweat and grinding teeth, we tottered to the site, where we were met by the master sergeant in charge of Survey Platoon. A juicer of the first rank, the chief disliked anything that kept him away from deliberations with his bottle. Thus he allowed us just seconds to catch our breath before dispatching us to the camp's perimeter to hack out outposts.

We flew to our task with vigor. The chief, a Korean War veteran, had shaken us with warnings of a probable mortar bombardment and we had no reason to doubt him, having assumed that we would be embroiled in fierce hand-to-hand combat the minute we disembarked from the ship. So we dug away at the hard earth until a horseshoe-shaped machine gun position took form. After a meal of cold C-rations we prepared for our first night in Vietnam and in war.

The dark hours passed without event, other than a furious assault on our position by a caribou-sized rat. The first of many determined enemies we were to encounter in this hostile land, the guerrilla rat seemed totally unintimidated by the blows we delivered with entrenching tools and rifle butts. After the rat finally staged a strategic retreat, the night lay passive around us, but our imaginations filled the darkness with foes. Several times the man on guard would awaken the others after hearing some strange and unfamiliar noise or after seeing a shadow suddenly form into the dark shape of a creeping enemy. Apprehension floated in the warm night air like mist.

The night was made no less eerie by the dun-colored geckos that infested the area. They serenaded us with shrill taunts that sounded like "Fuck You! Fuck You!," as if they too resented our presence as invaders in their country. Naturally we labeled these leftovers from the prehistoric past as "Fuck You Lizards."

The first days were easy. We spent the morning hours improving our positions, with the hot afternoons reserved for acclimatizing ourselves. Bundles of mail were passed out and the battery dispatched jeeps to barter with the locals for beer, sodas and ice. Thus far it hadn't seemed like a bad war at all.

My first contact with the Vietnamese occurred the morning of the second day. Three kids and a woman with the orange gums and blackened teeth of a betel nut chewer approached us with baskets heaped with bottles of beer, sodas and bananas. Each thrust a bottle toward us and pleaded through hopeful grins and rotted teeth, "You, you, G.I.! You buy number one beer, Coke?"

We had been warned of incidents in which Viet Cong agents had dropped slivers of glass or drops of battery acid into the beer or soda sold by such innocent-looking peddlers. But thirst overcame caution and I ventured out from my post to barter with them.

Taking a quick gulp of the Vietnamese brew I had purchased, I realized why it was referred to by G.I.s as Tiger Piss. I passed the bottle to my buddies, who, being dedicated guzzlers, managed to gag down the beer without barfing.

We were soon swamped with Vietnamese peddlers. The market day atmosphere quickly changed, however, when our fire-breathing, granite-jawed first sergeant came charging the mob. He had a pathological hatred for Orientals, or slopeheads, as he called them, and felt that the only way to win their hearts and minds was to rip out their hearts with bayonets and bash out their brains with rifle butts. No man dared oppose El Cid, as we called him because of his first name, Sidney, and his heroic pretensions. Everyone in the battery lived in awe and terror of him and no one was about to argue with him on behalf of the gooks.

Grabbing their goods, the Vietnamese fled in panic as a triumphant top sergeant harangued us against dealing with anybody dressed in anything but olive drab. The next three troopers he caught communicating with the gooks found themselves digging a garbage sump for the battery. So much for civic relations.

The easygoing days ended at sunset. The dark nights, with only the mocking of the Fuck You Lizards to disturb the silence, descended with an unnerving suddenness. The moon frowned down with an ivory malice. Tightly wound nerves teetered on the edge, fingers tightened nervously around triggers, eyes strained to search the depths of the darkness, hearts pounded at sudden shufflings in the brush that could be an animal thrashing about for food or a crawling man, grenade in hand, intent on murder.

The black quilt of the night would often be ripped by the scarlet flame of an M-16 rifle fired by a jittery sentinel. One night a single, nervously fired round escalated into a volley. For several mad minutes red tracer bullets laced the darkness. Then cries for a cease-fire rang down the line of outposts on the edge of the perimeter as the realization struck that we were waging a firefight with an infantry company which had just moved into an area directly opposite our southern defenses. Fortunately, only the vegetation above our heads suffered from the exchange of fire. This was the first of many such incidents.

The vacation lasted four days. Then the job of the Survey Platoon began. With thirty-meter steel tape, theodolite, aiming circle and aiming stakes, we surveyed in battery positions through the thick yellow dust and thorn bushes. Then we were handed shovels and sandbags to begin construction of a line of bunkers.

The scene became one of sunburned backs streaked with sweat and mud; of bloody hands necklacing the camp with a steel bramble of concertina and tanglefoot barbed wire; of ax-wielding arms chopping at the undergrowth to clear fields of fire.

Slowly we transformed a piece of thorny wasteland into a military base, our only rewards being C-rations, a steel pot full of water to take a whore's bath in, and an inflated air mattress to rest our weary bones. We would be awakened during the night either to stand the two hours of guard allotted to each soldier in each position, or to be startled from sleep by the sharp report of a weapon discharged by a nervous nellie who would later swear there had been a Victor Charlie (Viet Cong) where there was now only a tree stump.

At this stage of the war, our enemy was mostly the insects that crawled through the maze of vegetation. Fire ants and red-and-black tree ants were the fiercest. I experienced their regimented wrath one day when, swinging my ax against the bramble, I scythed a huge hive down from an overhanging branch and onto my head. Thousands of ants swarmed out of the multi-combed cone to launch a carnivorous assault on every inch of my body. I tore my clothes off in a panic and stood flailing away at the angry, checkered regiments. Two other G.I.s in the thicket rushed to my aid to slap frantically at my naked hide. With their help, I finally brushed the last insect from my body, which was already swelling with a hundred red bites.

Next to the ants, the termites were the most numerous. Scattered throughout the area were dirt pyramids constructed by them, some as high as eight feet. When I first saw them, I assumed they were ancient monuments to the gods built by the early primitives of the region.

The night continued to provide our only break from the monotony. The darkness enveloping our bunker of interwoven brown and gray sandbags exploded on the night of August 6 into a mad wake of streaking scarlet tracers splintering the trees above our heads. A raging firefight was soon in progress on the east side of the battery perimeter where the bunkers of Ammo and Communications platoons were located. The noisy spectacle was reduced after a quarter of an hour to sporadic rifle fire.

We learned the following morning that the battle had been another contest between friendly units. The opponent this time had been A Troop of the 2/17th Cavalry, the brigade's jeep-mounted reconnaissance outfit. The bullet holes in the gun bunnies' bunkers attested to the great amount of ammunition expended, but fortunately no one had suffered injury. Luckily, we were still as incompetent at hitting the "enemy" as we were at identifying him. Refusing to relinquish the honor of being the first in the battery to scrimmage with Charlie, several of the Commo "rats" and Ammo "humpers" insisted they had seen V.C. snipers initiate the firefight by firing on HQ Battery and the cavalrymen from positions in the intervening ground and then beat a hasty retreat before the converging volleys came from the aroused troopers. Anxious to believe we had actually clashed with the enemy, I was one of a few in the battery gullible enough to swallow the story.

On August 15 the 2/320th Artillery Battalion moved out of its half completed camp to support the infantry battalions on a search-and-destroy mission against a Viet Cong concentration in a hill mass west of the nearby port city of Nhatrang. Only the First Section of the Survey Platoon was to take part in Operation Barracuda; Tinker's section was awarded the dubious honor of providing for the stay-behind guard.

We unfortunate few from Survey Platoon were dispatched to boost the guard at Alpha Battery's position. Taking our posts, we began a weeklong ordeal of boredom and dizzying drowsiness. With just two men posted at each bunker, we got only snatches of sleep. There was nothing to relieve the monotony of jungle scenery; the hours of guard grew longer with each shift. My bunkermate's sole interest and topic of conversation was "Gettin' the fuckin' hell out of this mother fuckin' dink country!" After the cannon cocker's baby spider monkey died, unable to survive on a diet of C-ration dried instant cream dissolved in canteen water and fed to it through a condom, he became even less talkative.

The only event that punctured the balloon of boredom that week was the sight of prop-driven A-IE Skyraider dive bombers in action. In concert with Huey helicopter rocket ships, they pounded a V.C. company which was reported to have sallied forth from its jungle lair to probe our weakly defended brigade perimeter.

On the morning of the eighth day, when the battalion returned from its first mission, we were finally relieved and allowed to return to "Hindquarters and Hindquarters" Battery. Operation Barracuda had sparked little action, but it had netted the 101st Airborne Division its first enemy killed in action since the end of World War II twenty years ago. The bloody distinction confirmed it; we were really at war now.

Chapter III

An Khe

The return to base was short-lived. Preparations were made for the 1st Brigade, led by Colonel James S. Timothy, to undertake its first major campaign. Coded Operation Highland, the push would take the brigade up Highway 19 leading from the port of Quinhon west to the Central Highlands city of Pleiku. We were to secure the area around An Khe, located about midway along the highway, so that the newly airmobile 1st Cavalry Division, on its way aboard troop transports across the Pacific, could establish a base camp and a heliport there in the middle of II Corps Tactical Zone.

On August 24 the olive drab snake of U.S. Army trucks and 105 millimeter howitzers began to wind along the road to Nhatrang. There the greater part of the brigade was to board LSTs and sail north for Quinhon.

In straight leg outfits the gun crews and their equipment were carried in big deuce-and-a-half-ton trucks. But in the airborne, the TO&E (Tables of Organization and Equipment) charts allowed for no piece of transport equipment too large to "heavy drop" from aircraft. Thus we had to pile all our gear and ourselves on top of canvas-covered loads heaped aboard the two three-quarter-ton trucks and two jeeps of the Survey Platoon.

Teetering atop our loads, we drove through the countryside in steel pots and flak jackets, watching the peasant populace warily and observing the almost swastika-like Buddhist symbols atop various shrines and temples. Passing through Nhatrang, we saw our first beer can suburb. House after house had walls constructed of flattened out and tacked together Budweiser, Busch and Miller High Life beer cans. Whole blocks architecturally advertised American breweries. For hundreds of Vietnamese, home was a square beer can.

Lining up bumper to bumper on the beach, the convoy was slowly fed into the gaping abdomen of a Merchant Marine LST. Once again the sea whipped up its white-capped wrath.

The following morning brought us in sight of the harbor of Quinhon. The day was half done before our trucks were steered down the ramp of the landing ship to the beach paved with PSP (perforated steel planking), used for improvised airstrips and roadways. The disgorged cargo of the LST then motored the few miles to the brigade assembly area, a dusty plain next to an Army engineer base.

The next morning's assault westward along Route 19 toward An Khe Valley consisted of a series of leaps and bounds. As Patterson and I taped distances for our survey team, the guns of Alpha Battery were hastily unlimbered and directed toward a hamlet sprawled at the foot of a ridgeline. Having been a gun bunny for six months, I appreciated the speed with which the cannoneers unhitched their tubes from the trucks, spread the trails of the guns, cut powder charges and set fuses, and connected explosive warheads to powder canisters. In just a few minutes the 105 mm's were poised to fire thirty-three pounds of explosives each, requiring only the commands of quadrant and deflection (range and windage).

The telephone circuit was not yet rigged between FDC (Fire Direction Center) and the waiting guns. Consequently, the E-8 master sergeant who was the chief of firing battery had to shout out the commands as he received them from the chart operators in the FDC tent. He bellowed out mightily so that all six howitzers, arranged in a standard five-pointed star formation with the sixth howitzer in the center of the star, could clearly distinguish his commands. "Shell, HE ... Fuse, quick ... Charge, four ... Deflection, 2240 ... Quadrant, 180 ... Center piece only ... Fire at my command!" The gunner and assistant gunner cranked the tube into firing position and the gun chief yelled, "Gun Three, set and ready to fire."

Upon command, the assistant gunner corporal pulled the lanyard, releasing shell and smoke. Before the shell's detonation had died, the gunners were already setting FDC's corrections. Two more adjusting rounds were hurled toward the target. Then, zeroed in, all six howitzers roared to the command "Battery Fire!" Fiery blossoms bloomed with steel-tipped petals among the thatch-roofed dwellings of the hamlet. The target was 700 meters away, almost point blank range. The huts were hidden behind a screen of smoke, with burning debris shooting skyward.

The target was a gook squad of seven men spotted by aerial recon as they moved through the ville. The cannon cockers of Alpha Battery blasted the hamlet with eighty-seven high explosive shells, but the return for this expenditure was but one dead V.C. The score was a cheaper kill, though, than the average ration of shells expended to enemy killed for the war.

An hour before dawn on the 27th, SSgt. Tinker's survey section motored closer to An Khe to undertake its third survey in two days. As we were completing the survey, the guns of Alpha and Bravo batteries arrived, and within a few minutes the artillerymen were lobbing shells along the sharp slope of a mountain towering over the site.

As the climbing barrage grew in intensity, two F-105 fighter-bombers soared overhead and dove toward the peak. The Thunderchiefs flicked their rockets against the mountain. Then came the guttural growl of the aircrafts' 20 mm cannon blasting out 6,000 rounds per minute. The cannon fire ripping into the mountain sounded like a great cosmic fart.

Finally, as the fighter-bombers broke away from their strafing runs, two slate-gray eggs tumbled from the bellies of the jets to detonate into fiery pillows of napalm. One entire ridge inflated into balloons of jellied gasoline.

The battalion's next push took us through dangerous An Khe Pass on Route 19 along which the elite French Mobile Group 100 had been nearly destroyed by the Viet Minh in 1954. The road twisted through forbidding-looking mountains, and at the summit of the pass curled around a ridge that blocked out the magnificent view of harsh highlands dropping down to the green kilt of rice paddies. We shared a common bond of anxiety as our trucks strained up and over the pass. The road was protected by the roving patrols of 2/17th Cavalry jeeps mounted with M-60 machine guns and 106 mm recoilless rifles, but still the suspense was not lifted until the convoy had curved around the last mountain onto the rolling plateau where the 1st Cavalry Division's future base camp sat.

On the 28th, Battalion HQ and HQ Battery moved into a semi-cleared patch of jungle to set up the TOC (Tactical Operations Center) for the 2/320th Artillery. The privates and bird corporals (Specialist 4s) were immediately put to work spading out foxholes and erecting sandbag OPs along the edge of the battery perimeter.

From our wilderness base we carried out our part in operations Talon, Venture, Bayonet and Cacti, bouncing over the roads to survey new sites for the gun batteries, and then usually returning to TOC to endure another night of waiting, watching and weariness. Usually the false peace of the night would be interrupted by alarms, bursts of gunfire, and flares popping into sudden hissing brightness. Fleeting shadows crept and stalked; strange cries sent minds into a waltz of terror; stomachs tightened and throats dried. The night pulsated with the heartbeat of fear.

When imaginings failed to summon forth gunfire, inventions served the purpose. On the night of September 4 several inmates of the Ammo Platoon asylum conspired with the flakes of Survey Platoon's First Section to liven things up. They leveled the muzzles of their M-16s at a nearby mound and opened fire. Soon a highly agitated first sergeant appeared to direct the defense. Displaying sudden, deep cracks in the armor of his fierce exterior, El Cid, an iron man corroded by the rust of fear, saw, through the panic obscuring his vision, the movements of armed men. No one else was able to penetrate the darkness with a laser generated by terror, but because it was the indomitable first sergeant who spotted the foe, no one doubted its existence. Even the perpetrators of the hoax believed that by some ironic twist of fate their sham battle had coincided with an actual attempt by the V.C. to infiltrate the perimeter, so formidable was the first sergeant's reputation. The impression of El Cid's infallibility was increased the next morning upon discovery of a log thrown across the tumbleweed maze of concertina barbed wire lining the perimeter, strongly suggesting a bridge for infiltrators.

Other incidents occurred along the easily spooked line of outposts. The wild dogs that roamed the area gave us several scares. One night, Ammo's and Survey's bunkers unloaded a couple of hundred rounds of machine gun and rifle fire and two frags (fragmentation hand grenades) when one of the hounds tripped two flares. The dog escaped unscathed.

The Viet Cong curs struck again a few nights later and this time caused our first casualty. Two flares were popped by the dogs and SP/4 Dillhoefer, a short, wiry-haired mechanic attached to the Commo Platoon bunker, tramped out with Max Patterson to the perimeter's edge where the stubble-strewn clearing ended up against a jungle wall. After replacing the trip flares, Dillhoefer seemed suddenly to dissolve into a blinding flash. A flare he had been carrying in the chest pocket of his jungle fatigue shirt had ignited. Dillhoefer had neglected to bend back the tips of the flare's safety pin and it had jostled loose to release the firing lever. Hysterical hands tore at the blazing shirt while Dillhoefer, yelping in fright, wildly wiggled under a spray of magnesium sparks. Somehow in the panic, the fatigue jacket was ripped off Dillhoefer. He survived the ordeal with only scorched skin and the loss of the few hairs he had supported on his narrow chest.

There were a few reminders that a world outside our circle of fear and frustration did exist. Mail call was the favorite event of the day, an amphetamine for morale. Letters were our lifelines to the "Real World." Payday brought MPC (Military Payment Certificates) in place of greenbacks, to reduce the loss of American dollars and the rate of inflation in the South Vietnamese economy. Though it was supposed to be non-negotiable in the Vietnamese market, black marketeers were easily available to exchange piastres for the scrip. Soon, many bars and "boom boom" houses were taking the "funny money" as direct payment rather than the Vietnamese Ps. Of course, greenbacks remained the preferred currency and many G.I.s supplemented their combat pay of $65 per month by selling U.S. dollars on the black market.

Chapter IV

Operation Gibraltar

The war for the Screaming Eagles had thus far been little more than a dangerous game of hide-and-seek. What V.C. had been encountered had seemed little better than rabbits running from the hunter. But all this frustrating thrashing about in the thickets for an elusive foe was to come to an abruptly violent end on the morning of September 18. From that moment no man among us doubted that we were opposed by a strong and formidable foe who knew how to wage war as well as any soldier on earth.

Tinker's survey party was attached to Charlie Battery to survey a battery position to support the heliborne assault by the 2/502nd Infantry Battalion. Earlier, as we had completed our survey of Bravo Battery's firing position, we heard the cries of "Medic! Medic!" A loader on one of the howitzers had remained too close to the breechblock of the gun after loading a new shell. When the 105 mm fired, the recoiling tube slammed into his hip.

It was the second injury the battery had sustained in the last few days. A lanky, Australian-born Pfc. called "Bones" was also hurt while loading a shell into the howitzer's breech. His finger was mashed to pulp by the weight of the breechblock as it was slammed closed by the assistant gunner. Bones had shoved the artillery round into the breech with fingers extended, instead of properly doubling his fist against the base of the shell so that the assistant gunner could speedily and safely slam the breechblock closed.

The first rains of the autumn monsoon had melted the road into a morass. The trucks of Charlie Battery inched along the muddy grades, with progress interrupted as wench and cable were employed to rescue vehicles bogged down in the brown glue. During one of these hold-ups we heard from the garbled buzz of a radio set news of a major battle erupting. Pleas for artillery support brought renewed effort to push the guns forward to within firing range of the beleaguered infantry. But the mud was an enemy with whom we could not contend, and C Battery had no choice but to turn back and attempt another route.

As we were beginning to retrace our muddy tracks, a C Battery corporal passed our truck to give us the straight poop. "The Five O' Deuce landed right in the laps of half the Charlies in 'Nam. They're getting the shit stomped out of 'em!"

Charlie Battery plowed its way back to B Battery's position, leaving the isolated companies of the 2/502nd Infantry without artillery support. The 2/320th battalion commander, Lt. Col. Braun, tried unsuccessfully to obtain the support of the newly arriving 1st Cavalry Division's double rotary CH-47 Chinook helicopters to lift the guns into position. The airmobile division's failure to help the 101st was the first of a series of events that bred an oftentimes unfriendly rivalry between the two units. Later that evening, the Cav's Chinooks finally were employed to carry a battery close enough to support the O'Deuce grunts.

Throughout the night the southeastern span of the horizon was aglow with 600 flares dropped by C-47 Dakota flareships and artillery illumination rounds. The rumble of sporadic gunfire could be heard coming from a blood-soaked rice paddy field where only the dead slept that night.

The bloodying of the 101st had begun at 0700 that morning. Twenty-six UH-1D and UH-1B Huey and Marine CH-34 Choctaw helicopters had deposited in two waves Charlie Company and two platoons of Bravo Company onto the crusty floor of a dry rice paddy near the village of An Ninh, fourteen kilometers north of Route 19. Then, before the remaining platoons of B Company could be landed, the 224 paratroopers on the ground, under the command of battalion CO Lt. Col. Wilfred Smith, were swept by an arc of fire and flame. The men of the 2/502nd Strike Force Battalion had been set down almost on top of a Viet Cong main force command post and training area. It had taken only a few minutes for the startled enemy to drop their breakfast rice bowls, leap into prepared positions, and open fire.

For the men of the Five O' Deuce the world suddenly became reduced to a fire-swept rectangle of rice paddy 150 yards wide by 400 yards long. In those moments every other reality was lost; memories were forgotten and futures held in abeyance. All that existed was the pandemonium of combat.

The helicopters ferrying the remaining two platoons of B Company attempted to approach the landing zone. Captain Robert Rawls, Charlie Company commander, rushed to the center of the convulsed LZ to wave away the Hueys from imminent destruction. A few minutes later, the captain's blood mixed with the blood of those already cut down by the sword-swipe of machine gun fire.

Twenty minutes later a third wave of Alpha and Bravo Company grunts tried to land 400 yards south of the initial LZ. Only thirty-six men got off the choppers as intense fire knocked three helicopters down, their wreckage adding to that of the two downed in the first waves. Led by two sergeants, the thirty-six troopers repelled three enemy assaults from their isolated positions, until they were able to link with the rest of the battalion on the morning of the 19th.

COs shouted in radio sets for arty fire to smother the enemy attack, but the Viet Cong had an invaluable ally in the barriers of mud which had resisted our efforts to advance the howitzers within range. For nearly two hours, tactical air support was also unavailable. Only the rockets of nine UH-1B gunships were ready to support the grunts. The infantrymen of the 2/502nd were on their own.

In these first volcanic moments, the 2/320th Artillery suffered its first combat deaths. Lt. Fox, artillery observer from Charlie Battery, and his RTO (Radio-Telephone Operator) were the first artillerymen of the 101st to die in battle in Vietnam. To the list of the officers killed in action was added Major Herbert Dexter, the battalion operations officer. Leading an assault on Viet Cong gunners in tiger-striped fatigues blasting at the Americans from a position atop a fifty-foot knoll, Dexter fell riddled by machine gun bullets. The maelstrom of fire also wounded the commanders of A and B companies and a platoon leader in Charlie Company.

The battle was not all one-sided, however. The surrounded Strike Force troopers soon shook off their initial shock to return fire with telling effect. The two Viet Cong battalions from the 2nd NVA (North Vietnamese Army) Regiment maintained a heavy fire, including 60 and 82 mm mortar fire, that kept the paratroopers pinned down throughout the day, but the V.C. did not attempt to storm the trapped G.I.s and annihilate them.

As night fell the battle tempo slackened somewhat. The V.C. probed the perimeter six times in groups of up to platoon strength but made no serious assault. One G.I. was killed by a Charlie who had crept through the brush to within five feet of his victim. A sulphurous sky colored by flares, which we witnessed from our arty position several klicks (kilometers) away, held the darkness at bay. The cacophony of battle was reduced to the hiss of burning flames, the moans of the wounded, and the sporadic ratcheting volleys of machine gun fire. The night seemed to last forever.

The ordeal ended for the paratroopers the following day. Their relief was twofold, as the rest of A Company from the 2/502nd and a company from the 2/327th arrived on the battlefield soon after the first spiraling rounds of the 2/320th began to sew a protective curtain of exploding metal around the surrounded infantrymen. Leaving behind their dead and a huge crimson banner bearing a golden hammer and sickle, the V.C. retreated.

The redlegs had hustled to the commands of "March Order!" at first light, and with our survey team accompanying, the twelve field pieces of two batteries lumbered out toward the intended positions of the day before. This time "General Mud" offered little resistance. The combat engineers of the brigade's Alpha Company, 326th Engineers, had dueled the roadblocks of mud through most of the night, enabling the convoy of artillery vehicles to plow across the reconstructed roads to their objectives. We started our survey under volleys blasting in red arrowheads of flame and gray smoke from the recoiling tubes of the howitzers. A battery of silvery-tubed 155 mm howitzers pulled into position, as did a pair of Pershing tanks, all from the 1st Cavalry Division.

The bark of command rang out and sweating cannoneers heaved the gun trails to shift the barrels toward a dun-colored hill several hundred meters southeast of the road. The hilltop was rapidly clothed in a robe of bursting gray. Completing the survey, we prepared to move back to TOC, when more commands set the straining cannon cockers to the gun trails again, this time turning the howitzers in an arc of almost 180 degrees. Sniper fire had smacked into the cannoneers from a low ridge behind the howitzers. Lowered to point blank range, the gun tubes shattered the ridge with HE (High Explosive) and the white-hot streamers of Willie Peter (White Phosphorous) shells. The sniper fire ceased.

The two-day Battle of An Ninh had been the first major ground action of the Vietnam War involving a U.S. Army battalion against a main force communist unit. (The U.S. Marine Corps had already tangled with the enemy, killing nearly 700 V.C. during Operation Starlite in the Van Thuong Peninsula near Chu Lai in August.) The men of the 2/502nd Strike Force had paid for their induction into history with the lives of thirteen paratroopers and two helicopter crewmen. Twenty-eight more grunts and several chopper jockeys had been wounded. The soldiers of the National Liberation Front had suffered a stinging defeat in this first trial of arms with the United States Army. The body count, the Army's yardstick to measure the extent of victory, numbered 257, many of whom were victims of the 100 tactical air strikes and the 11,000 artillery rounds fired.

The days following the battle were largely quiet, though beset by constant rain that threatened to wash our outpost away. With the brigades of the 1st Cavalry Division arriving at their base camp, the area seemed more secure. The line of OPs protecting TOC rarely disturbed the night's slumber as they had earlier in the month. Instead, we sneered at the frequent rumble coming from the nervous outposts along the cavalrymen's perimeter. We laughed at accounts of firefights erupting between green units of the airmobile division, easily ignoring the fact that only a few weeks before we had been committing the same blunders. After the 1st Cav's initial reluctance to come to the aid of the Five O' Deuce on the first day of the Battle of An Ninh, everyone wearing a Screaming Eagle patch on his left shoulder harbored resentment toward the heliborne cavalrymen bearing the big yellow and black horsehead patch on their uniforms.

One last incident occurred before the brigade's departure from the AO (Area of Operations) to intensify the feud. On the night of the 28th, the locomotive swish of shells streaked over the battalion camp to explode directly across the dirt road fronting the Ammo and Commo platoons' bunkers. Shouts of "Mortar attack!" and "Everyone into the bunkers! We've got incoming!" rebounded. As sleepy "spoons" (Army cooks) and FDC men stumbled toward cover, more shells arrowed what seemed like inches above our heads.

Several anxious minutes passed. A frightful vision assaulted my mind of a shell ripping the air in its flight towards my crowded hole. There would come a blinding, red-orange flash, then the screams of men disintegrating, and finally a dreadful silence and the curling towers of smoke rising over a charnel house. In near panic, I wiggled clear of the bunker and into the open.

But that fateful next shell never exploded; the bombardment was over. I had undergone my first shelling, and it had left me feeling terrified and helpless. But surely, I consoled myself, in a small arms skirmish where one could fight back, things would be different. I would redeem myself for my moment of panic ... in battle against an enemy on the more or less equal terms of rifleman against rifleman, instead of against the shells of unseen guns fired by men miles away.

There immediately arose doubts as to the identity of our assailants. Several Korean War veterans disagreed with the assumption that we had been the targets of enemy mortar rounds. They claimed that the shells had come in too low, too straight, and too fast to be incoming mortar shells. The sound and size of the detonations were suspiciously similar to our own 105s. They had to be artillery rounds, and the enemy possessed no artillery in this AO. The following morning we learned who had bombarded our camp and the doubters' suspicions were confirmed. Through a mix-up in communications, gunners of the 1st Cav had aimed their pieces at what they believed were the freshly vacated positions of the 2/320th Artillery, in the hopes of blasting V.C. foragers who might be scouring the site for loot accidentally left behind by the departing paratroopers. Another black mark was chalked up against the airmobile cavalrymen.

With the Viet Cong quiet around An Khe, the brigade was given helicopters from which soldiers harnessed to bulky bundles of nylon could be dropped. A minimum of one jump every three months from an aircraft in flight was required to retain jump status and collect jump pay of $55 a month, so for several days troopers were busy sliding out of Huey helicopters on their rumps, counting the long four seconds (and often closing both eyes tightly) and waiting for the snap on the shoulders and jerk on the neck to announce the opening inflation of the parachute. This was to be my thirteenth "blast," and, true to the number's evil reputation, it was very nearly my last.

It was my first jump from a helicopter, and I was unfamiliar with the proper way to exit the chopper. When the heart thumping tap fell on my shoulder indicating it was time for me to jump, I kicked back with my legs to provide the momentum needed to extract myself from the chopper — instead of lifting myself up with my hands and sliding out on my bottom, as was the proper procedure. Thus, instead of falling out and away, feet first, from the helicopter, I did an aerial bellybuster.

I fell, with my face staring at the ground more than a thousand distant but very fast feet below, wrapping my flailing legs around the helicopter's landing skid. I unwove one leg immediately, but the second seemed lashed in a secure knot to the long ski of the Huey. I twisted in crazy contortions as the chopper carried me over mirroring rice paddies. Each pounding of my heart, each second of my consciousness seemed like a dozen lifetimes as I struggled for freedom.

My bondage must have lasted but a few seconds, though it seemed I was held captive for all eternity by that Huey and by a leg that no longer obeyed my commands and seemed no longer a part of me. Finally the knots released and I fell free, my parachute popping open almost immediately. After such a unique exit, I expected to look up and see great holes in my chute and to land in a tangle of concertina wire, but the rest of the jump was anticlimactic as I floated like an autumn leaf to a feather soft landing on the DZ (drop zone).

Prior to leaving the An Khe AO, the battalion lost two more men, both forward observers. While humping up a harsh hill with an infantry platoon from the 1/327th, Lt. Kelley and Pfc. Logan, one of the men with whom I had shared the lonely vigil at Alpha Battery's Cam Ranh Bay camp, encountered death suddenly and ingloriously. The troopers had briefly sagged to the ground to rest before proceeding on uphill. Then, as the platoon stumbled to their feet to resume the climb, grunting under the load of heavy rucksacks, a series of blinding flashes seemed to swallow Logan in fiery smoke. A bandolier of M-79 grenade launcher shells strapped to Logan's rucksack had exploded.

Logan's life was blasted to eternity almost instantly. Lt. Kelley died moments later, as did a third man, before the whirling iron bird bearing the red cross could fly him to the hospital. Another thirteen crunchies (infantrymen) felt grenade shrapnel tear into their flesh. What caused the string of 40 mm grenades to detonate was open to debate. Some witnesses claimed a sniper bullet set off the chain reaction of rioting metal. Others felt that the tangled brush had threaded its green grasp around the safety cotter pin of a hand grenade attached to Logan's LBE (load bearing equipment, often sarcastically referred to now as the LBJ) to set off the catastrophe.

Chapter V

Quinhon

On the last day of September, Tinker's survey team heaped truck and jeep with their gypsy cargo and moved out with the firing batteries in convoy toward the new AO. An Khe and its mountains were left behind as we entered the flat, more open area around the port city of Quinhon in Binh Dinh Province. The most striking change from the relatively cool mountains only sixty klicks west was the yellow punishment of the sun. Gratefully, the furnace that was to be our campsite was cooled by periodic drizzles. The all too brief sprinklings were welcomed by sweaty troopers as they filled sandbags with the dry red dust. But always the torture would resume as the sun reaffirmed its reign with temperatures sometimes approaching 120 degrees. Within a few weeks though, the roles of represser and rescuer were reversed, as we praised the Southeast Asian sun whenever it made one of its rare attempts to tear through the closed curtains of the monsoon.

Other than providing security for our South Korean allies of the ROK (Republic of Korea) Capital "Tiger" Division coming ashore at Quinhon, the brigade accomplished little. In nearly six weeks of patrolling no major enemy unit was encountered. The all-important body count in this Operation Sayonara numbered a meager eighty-one. Although an advance element of Bravo Battery scouting a firing site briefly came under machine gun fire, the only encounter we in Survey had with the enemy was in the form of three-pronged barbs called Devil's Teeth that were strewn about the area to puncture the tires of our vehicles.

As the pace of the war slackened for us, the battalion started issuing passes into Quinhon. Each party of olive drab tourists was warned by "first sleeves" (first sergeants, also often called "first pigs") to steer clear of booze, brawling and, most particularly, broads.

"All right, men," admonished El Cid, "I want you all to go ahead and let some steam off, and you cocksmen with balls for brains go on if you must and get your nuts off with them slopehead bitches. But, by God, I want you all to remember this! Out in the sticks your enemy is the V.C., but in Quinhon or any other fuckin' slopehead city your enemy is V.D., not some grenade throwin' terrorist. Ninety-nine percent of them whores have got the clap or syph or worse. These bitches have cunts just crawlin' with diseases nobody has ever heard of before. I've seen young fuckers just like you come back from visitin' these 'ladies' with their balls turned blue and swollen to the size of tennis balls; their dicks rottin' off. And gentlemen, because there ain't no cure for some of these things, I've seen soldiers assigned to permanent, and I do mean permanent, duty stations in the 'Nam!"

Then, as an afterthought, the first sergeant conceded, "Now, for those who just got to go ahead and grab a piece of slant-eyed ass, make damn sure you carry an insurance policy. You can pick 'em up with your pass when you leave. Remember, you don't get no fuckin' Purple Heart for a syph swollen prick!"

As we broke formation to board the trucks that would take us into Quinhon, El Cid tossed one final zinger. "One other little detail, gentlemen. A lot of these gook hookers are Charlie's bitches, who have razor blades stuck up their snatches to give you a fuck you won't never forget!"

Several of the troopers winced at those words of warning, only to hop aboard the truck and quickly forget them as lust took over from logic during the ride into Quinhon, where they paid the going price of 300 piastres for a few moments of pleasure and then returned infected. A surveyor was among many in the battery to feel the bite of the clap bug. He relished the affections of three cyclo girls (motorbike-borne whores) and a few mornings afterwards was reminded of their ministrations when he employed one of the cylindrical black cardboard shell containers stuck at an appropriate angle in the ground and fondly referred to by their G.I. patrons as "piss tubes."

My first trip into the city was more or less typical: bar hopping from the Tokyo Bar to the Blue Moon Bar to the Playboy Bar; taking in the sights and smells of the city from the seat of a pedicab or rickshaw. Cripples were everywhere along the avenue, begging, pickpocketing or peddling pornographic photos and joints of marijuana. Adolescent procurers banged clenched fists against open palms in their lewd sign language as they hustled for mothers and sisters. Pint-sized pimps pulled at the sleeves of G.I.s to proposition.

"Hey, G.I., you want number one boom-boom? I show you number one baby-san. She number fuckin' one cherry. She boom-boom you only three hundred Ps. Hey, big bargain. Hey, G.I., this baby-san number one ripe cherry in Quinhon."

With promises of extra piastres to the winner, we goaded our pedicab drivers into races from bar to bar. Like chariot drivers in Imperial Rome, we darted in and around the traffic of the Vietnamese city, whipping the sweating pedallers with red and yellow piastre notes. Once in the bars, we would be instantly accosted by bargirls pleading, "Hey, G.I., you buy me Saigon tea. You buy me Saigon tea, I love you too much!"

Saigon tea usually consisted of nothing but colored water or a diluted creme de menthe and cost 180 piastres, but the hustle usually worked on the hordes of horny G.I.s. I fell for it even harder than most when an Oriental Aphrodite calling herself Helen approached. I pursued the beautiful bargirl during several subsequent visits to Quinhon, but our ridiculous romance soon foundered over a rivalry with a carrot-top leg engineer lieutenant, with whom I nearly came to blows.

I took my hurt feelings out on one of the back alley whores whom I had resisted until now. Like so many other young men before me who had gone off to war, service to my country had also included being serviced into sex by paid, painted women light years removed from love. Uncle Sam is indeed one of history's greatest pimps.

I tried desperately to forget Helen, but I reeked of a painful naivete towards both love and war. And I was paying the price for my illusions of the one now, just as I later would be presented with an even bigger bill for the other. I had been swept along on a tide of uneducated lust and slammed against bitter shoals by an unrequited love, again, as I would later be hurled even more painfully by the glory and honor I had tried giving a war that would accept neither.

A few days after we in Survey had calibrated the battalion's eighteen howitzers from a mountaintop defended by a platoon of Vietnamese "Ruff Puffs" (Regional and Popular Forces), a sky pregnant with rain gave birth to the monsoon. We were totally unprepared for the liquid fury. The fighting holes and horseshoe-shaped machine gun pit became overflowing ponds. The sunken road that cut through the center of the camp was transformed into a river of ocher-colored mud. We wallowed in the slop of a brown waterfall.

The rain sounded like the weeping of a thousand exiled angels but its power was like that of a god. While it held sway, the despotism of the rain was unchallenged. The monsoon dominated all; contemptuous of even the mightiest of man's war making machines, it mocked with wet disdain our puny attempts to press the offensive.

The ordeal of us artillerymen was hardly more than an inconvenience, though, compared to that of the miserable grunts. Shame often struck me in mid-sentence as I complained about the distressing conditions under which we lived. I would think of the poor rifleman making his bed each night in a mattress of mud. But then my pity would be swept away by profanity-provoking thoughts of the lucky leg engineers, like Lt. Carrot-head in Quinhon, sleeping in tents with wood floors and even a generator to provide the poker players with light. And I am sure that those engineers harbored similar envy toward the REMFs (rear echelon mother fuckers) who pounded typewriters in Saigon and lived in barracks or even hotels with running water, real beds with real pillows, and gook maids to clean their rooms, starch their fatigues, and often warm their racks.

But the resentment wouldn't stop with the Saigon warriors. They undoubtedly felt bitter about the middle class college deferees whom they imagined to be freaking out on acid trips, plunging into wild orgies and burning draft cards. There was certainly a class system of misery in Vietnam, and my comrades and I felt not too far removed from the muddy beggars at the bottom. Although I had no great affinity for mud, I had no real desire to join the khakied aristocracy at the top either. With my mania for the glory carried on the back of every infantryman, I would not be satisfied until I was with those deep in the muck.

No one had the decency to call a halt to operations. A helicopter-borne artillery was still several months in the future for us, and no vehicle existed which could navigate the morass. But that is not to say it wasn't attempted! My memory of that first monsoon is largely one of swallowing globs of mud from the spinning tires of marooned trucks as I added my weight to the efforts of others attempting to free them. All our grunting and groaning failed to make any impression on the impassable barrier which the monsoon had erected. For weeks there was almost no reprieve.

To compound the misery of the monsoon was my first of several bouts with diarrhea. Eventually both the rain and the shit stopped pouring, and the world looked a little better from my foxhole and slit trench perspective. The combination of the two had been more than I sometimes thought I could bear.

Gradually the weather cleared enough to allow the brigade to schedule more jumps. The gray skies around Quinhon were soon dotted with white nylon mushrooms under which oscillated the paratroopers of the 101st. The jump was routine for me this time, if any parachute jump can be called routine. A blissful feeling followed the mad moment of the prop (or in this case, rotary) blast. After the gut-grinding terror of the minutes leading up to the jump, the descent earthward held for me a keen sensation of freedom and invincibility, even though I was strapped to a harness which for seconds held the power of life and death. Jumpers were supposed to remain silent in the air, but I could never restrain myself from letting loose with a little shout of conquest, releasing the voice of a spirit freed with this canopied dare to the laws of gravity.

The rapture lasted only seconds, however, for the approaching drop zone demanded preparation for contact with the often inhospitable earth. After a quick check to avoid landing atop another paratrooper or into the branches of a tree, the final second came when the tenseness was forced from legs to be telegraphed in tightening knots up into a man's guts. Then came the thump of impact, the silk panels settling lazily to the ground, the tumbling into a backwards somersault or the plopping on knees or flopping down on the ass; but rarely the execution of a real parachute landing fall taught in jump school at Fort Benning, Georgia.

While the jump was an almost perfect reparation for the harrowing events of my last leap, misfortune seemed to plague many of my fellow jumpers. Several chutes popped open into the bra cup-shaped Mae Wests (a malfunction occurring when one or more panels of the parachute are blown inward through the suspension lines to pop open on the opposite side, thus creating two smaller canopies resembling a king-sized bra, and bringing on an often bone-cracking rate of descent twice that of a normal canopy). All six members of one heliborne stick of jumpers were blown by a sudden gust of wind several klicks beyond the heavily secured drop zone to plop into the far less friendly hills. Our platoon leader came crashing smack into a very unyielding tree. Too panic-stricken to attempt a slip to the right or left (executed by raising up in the parachute harness and pulling down on either one or two of the four risers that connect the harness to the chute's suspension lines, thus forming the canopy into a sail which the wind will push along in the desired direction), our stalwart leader molded his face into the tree trunk with a jarring collision that echoed across the DZ. The acrobatic feat of the day was accomplished by a trooper who made a perfect landing astride the back of a water buffalo.

Our South Korean allies began arriving in the last week of October. A brigade of the elite Capital (Tiger) Division came ashore at Quinhon from the same ancient hulk, the *General Leroy Eltinge*, from which we had landed only three months before. Compared to the puny looking ARVN (Army of the Republic of Vietnam) soldiers, these cocky Koreans seemed like real soldiers. They too were members of one of their country's special fighting units, wearing the colorful shoulder patch of a fierce looking tiger and practicing the Korean martial art of tae kwon do. The South Koreans lived under a harsh code of discipline. When one soldier failed to properly execute his duty, all those along his chain of command suffered. According to the scuttlebutt we heard, the Tigers would form a line consisting of all members of the offender's chain of command from battalion commander on down. The battalion CO would initiate the proceedings by smashing either his fist or his commander's baton against the upraised chin of the company commander. The wobbly company CO would perform an about-face and avenge himself against the platoon leader. The platoon leader then had his chance to swing at the grim jaw of his sergeant standing at rigid attention, and so on down the ranks until the guilty private at the bottom absorbed the final blow.

The fighting qualities of the Capital Division were soon to be demonstrated with a professionalism that aroused the envy of American commanders. After a few months of active campaigning in Vietnam, the Tigers were generally acknowledged as the finest warriors in country. The kill ratio of enemy KIAs (killed-in-action) to friendly KIAs for the South Korean division was a phenomenal 16:1. However, one small detail concerning this fantastic kill ratio was often overlooked. The South Koreans waged war with a savage totality. The ROKs rarely bothered to take prisoners. When an area was swept, it was often literally swept clean of all life and property. Gender and age were rarely safeguards against the pitiless columns of our allies. On one occasion, an entire village in our AO was razed and most of its inhabitants summarily executed as punishment for allowing snipers to fire on a South Korean company from concealed positions within the ville. The body count thus was often inflated by the Korean policy of counting all Vietnamese killed by their forces as enemy soldiers (something practiced by U.S. units as well, but usually on a much smaller scale).

When the countryside had dried sufficiently to allow us movement, the battalion headquarters shifted camp several miles northwest. Situated near the entrance to G.I.–dubbed Sniper Valley, the new location was overlooked by pagoda-capped hills and a fifteen-foot-high white stone image of a brooding Buddha. Very little excitement transpired at this position for the first several days. But then an event did occur which seemed almost a landmark in my life. Someone other than my allies finally took the time and trouble to shoot directly at me. A great weight was lifted from my mind. I had been nagged by the dreadful thought that I would have to return home and admit the shame of never hearing the crack of a bullet rocket past my ear; at least not that of an enemy fired bullet.

My supreme moment came as I was sitting on the sandbags of my guard post, situated to the rear of a former Buddhist monks' dormitory that now housed battalion HQ. Munching on a bag of sunflower seeds sent in a "Care Package" from home and reading a paperback, I was about as alert as a stone. Suddenly a steel-tipped whip cracked the air above my head and flailed chunks of stucco from the building to my rear. Several sunflower seeds later, it occurred to me that I had been fired upon, or at least had been in the path of a bullet intended for the open window of battalion commander Col. Braun's office. The bullet's echo had hardly died before a yelping bunch of baboons in olive drab, led by the sergeant-major, tumbled out of the mission and stumbled up the incline where my sentry box sat. Valiantly, the sergeant-major ordered me to accompany an FDC sergeant to scout a sandy knoll some thirty meters from my post while he heroically covered our rear. We stormed up the hill, John Wayne style, snooped around, and discovered nothing, which was fortunate for my well being considering the fact that I had absent-mindedly rushed to battle without an ammo magazine in my M-16 or a single round in the weapon's chamber! My first moment of glory might well have been embarrassingly fatal had Charlie lingered behind.

Rattled by a rash of accidental discharges of weapons within the battalion, Col. Braun had ordered that all ammo magazines must be removed from weapons, even those of the men on guard duty, and not inserted until fired upon. The colonel thought we were a greater danger to ourselves than were the V.C.

The only other combat around Quinhon for us was the ambush of our arty truck convoy one day by the "Mad Mama-san." The crazy old woman had earned her reputation by staging repeated hit-and-run attacks on practically every vehicle that attempted to negotiate the dirt road from our camp to Highway 1. The convoy I rode in was one victim of her delirious fury.

The ambush occurred as the lead truck in the column was about to turn onto the highway. The convoy ground to a halt as a maniacal disturbance broke out at the head of the line of stalled vehicles. Word was passed back that the battery was under attack by the Mad Mama-san. After four troopers were unable to tame the convulsive female without lighting her up, the order was given to proceed past the mama-san, even if it meant running her over. As we roared past I caught a glimpse of this woman who had dared do battle with a U.S. artillery battery. Fiercely swinging a splintered straw broom, the ancient shrew was completely nude except for a filthy burlap sack wrapped around her head. Her face was a ruin of wrinkles and a brilliant orange mouth displayed the rotted remains of teeth and gums that had chewed too much betel nut.

Our driver gunned the truck past the screeching tigress, saving us from her flailing broom. But several G.I.s in other trucks were less fortunate, as steel pots went flying. We never learned what became of her, but I couldn't help wondering if the less tolerant ROKs hadn't secured an immediate end to her depredations once she turned her broomstick on them.

Casualties were comparatively light within the brigade during the soggy operations in the Quinhon AO. Although the grim production line in this bloody factory did slow, it never entirely ceased operation. Some men did die and what was particularly hard to take was that some of the dead fell victim to friendly fire. Six troopers from a squad of the 2/327th Infantry, including two cherries (replacements) who had just arrived in country two weeks before, were killed by a short round from one of Alpha Battery's guns.

Sometimes it seemed as though Charlie was unnecessary; that Lt. Colonel Braun was right, that we were a bigger danger to ourselves than to the enemy. Given enough time we would kill ourselves without Charlie having to squeeze a single trigger.

Chapter VI

Phan Rang

By mid–November the 101st's primary mission of securing the Quinhon area for landing and deployment of the Tiger Division was complete. The brigade now prepared for movement, again largely by LST, to the small port city of Phan Rang, about sixty kilometers south of Cam Ranh Bay. The new objective was to become the permanent base camp of the 1st Brigade.

We came ashore at our new home on November 11. At Phan Rang the airborne eagle was to construct its eyrie, a home for its chicks ... the cherry replacements arriving from stateside. It was to become a home which few of the men of the brigade would see much of after they had joined the 101st in the bush ... not until they had survived long enough to earn the distinction of being a short timer with only a few days remaining in the war and in the country. The 1st Brigade remained at Phan Rang for less than three weeks that first time, all of which were spent clearing and constructing. Then once more we were dispatched to the endless hunt. The entire brigade was to return to base camp for only two brief breathers from December 1965 through the spring of 1967. No other brigade-sized unit serving in Vietnam could claim so much time in the bush.

Phan Rang seemed even more desolate than Cam Ranh Bay. With so much jungle to pick from, the brass had found a desert on which the men of the 101st were to build their base. Red dust blanketed everything, quickly covering tents and creeping into men's eyes and mouths as it was carried by an always brisk and searing wind. After a few days in this desolation, we almost longed for the claustrophobic jungles.

Naturally, along with our base-constructing duties we were also to man a sandbag OP. For those who escaped a night of listening to the taunts of the Fuck-You Lizards, there were poker and blackjack games, the nightly flick at an open-air theater, and an EM (enlisted men's) club serving beer for a quarter and soda pop for a dime a can under the shelter of a hex tent.

Other than letters from home the only contacts with the world outside our bleak encampment were the *Stars and Stripes* newspaper and the few transistor radios scattered through the battery. The most popular radio broadcast was that of Hanoi Hannah and her gleeful predictions of American annihilation. Hannah was North Vietnam's version of Tokyo Rose and Axis Sally. Her musical selections included American golden oldies, Marxist marches and Vietnamese anthems. Hannah's approach to wrecking our morale was through an appeal to the G.I.s' conscience. She harangued us on American atrocities, on the imperialist designs of a Wall Street–dominated government. She pleaded compassion for a valiant Vietnamese people waging war against capitalist exploitation. She stressed the social, economic and racial divisions within American society. The black soldier, who made up a disproportionately large share of U.S. combat forces in 'Nam at that time, was often her prime target.

In a soft but penetrating voice, Ho Chi Minh's sweetheart would scold the black G.I. "Why do you fight us? Why do you kill us? Are you still little better than chained slaves to your white masters? Do you still jump and meekly say 'Yes Masser' when a fat white politician hands you a rifle and orders 'Here, Boy, go kill those commie gooks to protect us white folks' freedom!'? Don't you realize that you are killing a people who you should treat as allies; a people who are fighting, just as your soul brothers in Watts fought, to be free of the white man's imperialist yoke? Are you to betray your brothers who died in Watts by serving the evil interests of the white capitalists?

"You have guns. Turn them on the real enemy; the enemy who attempts to crush freedom from the hearts of 'Niggers' and 'Gooks' alike. How can you kill Vietnamese patriots who have never harmed you or your loved ones, while the blue-uniformed white Gestapo and their KKK allies murder your brothers and defile your sisters. Black soldiers! Join your yellow brothers in the anti-imperialist crusade against white American aggression!"

Hannah won few converts among either black or white G.I.s. But she did amuse us with outlandish claims of total victory over the decadent capitalist armies. Among Hannah's broadcast triumphs was the annihilation of the 1st Brigade in two separate battles within a six-month period. One time we were "exterminated" was during a brief stay at our base camp in an area nearly devoid of enemy activity. These bombastic claims made us incredulous of Hanoi Hannah's newscasts and made it easier to reject her editorial comments on American society. We were, after all, largely the patriotic sons of working class fathers, mostly volunteers, engaged in a conflict that had escalated to a ground combat war for America only eight months ago. Later on Hannah's broadcasts must have reached far more receptive ears among the many bitterly anti-war draftees and Afroed black militants for whom the war was such an abomination.

Hanoi's brainwashing broadcaster delighted in pouring salt into the raw wounds of the American social scene, and one of her favorite sore spots was the Watts riot of August 1965. Labeling the six days of looting, arson and anarchy as a genuine people's insurrection, she tried with little success to sow racial dissension within the American ranks. Regardless of the chasms separating the races in America, the white and black G.I.s who shared a common bond of suffering were forced into a brotherhood of the beggar. Within the rear echelon and support units there did exist a de facto segregation during off-duty hours. In Saigon a multi-block area of bars and brothels along Tu Do Street became exclusively patronized by black G.I.s and was known as "Soul City." But for the boony trooper, living for eleven of his twelve months of 'Nam duty in the green jungles, there was no separation of the races. The only color that mattered was olive drab.

There were few references to "Niggers" or "Honkies" within the platoons trudging a trail of sweat along the jungle paths. There were no segregated restaurants or housing; everyone ate out of a C-ration can and slept under a leaky poncho. There was no job discrimination; all were employed in the same dirty, dangerous occupation with the worst working conditions in the world.

The color of a man's skin was of little significance under the indiscriminating clatter of a machine gun or the unbiased whine of mortar shrapnel. The sun, rain, insects and terrain left men with neither the time nor energy for hating the guy who shared the task of hauling an M-60 machine gun up and down the mountains of Vietnam.

Hannah also emphasized our largely working class origins. Wielding the scimitar of class conflict, this Aimee Semple MacPherson of revolutionary evangelism would preach the perfidy of capitalist class exploitation by pointing out that we proletarian sons were forced to carry guns while the sons of the bourgeoisie carried briefcases. Her claim carried the weight of truth. The men with whom I shared the Vietnam War were overwhelmingly the sons of steel-workers, truck drivers, mechanics, small farmers and sharecroppers, men from small towns and rural routes in the South and Midwest or from big city ghettos. From my small home town of Plainville, Kansas, all but two of a dozen high school buddies would eventually serve in Vietnam and all were of working class families, while I knew of no middle class sons of the town's businessmen, lawyers, doctors or big ranchers from my high school graduating class of 1964 who experienced the testing, trying time in the 'Nam.

But while Hannah's hymns of class warfare deepened our antipathy toward the "common enemy — the bourgeoisie," they also intensified our hostility toward the other army of young soldiers the Vietnam War had recruited

... those soldiers for peace who brandished flowers instead of firearms; whose uniforms were long hair and Levi's, with the circled spaceship of peace as their medal and the flash of a two-fingered V their salute. They did not face the machine guns and mortars of black-pajama-clad communists, but the clubs and tear gas of blue-coated cops and the darkening of a nation's spirit.

Though the marching mobilizations for peace were shouting for our immediate return home — something most G.I.s desired, except for the few of us whose vision was obscured by the glory dust stinging our eyes and whose hearts were hardened by the poisoned blood of machismo coursing through our veins — the anti-war demonstrators were usually condemned by the objects of their concern as reinforcements for the enemy. To many of us, the peace phalanx parading American streets represented only the spoiled, gutless middle class kids who cowered in college classrooms to escape the battlefield and campaigned to discredit whatever honor and prestige we might earn through courage and sacrifice in battle. The peaceniks might not be attacking the integrity of the American soldier directly (that would come later with My Lai and taunts of "Baby Killer! " hurled at returning vets), but they were prose-lytizing against the war as a contemptible and dishonorable venture, and we offspring of this conflict therefore felt we too were being held in low regard.

Few of us felt any loyalty to this war, but we did possess a deep loyalty and kinship to each other and to our units. We were like sons with little love left for a cruel mother, but nonetheless determined to defend her name and honor against all slurs. Were we to allow the finger of shame to be pointed at her, we would also be accepting that shame.

We often reacted bitterly against the advocates of peace, often our middle class schoolmates who had packed their sport coats and blue jeans and left for rooms in dorms and Greek houses after high school graduation, while we stuffed duffel bags at Army reception centers with fatigues and khakis and were marched off to boot camp barracks. They let their hair grow long and their minds expand to more liberal horizons; we had our skulls shaved to an Army burr and our intellects lobotomized of all but trained responses to the military's concepts of duty, honor and country. During the time they were studying Freud and Joyce and Rousseau and Marx, we were learning how to most effectively garrote an enemy soldier, how to disembowel a man with a bayonet, how to place a pattern of 7.62 mm bullets into the heart of another human being. Our middle class schoolmates turned first against the war and then against their middle class culture, facing their parents from across the canyon of a generation gap; we found ourselves alienated from those elders who took pride in our defense of the democracy of their American Legion and Fourth of July speeches — while we took pride only in one another's courage and in the collective courage of our platoon, battalion or division — and from those student radicals of our own generation, from whom we were separated by a class gap, a philosophical gap, and a gap of 6,000 miles and 365 days.

A favorite tactic of Hanoi's disc jockey was to demonstrate the American public's disapproval of the war by broadcasting tape recordings of student peace demonstrations. But Hannah's admonitions were usually received by her G.I. audience with only jeers. It required extra effort to be a dove in Vietnam, where the enemy was real and the bullets he fired carried greater impact than an olive branch. Faced with the possibility of killing or dying for Vietnam, we were unwilling to accept the label of aggressors of an imperialistic government. (This was to be the first war in which substantial numbers of American soldiers openly opposed the conflict. But that was to come later, after the 1968 Tet Offensive shut out the light at the end of the tunnel.) In 1965 and 1966 most U.S. soldiers were as patriotic as our fathers in the "Big One." The nationalism we bore like a birthmark was not that of super patriots; we had been born and raised with it, like others with their religion. We did not evangelize for it, felt no crusading fervor about it, but neither did we have any reason to question it. We went to Vietnam in 1965 with a fundamental faith in America's righteousness. Within a few years that faith would become more difficult to sustain, but in 1965 it was part of our identity, not yet really subject to doubt.

Though we had time to tune in to Hannah, the men in other units were not so inactive. While the paratroopers of the 101st were building a home in the wilderness, the air cavalrymen of the 1st Cavalry Division were engaged in the Ia Drang Valley in the first major clash with North Vietnamese Army regiments. At Landing Zone X-ray and LZ Albany — where a battalion of the 7th Cavalry Regiment nearly met the same fate as it did under Custer on the Little Bighorn — the air cavalrymen lost in one bloody week in November nearly 300 killed and over 500 wounded (only the Battle of Dak To in November 1967 would claim more American casualties in the Vietnam War). By body count the North Vietnamese suffered more than 1,500 killed.

American commanders, determined to fight a conventional World War II–style war in Vietnam regardless of the guerrilla tradition of the French Indochina War and all the lip service paid to "counter-insurgency operations," had won their first big set piece battle, prevailing largely because of vastly superior firepower and heliborne mobility. Periodically, the North Vietnamese would offer the American generals their much desired conventional battle and would usually suffer much heavier losses. Ironically, the North Vietnamese, with their full mobilization and united home front, could more easily afford these higher casualties than could the mammoth enemy with ten times their population. The U.S. Army, a huge but cumbersome creature, with its million-man tail and its weak bite of but sixteen combat divisions, had difficulty replacing its losses. Along with the strange insistence on fighting a war with an army claiming more bureaucrats than boony rats, and the government's reluctance to mobilize the reserves for fear of increasing the unpopularity of an already unpopular war, the Army was further weakened by its policy of annually molting itself of its trained, hardened combat veterans.

Though naturally popular with the men who knew their ordeal would last only 365 days, this rotation policy presented the Army with a major replacement problem and meant that even in units with low casualty rates there was always an average of at least one-third of the outfit's men who were cherries. It was even questionable in the long run whether the policy had a positive effect on the G.I.s' morale. It did prevent men from despairing that death or injury alone would liberate them from the 'Nam, but it also meant that men were more concerned with surviving their year in country than with defeating the enemy. More importantly, it lessened the special bonds of loyalty and comradeship that arise between men in war and that are a necessity in forging good soldiers and good armies. Particularly in the last few months before rotation, the strong need to retain the respect of a man's comrades assumed less importance than simply staying alive, even if this meant losing a hard-earned reputation for dependability in and out of battle. When a man owns nothing but the respect of his bush buddies, he is willing to risk his life to hold onto his friends' and his own good opinion of himself. With the incentive of rotation, the instinct for survival overwhelms the need for the esteem of one's comrades-in-arms.

The rotation policy was instituted, I suppose, by Pentagon planners who assumed that no more than two or three years would be required to defeat a weak enemy. It would also insure that a greater number of career men would receive combat experience and a shot at earning the medals and campaign stars that were a prerequisite for speedy promotions. But as the war dragged on year after year, the policy became increasingly self-defeating. Some form of rotation was certainly necessary, for it would have been inhuman and destructive of morale to subject men to an endless purgatory in Vietnam. But it would have been better to rotate brigades and divisions in and out of Vietnam, or at least in and out of a direct combat role, instead of leaving a unit's flag in country while replacing all its personnel. That way, a soldier's sense of continuity and pride in his unit and comrades would be strengthened and sustained. World War II was fought and won with such a policy, and as a result the average number of weeks that G.I.s actually experienced combat in the Second World War was fewer than that experienced by American soldiers in their one-year combat tours in Vietnam. The rotation of units instead of individuals would also have lessened the amount of time spent in training. (It was not unusual for a division's best NCOs to be back in the rear area base camps training newly arrived cherries rather than out in the bush with the battalions.)

The men of the 101st heaved themselves into the steel bellies of C-130 Hercules transports on the morning of November 30 to be flown to III Corps Tactical Zone, the provinces surrounding Saigon, where they were to take part in a search-and-destroy operation around Lai Khe and Ben Cat. I too boarded a troop carrier that morning, but my destination was different. I was scheduled for five days of R&R (rest and recreation — translation: Thai Whiskey and Siamese whores) in Bangkok, Thailand, but managed to stretch the five to fifteen in the Thai capital and in Saigon by taking advantage of the nonavailability of return flights to Phan Rang. I beat the brigade back to base by only a few days, officially AWOL and with a case of the clap.

Operation Checkmate, carried out in coalition with the 1st Infantry Division, the 173rd Airborne Brigade, and the Royal Australian Regiment, netted the 101st its most disappointing results thus far: only six V.C. killed by body count versus seven paratrooper KIAs. The only "highlight" of the operation was the deployment of Hatchet patrols by the 2/502nd's CO, Lt. Col. Henry "Gunfighter" Emerson. Inspired by the mutilation of a fallen Five O'Deuce trooper by insurgent soldiers, Emerson equipped each patrol member with a hatchet and offered the incentive of a case of beer and a three-day pass to Saigon to any man who would bring back from the hunt the trophy of a Charlie's head. Pickings were sparse, however, but finally Emerson's reward was earned by a young trooper who happened to stumble over a dead enemy soldier. The Viet Cong extracted quick revenge for this decapitation by ambushing a six-man patrol of 2/502nd headhunters. Three Strike Force troopers died before they had a chance to use their shiny new hatchets, and two of the survivors were wounded.

My own battalion, the 2/320th Artillery, saw even less action; the only violent incident occurring when several command-detonated mines exploded under the vehicles of an arty motor convoy, wounding a lieutenant and three cannoneers from Charlie Battery. On the whole, the operation had been less dangerous than the wild rides I had risked in the traffic of Saigon with a lunatic cab driver at the wheel, while stretching out my R&R.

Christmas Day was hardly a joyful occasion, even though the brigade was in base camp and temporarily removed from the war. I spent half the day watching the lizards scurrying in and around the sandbags of my platoon's bunker, and then was relieved to take part in the third police call of the battery area that morning. The word had been sent down that General William Westmoreland had helicoptered out from his Pentagon East headquarters at Tan Son Nhut Airfield outside Saigon, intending to overfly the brigade camp and honor us with Christmas cheers through a loudspeaker aboard the chopper. Naturally, the 101st, Westmoreland's pet unit, which he had commanded at one time, would have to appear spic-and-span. We were still busily picking up bits of trash and cigarette butts when the MACV (Military Assistance Command, Vietnam) commander buzzed overhead and wished us Merry Christmas. It may not have been so merry, but it certainly would have been less of a hassle if the four-star general and his Christmas greetings had remained in Saigon.

My best Christmas present came two days later, when I was one of the lucky sixteen privates and Spec 4s chosen by the battery to attend the Bob Hope Christmas Show at Cam Ranh Bay. The show was worth the fifty-klick, kidney-crushing ride. We joined a G.I. audience of 10,000 laughing at Hope's jokes and whistling and leering at Miss U.S.A., Carroll Baker and Joey Heatherton.

Rather than risk a night ambush along Highway 1, we stopped on the return trip at dusk to bed down in a Special Forces compound at nearby Dunba Tin. I was surprised at the relative comfort offered by the "Sneaky Petes" post. On this and subsequent visits to Special Forces camps, I was to discover that while a Green Beret outpost was no Versailles in the wilderness, neither was it the always perilous hellhole the American public imagined. Often they had nightly movies, a plentiful supply of cold beer, and hot meals cooked and served by a Vietnamese staff that also included housekeepers and laundry service, as well as electric lights and hot showers. In later years many base camps of the combat divisions were provided with such luxuries and more, like pizza parlors, swimming pools and miniature golf courses; even then, some support and logistical bases could boast of these things. But in 1965 and 1966 the men of the 101st and other combat units lived without frills and fancies.

Many of us felt that the Green Berets were overrated. Though their camps were frequently the target of enemy harassment and attack, such as at Plei Mei and A Shau, and despite the fact that the Sneaky Petes did lead Vietnamese Ruff-Puff patrols into Charlie's domain, the men of the Special Forces rarely underwent as much combat as the line infantrymen. To us, those who wore the green beret, yellow sword and lightning patch of the 5th Special Forces — the only group fighting in Vietnam which was celebrated by the American media and public at a time when it was still possible to stir hero worship for soldiers trapped in the Vietnam miasma — were not heroes but media stars of this Southeast Asian war epic. The Vietnam War's real heroes were, as in all other wars of all other ages, the haggard, overburdened foot soldiers, the Eleven Bravos, the brothers of the bush — not the Green Berets, regardless of John Wayne's, Sgt. Barry Sadler's and Robin Moore's efforts to prove otherwise.

After Christmas, replacements began to fill our ranks with new faces. Much of the "new meat" replenishing our numbers suffered a double dose of the usual harassment meted out to cherries, because they wore the double AA "All American" blue and red patch of the rival 82nd Airborne Division on their right shoulders, denoting combat duty with that division. Except for a few senior NCOs, the combat these nineteen and twenty-year-olds had seen was obviously not that of Salerno or Normandy, but of what we in the 101st had derisively termed the 82nd's divisional R&R in Santo Domingo in the spring of 1965. Though nearly a score of the 82nd's paratroopers had died in the Lyndon Baines Johnson corollary to the Monroe Doctrine, many men of the 101st looked with scorn on the 82nd's "little war."

This disdainful attitude was furthered by self-incriminating tales from the replacements: of the first Purple Heart of the campaign being awarded to a man who suffered a broken ankle when a mechanical mule rolled over his foot after breaking loose from its moorings during the unloading of a C-130 at San Isidro Airbase outside Santo Domingo; of the lieutenant who won the Silver Star just for crossing a street under sniper fire. These were typical stories of men earning medals I held to be almost sacred and desired with all my soul to have. I was appalled at this sacrilege. Later I learned that the 82nd held no monopoly over the practice of distributing medals on an almost assembly line basis.

New Year's Eve was cause for a more spirited celebration than our dreary Christmas, for it marked the beginning of a new year that would before halfway through find most of us removed from the war. When the clock struck 12:00 midnight, the howitzers of Charlie Battery announced the onset of the new year by blasting sixty-six illumination shells into the violet sky. The thundering howitzers were joined in their salute to the opening of a new Cong killing season by a celebration of tracer-spitting machine guns and automatic rifles, bursting fragmentation and white phosphorous grenades, and back-lashing recoilless rifles. The entire perimeter of the brigade camp was lit up with the yellow and red lightning of Ares exploding.

There was but one small gap of undisturbed blackness in the otherwise unbroken ring of military fireworks ... the stretch of perimeter facing HQ Battery, 2/320th Artillery. Anticipating the pyrotechnics, the sergeant-major had whined orders in his virago's voice for the battery to hold its fire. And so we held back from joining in for the first few minutes, our weapons silent but our mouths machine gunning profane bullets at the termagant terror with the sergeant-major stripes who had spoiled our fun. As the new year grew minutes older and the fireworks continued unabated, our collective voice growling for action, our theodolite operator finally grabbed the field phone at our OP to urge the adjacent bunker to join him in setting the sky on fire. Halfway through his gunpowder advocacy, the voice of El Cid interrupted.

"Just one of you shitheads touch a machine gun tonight like you was even thinkin' of firing it ... and I'll court-martial every swinging dick of you in the morning!"

HQ Battery's bunkers remained chastely silent.

But the battery EMs gained a measure of revenge on our battalion sergeant-major when, a few nights later, a band of night raiders sneaked stealthily up to his tent and tossed a CS gas grenade under his overburdened cot. Coughing and gagging, the sergeant-major barreled out of the asphyxiating tent and charged wildly in his underwear to the first pig's tent to demand that the culprits be apprehended and punished severely. Although El Cid conducted a vigorous investigation, the mad bombers were never brought to justice.

The sergeant-major's suffering was quite mild though, compared to what similarly detested lifers would experience in later years of the war in an army which would drastically change. In 1966 the sergeant-major was the victim of a non-lethal gas grenade; in 1970 he was more likely to have been "fragged"—blown to pieces in his sleep with a fragmentation hand grenade.

The first two weeks of 1966 brought little but monotonous labor as the slow, grimy process of building a base camp continued in full swing after the interruption of the Ben Cat campaign. Our leaders seemed intent on making Phan Rang a wilderness copy of Fort Campbell, with all the petty spit-and-polish garrison games played stateside. The old routine of spit-shined boots and polished brass, formations and police calls, and all the other Mickey Mouse harassment of Army garrison duty was reimposed. We were soon longing for the boondocks, where we may have been beset by filth, fatigue and fear, but where we were at least removed from most of the Army's special brand of bullshit.

Chapter VII
Tuy Hoa

The daily doldrums and nightly poker games were finally terminated by the brigade's departure from Phan Rang to the coastal city of Tuy Hoa, located on the South China Sea between Nhatrang and Quinhon. Rumors had abounded soon after Christmas of a forthcoming operation. Several AOs had been mentioned along the G.I. grapevine, including the Marines' I ("Eye") Corps and the DMZ, the teeming, watery Mekong Delta, and a return trip to Quinhon — although no one had ever mentioned or even heard of Tuy Hoa. But none who served in the 1st Brigade of the 101st in 1966 would ever forget Tuy Hoa. There, in the mountains and paddies surrounding the city, men of the 101st would fight and die for eleven of the twelve months of the year. Though sections of the brigade would be hurled into other rugged corners of the country during the year, there would always be at least one battalion of Screaming Eagles fighting in this rice-rich province.

On the morning of January 16, after a stormy, seasick passage aboard another gray LST veteran of World War II island-hopping campaigns, we caught our first view of a patch of Vietnam that was to become the last place on earth for many of our men. The primary mission assigned to the infantry battalions during the first phase of Operation Van Buren was to protect the rice harvesters from the foraging parties of Viet Cong who annually collected nearly half the harvested rice. The Viet Cong and their North Vietnamese allies depended on the rice paddies of Phu Yen Province to feed many of their troops in the II Corps area, and it was this enemy harvest that the 101st, in conjunction with the 2nd "Blue Dragon" South Korean Marine Brigade, was ordered to prevent.

HQ Battery was encamped along with the brigade headquarters on the sand dunes fringing a PSP airstrip known as North Field. In a few months construction would begin on a new 10,000 foot jet airfield at an old French-built concrete runway called South Field. The long trip from South Field to North Field involved a slow passage through sand dunes to the craters of

Highway 1 and thence across the 1,000 meters of a thirty-year-old rail and motor bridge, one of the longest in the country. Between the two airstrips sprawled the city of Tuy Hoa, with a population of about 30,000.

From the sandy mounds of our North Field camp, we overlooked a sweeping assortment of shimmering green rice paddies, criss-crossed by a waffle-shaped pattern of mud dikes, culminating against the abrupt ascension of jungle-attired mountains. Our stadium provided a spectacular view of the daily aerial bombardments on the mountainous screen by flights of F-4D Phantoms, A-4E Skyhawks, and the steeply diving, propeller-driven Skyraiders. The unblemished green faces of the mountainsides soon wore the scorches and scars from canisters of napalm, high explosive bombs, and white phosphorous rockets.

Some of the brigade's first casualties of the campaign were suffered at North Field before the operation even began. A perimeter patrol of infantrymen had just returned to the base, when one of the boony rats stumbled and fell as he was hopping down from the truck. His M-16, carelessly flipped off safety, chambered with a round, and set on full automatic fire, went off as he fell. A soldier from Troop A, 2/17th Cavalry was killed and a half dozen others wounded because of one clumsy trooper.

An erupting opera of fire and light awakened our camp at midnight on the first day of Tet, the Vietnamese New Year. The ARVN and Popular Force soldiers in the Tuy Hoa area were splitting the night sky with every weapon at their disposal in a symbolic battle to drive the evil spirits of the old year away from the innocent year just born. The Vietnamese missiles and projectiles were launched directly overhead in what looked like an effort to blast the stars from their cosmic anchorages. It was all very grand and colorful, but unfortunately the streaking shells obeyed one of the major laws of nature ... that what goes up must eventually come down. The tracer bullets and artillery shrapnel, fired in festive spirit but potentially fatal upon collision with human flesh, fell directly on the 101st's North Field headquarters. Ironically, the men of HQ Battery came under the heaviest fire we had experienced in Vietnam so far — from the celebrating weapons of our Vietnamese allies. Spent bullets and the jagged sleet of shrapnel plummeted into the sand around our tents and ripped their walls. The supply sergeant's tent was shredded by descending metal, which cut viciously into his arm. Almost miraculously, he was the battery's only casualty of the hot rain of fireworks as we scampered to the foxholes we had scooped out of the sand dunes.

As in the outpost scare at An Khe, the first sergeant's armored exterior showed definite signs of cracking along the fault lines of crisis. Panic crept into his usually gruffly confident voice and his brown, granite-like features paled to a face of ice as he bunched his men into the sandy holes, which offered little shelter from the high trajectory descent of the Tet fireworks. I began to wonder if "El Cid" was an appropriate title to hang around the man's neck and to realize that courage should not be arbitrarily assigned to a man because of his pose or posture.

The noisy festivities continued at a slower pace through the morning and on through the three-day holiday. Five men were wounded around brigade HQ during Tet, but it was suspected by many that not all these casualties were inflicted by the stray bullets of intoxicated Tet revelers. It was speculated that enterprising enemy snipers took advantage of all the noise and nonsense to slither up to American security posts and take pot shots.

The explosive commemoration of Tet provided almost all the excitement in our first weeks at North Field. But before boredom could become firmly entrenched, Operation Van Buren shifted into high gear. The infantry moved out of their security posts in the green checkerboards of the rice-wealthy lowlands surrounding Tuy Hoa and into the mountainous interior to seek and destroy the Viet Cong. To support the groundpounders' movement into the highlands, the artillery penetrated deeper into the valley. Survey Platoon was attached to the firing batteries for the next three weeks, surveying for the rapidly leapfrogging howitzer batteries during the day and providing perimeter security by night. We splashed through rice paddies, tromped through burned and blasted villages, and climbed over the scorched foothills with our thirty-meter steel tape and T-16 theodolite. The days dissolved into an eternity of constant movement, toil and heat, with air strikes and artillery bombardments our only frames of reference.

Our destructive promenade followed the craters of a road scraped out along the valley canal's edge, now choked with bloated bodies of enemy soldiers, peasants, water buffalo, pigs and other livestock felled by howitzer shells and Skyraider bombs. The swollen, fly-covered corpses floating in the bloody mire or sprawled in contorted postures of sudden, violent death along the muddy embankment were the first enemy dead that most of us had seen after more than six months in Vietnam. We demonstrated little outward revulsion at the sight of those killed, even though they had suffered horrible mutilation, not only from the metal that had slain them, but also from the sun's rays, the decay of the steaming humidity, and the maggot banqueteers feasting on death. The blobs of rotting flesh were, after all, only the enemy's, and soldiers are taught to withhold sympathy for the enemy or squeamishness at the sight of his dead. Regardless of our unfamiliarity with the sight of war's victims, we had, nonetheless, already managed to acquire an immunity of sorts to the human reality of those decomposing figures.

If we were reluctant to show remorse over the corpses of the enemy, we did react with degrees of shock or horror to other scenes of death and maiming. One such sight was the discovery of the bodies of a Vietnamese woman and her baby, clutched firmly to her breast in the havoc of death, lying among several other corpses found in a B Battery position. Even more pitiful was the sight of a blood-spattered Vietnamese mother holding tightly her wailing four-year-old daughter whose left arm had been blown off by a grenade thrown by one of the infantrymen sweeping a burned-out village ahead of our survey party.

Though the gales of combat blew hot and harsh in the infantry's face, only a few members of the artillery came under direct enemy fire during the operation. One rare incident involving the Survey Platoon happened as the First Section attracted sniper fire while they surveyed past one of the many bombed-out hamlets in the valley. Lying low and assuming that a surveyor's duty was to survey and not to undertake heroic charges that might cost him his life, the survey chief radioed to a jeep-mounted patrol of the 2/17th Cavalry for assistance. Then, as the surveyors looked on, the cavalry jeeps surrounded the hamlet and proceeded to rake the ruins with a steel sweep of .50 caliber and M-60 machine gun fire. The cavalrymen then conducted a recon through the ville, torching the few shacks still standing.

Later in the day, Second Section's H.T. Tinker captured two unarmed, undernourished Viet Cong stragglers. While zipping around in his jeep setting up traverse stations for the survey team following behind on foot, Tinker was intercepted by a mob of frantic Vietnamese peasants. The rice farmers claimed they had caught two stray Charlies in the act of stealing their pigs and had chased them into a barn. Tinker gunned his jeep down the road to the barn, from which the two scrawny foragers sprang and started running along the nearby rice paddy dike. Tinker fast-drew his .45 pistol and fired three shots over their heads, inducing them to surrender. The sergeant tied the pair together and then roared back to triumphantly display his conquests to the surveyors. He huffed and puffed for days afterward, his puckered mouth and plump jowls overworked in describing how he had practically single-handedly broken the back of the 95th NVA Regiment with this one incredible act of supreme heroism and unsurpassed audacity ... the capture of two tattered stragglers, unarmed and almost comatose from malnutrition.

The grunts were meeting with some success in their hunt for V.C. game. On the afternoon of February 6 the platoons of Charlie Company, 2/502nd, stumbled into an entrenched hamlet in the village complex of My Canh, manned by the automatic rifle teams of the 5th Battalion of the 95th NVA Regiment. The same men who had leaped from helicopters into the machine gun crossfire at An Ninh in September 1965 found themselves engaged in the fiercest battle the brigade had fought since that bloody tournament in the Central Highlands. Reinforced by a task force from the 1/327th, Charlie Company blasted the enemy from their spider holes and bunkers constructed of thick banyan logs, at one point engaging the soldiers of the 95th Regiment in hand-to-hand combat, a rarity in modern warfare, even in the close-quarters fighting of the Vietnam War. When the North Vietnamese withdrew into the sanctuary of jungle darkness, they left sixty-three of their comrades dead in the tangled brush enclosing My Canh village; the paratrooper victors suffered twenty-six KIAs.

Victories such as My Canh were rare. Mostly, the operation was a slow anabasis through the mountains in search of a slippery phantom who was seldom overtaken by the chasing bloodhound packs of 101st infantrymen. But the columns of crunchies hung doggedly onto their elusive prey's tracks, and when another mountain was crossed which put the foot soldiers out of range of their 105 mm big brothers, the howitzers were thrust forward several more kilometers. With at least one of the three firing batteries rolling forward each day, our two survey parties were constantly on the go. Where boredom had once nagged us, exhaustion now threatened to overwhelm.

Thankfully, on February 21 Operation Van Buren was consigned to the small print of official military histories, and the tired, grimy men of the 1st Brigade returned to their rear area camps to rest and refit for the next hunt. The six-week-long campaign had certainly not administered a crippling blow to the enemy in the Tuy Hoa region. But it had given a bloody nose to the 95th NVA Regiment and set many communist soldiers' stomachs to growling by protecting the rice harvest from the provisioning teams of the enemy's quartermaster corps. The NVA/V.C. body count totaled 348, the highest count of corpses yet by the brigade in a single operation.

On the last day of February the brief "rest" period ended and Operation Harrison began in full swing as the new brigade commander, General Willard Pearson, with body-counting fingers, grasped for more stars to build a constellation on his collar. For this operation we forsook the three-quarter-ton trucks and mutant roads for the immeasurably greater mobility of helicopters and the Vietnam sky. With the 105 mm howitzer slung on a swaying cable underneath and with the nine-man gun crew and the basic gun load of sixty-six rounds of HE, Willie Peter and illumination shells loaded inside the cavernous interior, the "Shithooks" (Chinooks) could move an entire battery several klicks in half an hour.

We in Survey Platoon usually accompanied the battery commander's jeep and the personnel of battery HQ in one of the lead Chinooks so we could jump immediately to our task and complete the survey as soon as possible, hopefully not long after the final sortie had deposited the last gun in place and the crew had laid the piece and started construction of the sandbag parapet that would ring the howitzer. Then, our survey completed and the 105 mm howitzers planted in their diamond- or star-shaped pattern, we would be dragged out to the edge of the bustling LZ to dig an OP hole.

Small poncho hooches were raised to protect us from the sun and night-time showers, but they had to be reconstructed several times daily as resupply Chinooks descended to whip up winds that scooped up clouds of dust, piles of brush, poncho liners and anything else that was not firmly anchored to the ground. Then, with all the sandbags filled and holes dug, we would likely repeat the whole process the next day in a different clearing on a different mountainside. We moved three times during the first three days of Operation Harrison. Then the pace slackened as Charlie Battery, to which we were attached, settled for a few days near a dirt airstrip outside the seaside MACV compound at Tuy An, north of Tuy Hoa.

The infantry, too, employed new techniques in their deadly art. One was the deployment of camouflage-coated, long-range reconnaissance patrols (LRRPs, pronounced "Lurps") and special recon and quick reaction platoons from each of the three line battalions: the Recondos of the Five O' Deuce; the Hawk Platoon of the 2/327th; and the Tiger Force from the 1/327th. Much more extensive use of night ambushes and patrols was also undertaken during the operation, and the 2/502nd conducted history's first battalion night heliborne assault. In the operation's one major contest, the 1/327th mauled a battalion of the NVA 95th Regiment in a chance engagement near the village of My Phu. The battle results were good enough to start our brigade commander salivating. While absorbing only light casualties, the men of the "Above the Rest" Battalion killed 118 communist regulars according to the body count.

On March 5 the 2/320th was choppered to a rendezvous point on Highway 1, where the battalion's vehicles were assembled. Hitching the gun trails to the three-quarter-tons, the firing batteries once again bounced over the horrid roads of Tuy Hoa valley, traveling the same terrain we had assumed to be cleansed of the foe by Operation Van Buren. To the subjective mind of the combat crunchie and cannon cocker, executing with his legs, sweat, and often his life, the grand designs of the search-and-destroy strategy, it seemed by the constant crossing and recrossing of the same mountains and jungles that we were getting nowhere fast and accomplishing nothing other than slaying a few unlucky representatives of an infinite race of little yellow men carrying big black rifles.

The position Alpha Battery occupied on the evening of March 5, with both survey sections and most of battalion FDC attached, consisted of a square of dry rice paddies already held by Bravo Battery, 1/30th Artillery's 155 mm howitzers and protected by a ring of infantry-manned outposts. A few minutes after midnight, I was startled from sleep by the crumping explosions of mortar shells bursting in clumps of orange-red flame and cordite-gray smoke. The voice of alarm swept across a sleeping camp suddenly sprung into anxious, apprehensive motion. The rush of scurrying cannoneers and the flurry of shouted orders competed with the quakes of a bursting mortar barrage. Looking across the quilted pattern of rice paddies to a thick belt of trees 300–400 meters distant, I saw the flash of 60 mm and 82 mm mortar rounds rocketing from their tubes and heard the rushing whoosh as the shells arced in their high trajectory flight toward our camp. Turning my head to glance back into the battery area, I watched the projectiles plummet into the sun-baked floor to suddenly flash with brilliant, crimson corollas.

The infantry outposts, now stirred to life, began lacing the treeline with scarlet stitches of M-60 tracer bullets, and a grunting gun crew was laboring a howitzer into position beside our tent to deliver direct point blank fire at the enemy mortarmen. The shells continued to fall in coughing salvos, most of the rounds bursting in the center of Alpha Battery, thirty to fifty meters from my platoon's tents. But one smashed into the battered earth not fifteen meters away, showering our tent with chunks of catapulted clods and the iron spittle of shrapnel. Then, as suddenly and unexpectedly as it had begun, the shelling stopped, before the cannoneers could retaliate with a single 105 mm warhead.

We found ourselves surprisingly calm and unrattled by the experience ... one that in the beginning we had daily anticipated, but which we had gradually grown less apprehensive of, after seven months in Vietnam had dulled the sharp edges of our fear. Still in our underwear, we dashed out of the hexagonal tent to sit along the crumbling walls of a rice paddy dike and observe the howitzer's point blank revenge on the stand of underbrush from which the Viet Cong mortar crews had already undoubtedly fled. The gun crew slammed a dozen high explosive and Willie Peter rounds into the vacated V.C. mortar pits, the booming detonations of the shells roaring almost simultaneously with the concussion of the recoiling gun's firing because of the short range separating the howitzer from its direct fire target. It was a fascinating artillery show, with sheets of yellow-knitted fire and curling claws of gray smoke from bursting HE shells and the rapier spikes of white phosphorous flowers ... but a show was all it was. Charlie had scampered from his firing pits before the last round had spiraled into Alpha Battery's star pattern, and the artillery shells were now accomplishing nothing other than the further scarring of Vietnam's green countryside.

Early next morning we learned the extent of the damage inflicted by the midnight mortar attack. One artilleryman, a leg cannoneer from the 155 mm battery, was killed. Another four redlegs from that battery were wounded. Eleven troopers of the 2/320th Artillery had felt the bite of shrapnel during the forty-round bombardment that had lasted less than ten minutes, including five members of a nine-man gun crew, wounded when an 82 mm round exploded a few feet from the sleeping crew's tent. The worst casualty in the 2/320th was an FDC radioman. Shaken from his sleep in mid-barrage by a buddy, the radioman was emerging from his hex tent when a mortar round scissored through the green canvas roof and detonated in the cot he had just vacated. He was blown through the tent's opening, his backside from head to heel shredded by slashing steel. Blackened, bloody strips of flesh splattered the burning remains of his tent. When he returned from the hospital nearly three months later, he bore jagged scars across his back ... the raised purple tracks of railroad spurs on the topographical map of his flesh.

A few days later the command was given to "March Order," and we were soon bouncing along the canal road to reoccupy the series of positions we had held in February. The war slowed down considerably for us during the remainder of March. The only excitement came when a Caribou transport, skimming across the dry paddies while making an extreme, low-level cargo drop, dipped a little too low and crashed into a paddy dike. None of the crew were hurt seriously, but the Caribou had both wings sheared off and its blunt nose crumpled. Two days after the crash, a giant Flying Crane "Mosquito" helicopter lifted the Caribou's broken body from the paddy square and sky-towed it back to South Field.

At the same position, snipers harassed our infantry security force with grenades and machine gun fire for three consecutive nights, wounding three perimeter guards. One member of the infantry detachment guarding our perimeter was killed ... not by enemy bullets, but by his own carelessness. A FNG ("fucking new guy"), the soldier had attached a grenade to his ammo pouch by routing the pouch straps through the ring of the grenade's safety pin, a common error committed by cherries. It was not unusual to see a trooper march by with his grenades dangling from ammo pouches by the safety rings alone; the inserted grenade clamp handles having worked their way out of the slitted pockets on the sides of the pouches. Fortunately, most soldiers at least had the foresight to bend back the ends of the grenades' safety pins before attaching them to their gear, so that the pins could not be pulled out by the weight of the grenades hanging at the end of the pouch straps. But this trooper had not even taken that elementary precaution and it cost him his life.

We in Survey came under fire twice more during the month; once while conducting a survey through a muggy stretch of mosquito-patrolled swamp, and again while plotting a battery center for Charlie Battery on a bowl-shaped hill north of Tuy Hoa. Both incidents were minor and hardly serious enough to warrant notice; each time only a few ineffectual sniper rounds fired from long range. But to me, anxious as I was for a combat glory which seemed in meager supply, each incident was important. The mortar bombardment had been my supreme moment in Vietnam thus far. Too fascinated by the brief shelling to be frightened, and with most of the rounds bursting at a relatively safe distance anyway, I had felt joyfully relieved of the burden of seven months' experience in a war with but a few sniper rounds as my only testament to battle.

Operation Harrison ground to a halt late in the month, allowing the platoon to return for another "rest" of one shit detail after another at the North Field HQ camp. Gratefully, the war machine, refueled and relubricated, was soon again cranked into motion for a new thrust into the Phu Yen Province mountains, and once again El Cid was forced to relinquish his shithouse serfs to the firing batteries.

Operation Fillmore, as this new search-and-destroy mission was coded, in honor of another obscure American president, witnessed little heavy contact. The one significant action was fought by the 1/327th. The NLF body count totaled forty-seven, with another twenty-nine probables, compared to light paratrooper losses.

The 2/320th began the operation with a snaking motor convoy along Highway 1 to the MACV compound at Tuy An. Every one of the half dozen bridges between North Field and Tuy An had been blown up by V.C. sappers, but thanks to the toiling crews of the 326th Engineers and to 1st Logistical Corps pontoon bridge builders, we covered the thirty klicks to Tuy An in six hours.

After completing the survey, we were assigned to bunker digging at the foot of the mesa on which the guns were sited. We were about to thread our way down the boulder-strewn hillside, when that mission was scrapped and we were given the new one of radio watch in the FDC tent. Already hot and tired from the long ride and survey, we cursed our leaders for this shift from one detail to another. But a moment later those curses turned to blessings, when a ringing explosion hurled dirt clods and tree limbs from the very point where we were to have dug the outpost hole. A party of Bravo Battery odds and ends had been appointed to replace our survey team for perimeter defense and had climbed down the slope to begin digging a horseshoe-shaped machine gun pit. Seconds after reaching the site, one of the guards, Pfc. Rodriguez, Bravo Battery's clerk, stepped onto an anti-personnel mine planted by the garrison of the nearby MACV compound. We had received warning of the danger of mines in the area, but somehow the location of this mine was overlooked. Wherever the fault lay, one fact was certain and irreversible: Pfc. Rodriguez would have to struggle the rest of his life without a right foot.

We returned to North Field after less than two weeks in the sticks. There an incident occurred that had possibly tragic consequences. The platoon had always been overly keen in our desire to blast away with our deadly Army tools. It seemed unfair to have to lug our rifles around without ever getting a chance to fire them; it was like giving a child a toy but forbidding him to take it out of its box. And so we fought our war safely — against belligerent dogs and bellicose trees, expending an incredible amount of ammunition, but never firing at the enemy.

Practically by force of habit, a surveyor one day burped a full magazine on automatic fire into the bushes along the road north of Tuy Hoa from the bed of the section's three-quarter-ton. A short time later, as we were driving back by the same spot on our return trip, the soldier was horrified to see a sobbing party of Vietnamese mourners walking away from the site of his automatic burst, bearing with them the deathly still body of a small peasant boy, clothed in black.

Turning to me with a look of consuming dread etched deeply into his face, the surveyor asked, "Oh Jesus Christ, you don't think I wasted that kid, do you?"

"God, I hope not. I sure as hell hope not!" I answered, hardly consoling him. "If you did zap that kid, we'll be hearing about it before long. The Vietnamese will be burning Americans in effigy and screaming for some round-eyed soldier's head!"

"Damn," the man winced. "I just know I'm gonna get my ass burned for this. It'll be just my fuckin' luck. Hell, when we were at Ben Cat, I heard stories about those crazy fuckin' tred heads in the Big Red One tossing C-ration laxative at slope kids from their tracks and then running over the mob fighting for the candy. Just squashed them like a bunch of slant-eyed cockroaches. And not a fuckin' thing happened to those grunts. But I'll just lay odds that I'll be doing a stretch in the LBJ (Long Binh Jail) for this."

He drifted in a nebula of fear and guilt for several days, expecting to hear of protests filed by the district chief and investigations commenced by the CID (Criminal Investigation Division). But we heard nothing, so we gave up feeling guilty and instead rationalized that the boy had died of other causes and the funeral party's passing by the location of the surveyor's bullet blast was merely coincidence. Gradually, the man's stricken conscience healed, but he doubtless still grapples in midnight meetings with a ghostly guilt in the shape of a little boy who can never answer the question of who was to blame. The incident cured his itchy trigger finger, but many of his companions in Survey Platoon continued to use the Vietnamese countryside as one vast shooting gallery.

In early April I shook my tree of destiny a second time (the first being when I enlisted airborne in the U.S. Army), hoping its golden fruit of glory, honor and prestige would fall on me. (It would require a third vigorous shake of the tree before the prized fruit would finally come down, and then it would spatter me with all its worm-eaten rottenness. But that was to be months into the future.) On that day, I ignored jeers and accusations of insanity from my comrades and signed Army extension papers which lengthened my tour of duty in Vietnam by six months.

I was motivated by many reasons, though the only one most of my peers in the battery could discern was madness. Max Patterson certainly doubted my sanity.

"Did you land headfirst on your last jump or have you been drinking too much Tiger Piss? Is it an Airborne Audie Murphy that you want to become?"

"Look Max, I can get out of this damn Army if I just hang around here for an extra six months. They'll give me a ninety-day early out, man. I think it's worth it. I just can't take the Fort Campbell bullshit for another year after I get back from the 'Nam."

"Early out, my paratrooper's posterior!" Patterson said. "You're gonna get that early out by way of a body bag the way you're going. Do you want to get out of the Army by KIA instead of ETS? You've still got that crazy obsession about glory and honor, don't you? You're still thinkin' about going grunt, aren't you? Mike, I'm telling you, it won't pay out, even if you don't get your ass zapped. Nobody back home is gonna give a rat's ass about any glory you might grab. When I was home on emergency leave when my brother died, nobody wanted to talk about the war. Oh sure, they came up with a few stupid comments like 'Wow, I'll bet it was no picnic over there!' or 'Did you get shot at; did you kill any gooks?' but when I tried to really tell them what it was like they acted as if they could give a shit less.

"You know, it was kind of a twist on the old situation where the veteran is reluctant to talk about his combat experiences with his civilian friends once he gets back home.... Well, hell, I wanted to talk about it, to get my head straight about what I'd seen and what I was a part of, but nobody wanted to listen ... except for a few college punks who weren't interested in what I had seen or experienced, but only wanted to soothe their conscience for hiding in textbooks to escape the draft by getting me to agree with them that we're all a bunch of kill-crazy imperialist running dogs.

"People back home just don't care, Mike. They don't understand this war, and so they don't make any effort to understand those men who are fighting it. They're only interested in how many horsepower is under the hood, in suckin' up suds and chasin' skirt. They won't want to look at your medals, Mike; they won't want to see the scars of your wounds; they won't want to listen to your war stories. They just don't give a damn!"

I tried to explain. "But I'm not really interested in 'Coming Home' parades and all that shit. The only respect I really want to win is my own and that of the guys out here in the bush. Whether anyone at home knows that I've found a bit of courage inside myself is not that big of a deal, just as long as I know it's there, that it's been tried and tested. And besides that, old 'Stick n' Stuck' tapeman buddy, I don't believe your claim that you're beyond all this prestige and pride stuff. If so, you wouldn't be a paratrooper. You know damn well that's part of the reason you volunteered to throw yourself out of perfectly good airplanes."

"Yeah, sure," conceded Patterson. "I'll admit I dig the idea of strutting around town with those paratrooper wings on my chest, cunt cap with glider patch on my crown, and spit-shined jump boots on my feet, impressing all the ladies and makin' my old school chums ooh and aah over my wild-assed jump stories. But that's just showing off. You're going way beyond that, to a point where proving something to yourself and to others takes on more importance than your life. There's a helluva lot of difference between playing with fire and throwing yourself into the flames, just to show that you're man enough to take the heat."

Chapter VIII

Phan Thiet and Nhon Co

On April 8 SSgt. Tinker's survey section boarded a C-130 for a flight with the advance guard of the brigade to a new area of operations. The "Nomad Brigade" was once again proceeding on a combat odyssey that would take it across the length and breadth of the 'Nam.

Our plane skidded to a stop on the short, 1,500-foot-long airstrip that rippled like the rail humps of a roller coaster. A few miles to the north was the quiet fishing town of Phan Thiet, the birthplace of Ho Chi Minh. It was situated on the South China Sea coast seventy kilometers south of our base camp at Phan Rang. Regardless of the apparent passiveness of the region, II Corps Intelligence had uncovered a possible Viet Cong logistical and training base in the mountainous redoubt along the II and III Corps boundary line running through Binh Thuan Province, of which Phan Thiet was the capital. The wandering warriors of the 1st Brigade were assigned to destroy the redoubt or prove it a myth. One battalion, the 2/327th, remained behind at Tuy Hoa to continue operations against the 95th NVA Regiment and local force units of the Viet Cong. The rest of the brigade would unfairly brand this detached battalion the "R&R Battalion," evoking images of the "We Aim to Kill" (their battalion battle slogan) paratroopers lying on their backsides on the sand of Tuy Hoa beach swallowing truck loads of beer and laying the ladies of Tuy Hoa city.

Shortly after being notified of my promotion to Specialist 4, we were hustled aboard Chinooks, their rotary blades whipping up a sandstorm around the Phan Thiet airstrip, and choppered out toward the mountains where Operation Austin II would be carried out. As we suspected, the mountain fortress of the enemy proved to be a fantasy, as often the very existence of our enemy seemed to be. The three-week campaign in pursuit of a phantom was a thirsty ordeal for the infantry patrols probing deep into the waterless mountains. Not since the snooping about in exasperation around Ben Cat in December had the men of the 1st Brigade encountered such a distressing lack of human game to bag for the ever pressuring accountants of the sacred Body Count. Only twenty-one locally recruited guerrillas were slain in the patrols and sweeps through the heights west of Phan Thiet. A water procuring patrol, of which I was a canteen-lugging member, discovered one of the dead, his belly bloated to the point of bursting and his features waxen with disfiguring death, floating in a trickling stream from which we had just filled our water cans and canteens.

More than a week of almost daily Chinooking from one firing site to another brought only dust and drudgery, our bodies caked with crud and our tongues parched from the sizzling sun and a scarcity of water, thorny underbrush and ten-foot-high stalks of razor-edged elephant grass, and rocky hillsides populated by a stinging species of brown scorpions, one of which thrust the burning spear of its stinger into my ass as I was sleeping one night. It was war at its wearisome worst, with men listening for the animating whine of bullets to crack the armor confining them in this jail of brutal boredom.

We were slung and carried by Chinooks late in the operation to another hilltop clearing of powdery red dust and dry brush burnt brown by the sun. A lone guerrilla, clad in black and bearing a Thompson submachine gun, sauntered up the hillside unnoticed by the hole-digging, sandbag-filling artillerymen, and sprayed the rising howitzer parapets with a fifteen-round clip. Startled surveyors dropped their E-tools (entrenching tools) and shouldered M-16s to pepper the rise from which the guerrilla had already fled. Both sides' bullets struck nothing but the crusty red earth covering the hills. That was the extent of our combat.

The lack of potable water in these Indochinese Badlands continued to be our greatest hardship. Even liberal dosages of Halazone tablets to the water could not prevent an outbreak of worms. One surveyor, particularly hard hit by the squirmers, had to be evacuated to the HQ camp one morning, just in time for a Charlie mortar shelling of the Phan Thiet airstrip. Accuracy was not this V.C. mortar crew's forte, for only a single 82 mm round hit among the parked aircraft, damaging the wing of a Caribou transport, while four shells soared off course to plummet into HQ Battery. A truck went up in flames, the only other casualty of the salvo.

Still out in the sticks, the rest of Second Section daydreamed of ice water and cool showers, while the infantry, as always, suffered even more. One Lurp team wandered in a lunar-like range of moistureless mountains for over a week with only the juice of their C-ration fruit cans to drink. When they were finally found by a Popular Forces patrol, the Lurp squad were near agonizing death by suffocation from tongues swollen with dehydration. Finally, our thirsty torture ended on April 24, when the operation ended and we were helilifted back to the brigade HQ camp.

Our job completed around Phan Thiet, we hurried with preparations for another move by C-130. This leg of our tour of South Vietnam took us to the rain-ruled Montagnard village of Nhon Co, eighty-five miles northwest of Saigon and almost within sight of the boundary line separating the jungles of Vietnam from those of Cambodia. The airlift to Nhon Co began April 25 and was completed by May 1, the day my platoon arrived at the brigade camp-site, built on the cleared side of a bamboo-covered hill crowding the short dirt airstrip. The monsoon season was nearing its peak here in the Central Highlands; the sky was thick with angry gray clouds, mean with rain.

Operation Austin VI started off as disappointingly as had its precursor at Phan Thiet. For six straight days in early May, the rain-weighted boony rats of the 2/502nd and the 1/327th combed the muddy trails skirting the mountains without once encountering the enemy. All that time the rain continued to fall, a wet, silvered insistence. The guns of the 2/320th Artillery were slung from one jungle base to another to be there if needed, but except for routine H&I (Harassment and Interdiction) fires and illumination missions, they hardly fired a shell the first week. It was beginning to look like another fruitless snoop through the jungle.

Then, when a routine report was dispatched from Brigade Intelligence of enemy concentrations around the deserted Bu Gia Map airstrip in Phuoc Long Province, the complexion of the campaign suddenly changed. As the O'Deuce brushed with enemy detachments during the push westward from Bu Gia Map in the platoon checkerboarding tactics conceived by battalion commander Col. Henry "Gunfighter" Emerson, other allied task forces were concentrated at nearby Song Be and thrown into the now burgeoning operation.

The incident that spelled disaster for the enemy regiment deployed in the area was the capture of a North Vietnamese Army sergeant by a patrol of Strike Force troopers. With a little physical prompting, he revealed details of a four-company ambush lurking in a position toward which the American columns were marching. Acting on the information, Emerson dispatched Alpha Company toward the ambush site, while swinging his black-bereted Recondos around the concealed enemy's left flank to be in attack position from the rear as A Company tightened the vise from the NVAs' front. The 141st NVA Regiment fought for an hour to disengage themselves from the front and rear attack by the 2/502nd on May 10. The fleeing communist regulars left thirty-five of their number dead in the elephant grass and bamboo, as well as twenty of their weapons. The retreating North Vietnamese were given no respite, as Alpha and Charlie batteries of the 2/320th pursued them throughout the night with more than 2,000 rounds, many fused to burst lethally above the heads of the escaping enemy, in amongst the trees where the scything debris from limbs and bark would add to the slap of shrapnel.

The following day, May 11, the Battle of Bu Gia Map continued with a repeat performance of the preceding day's single envelopment maneuver. Alpha Company again struck the 141st frontally, while Task Force Brown, composed of troops from Bravo Company, 2/502nd Infantry and Alpha Troop, 2/17th Cavalry, swept through a leech-infested marsh on the enemy flank to smash again into their rear. The resistance of the badly mauled 141st Regiment quickly crumbled under this second assault from their rear in two days. The NVA soldiers fled toward the border, having lost an appropriate total of 101 men killed in their two-day confrontation with the 101st.

The broken regiment was not yet allowed to slink back into the green gloom of the Cambodian jungle. Their American opponents had one last torment, one more battle mace to bludgeon them in their withdrawal ... a B-52 aerial bombardment.

From open bomb bays, 750-pound bombs spiraled earthward toward an already shattered piece of jungle. Little yellow men in ragged black pajamas and tattered khakis endured terrifying seconds that stretched into eternity. Then came the mad moment when bombs and earth collided in a blinding, burning flash.

Like a monstrous string of firecrackers, a chain reaction of explosions rocketed across the tangle of bamboo thickets. Great red mouths opened in screams of violence. The jungle heaved and quaked in crazy convolutions; the misty horizon was ripped by yellow bolts of bomb blasts. A highway of bomb craters was blasted through the tormented rain forest.

We witnessed the awesome display of B-52 power from our fire base on a bald hilltop several klicks distant. It was the third such bombing we had seen; the other two had danced their ruinous red waltz in the mountains north of Tuy Hoa in March. They were fascinating, with their destructive kaleidoscope of bursting colors flashing in violent kinship to the Northern Lights. Modern warfare can be stunningly beautiful, with its volcanic splendor delivering horror and death.

However, the air strike's effectiveness did not match its flaming grandeur. The infantrymen, sweeping through the jungle on the heels of the strike, found few victims among the pathos of bomb craters teeming with infuriated armies of red ants blasted from their homes by the giant hail of 750-pound bombs.

The victory of Bu Gia Map, won at a cost of six paratroopers killed and seventeen wounded, was offset by a helicopter disaster a short time after the battle ... as if the never-satiated god of war was compensating the North Vietnamese for their losses with a sacrifice of American blood, thus balancing the sanguinary scales of war. Hit by ground fire or cursed by mechanical failure, one of the hard-working Chinooks crashed into the green patch of purgatory around Nhon Co, with the loss of all twenty-one G.I.s aboard, including the brigade chaplain and a half dozen cherry replacements for the howitzer batteries of the 2/320th.

Chapter IX

Toumorong

On the morning of May 14, I boarded a Caribou and flew to Phan Rang. I had been granted a leave home to Kansas as reward for my six months' extension. As I headed for home, Donny, my boyhood buddy who had fallen under the same sorcerer's spell from which only Vietnam could awaken us, was preparing to make the journey in the opposite direction as he began a two-year tour that would carry him from the bright light of glory's promise to the dark debris of a life shattered.

Flying by way of Tan Son Nhut and Yakota Airbase in Japan, my C-141 touched down early on the afternoon of May 19 at Travis Air Force Base in California. I had returned to the civilization from which war had exiled me for nearly a year, but immediately I felt out of place, alienated from this suddenly unfamiliar world. I felt keenly disappointed that I could not summon the expected, joyous glow of homecoming. Reunion with my homeland left me numb and strangely insecure. I almost turned around to reboard the plane, ready to fly back to Vietnam and to whatever fulfillment, purpose or meaning it could provide.

After long hours by jet and Greyhound, I reached the small farm town of Plainville, Kansas, that I called home. The first night I attended my sister's graduation at the same small high school from which I had graduated just two years ago, though it seemed a millennium. My family, the people I had grown up with, my high school buddies — all seemed like spectors in a dream, their faces fixed in smiles of cold indifference; reality existed for me only in the sun-scarleted faces of men thousands of miles away. A loneliness and emptiness I could not understand, that seemed so inappropriate to a homecoming, overwhelmed me; I did not belong.

The days passed by rapidly. While Donny was settling into his easy first tour as a mechanic in a helicopter battalion attached to the 1st Infantry Division, I was gradually regaining my equilibrium, recovering some sense of that part of me that had never left Plainville. The easy luxuries I had taken for granted until they were suddenly gone were again within hand's reach. I had looked forward to the simple pleasures of sleeping on a soft bed under a leak-proof roof with no threat of guard duty to disturb my rest, of eating home-cooked meals, of reading books and talking to family and friends. But now that I had these things, they seemed inconsequential. Something that had become necessary and vital was lacking. I found myself dreading the day I would begin the long trip back to Vietnam, and yet at the same moment desiring to hasten back to those jungles, to the heat, rain and insects, to the sweat of danger and stench of death.

The urge to descend once more into the green ghastliness of Vietnam strengthened when, in the second week of June, newspaper headlines and television broadcasts spoke of the greatest battle yet fought by the 101st in Vietnam ... one that I, sitting in my parents' living room thousands of miles from my unit, was missing. Every combat division or brigade in Vietnam would have its moments in the sun: the 1st Cavalry Division found it on the banks of the Ia Drang; the 1st and 3rd Marine divisions, at Hue and Con Thien; the 26th Marine Regiment, at Khe Sanh; the 1st Infantry Division, at Dau Thieng during Operation Attleboro in November 1966; the 173rd Airborne Brigade, on Hill 875, overshadowing Dak To. (Sadly, the 23rd "Americal" Division will forever be associated not with a great battle, but with the massacre of My Lai.) Although the 101st's most famous, or infamous, battle was to be the meatgrinder march up Hamburger Hill in May 1969, its greatest triumph, at least in its first year in Vietnam, took place near the same Central Highlands bastion where the paratroopers of the 173rd would undergo their ordeal on Hill 875 nearly a year and a half later, in November 1967.

The 101st's battle near Dak To was to produce one of the more famous moments of the war's early years, when a former West Point football great became a Vietnam battlefield hero by calling down an airstrike to splash flaming napalm on the enemy and his own men. And I, history-conscious and thirsting for glory, found myself watching it on TV and reading about it in the newspapers; electronic images and newsprint unable to convey the sweat and blood of men I knew — comrades-in-arms fighting for their niche in history. I felt no more a part of the 101st's "Rendezvous with Destiny" in the green mountains around Toumorong and Dak To than of the same division's glory days during the Second World War. It would be another page of history I could only read about or, at best, hear of from comrades who had experienced it first-hand.

The battle had come about soon after the brigade, minus the 2/327th "R&R Battalion" securing Tuy Hoa, was committed to the Dak To area in northern Kontum Province. The Dak To airstrip sat next to a CIDG (Civilian

Irregular Defense Group) camp in a teacup-shaped valley overlorded by a green ring of high hills. From this rugged amphitheater, encompassed by rising tiers of mountains, the Screaming Eagles brigade was helilifted into the vastness where the 24th NVA Regiment waited to play its role in the 1st Brigade's finest hour.

The objective of Operation Hawthorne was the relief of the Sneaky Petes outpost of Toumorong, sitting atop the high ground overlooking the bamboo bramble of the Dak Tan Kan Valley. The Special Forces camp was threatened by an enemy monsoon offensive aimed ultimately at Dak To and the provincial capital of Kontum City. Lt. Col. David Hackworth's 1/327th, along with the 42nd ARVN Infantry Regiment and the 21st ARVN Ranger Battalion, were selected to carry out this mission, with Bravo Battery, 2/320th in support.

On the afternoon of June 5, Bravo Battery was lifted by Chinook helicopters to a position astride a meandering brook, called the Dak Djram Creek, and at the very foot of an ominous looking ridge line capped by the abrupt peaks of Hills 1063 and 1073. To provide security for Captain Whalen's star-shaped pattern of 105 mm howitzers, Alpha Company, 2/502nd, commanded by Captain Brown, was deployed along the exposed western flank of the battery. The 1/327th swept over the ridge mass fronting the artillery pieces and, although they reported light contact along the jutting fingers of rock and bamboo, this raised little concern and less anxiety. The only casualties the brigade took on June 5 were the result of the mauling of a platoon of Hackworth's battalion by a short round. Again, as at Quinhon in October, the 105 mm howitzers, thundering allies of the infantryman, became his executioner. Six grunts died in the blast of an artillery round flashing tragically short of its target, and thirteen of the platoon's survivors were wounded.

The Battle of Toumorong broke out in full fury at 0230 on the morning of June 7. A battalion of the 24th NVA Regiment stormed Bravo Battery's firebase, intending to annihilate the cannoneers and their infantry security detachment and seize the howitzers. The cannon cockers, who had escaped the savagery of sustained action for many months, now found themselves the targets of one of the most determined assaults yet carried out by the enemy on a unit of the 101st.

The first warning of an impending attack was the cough of mortar shells exploding around the battery CP and the FDC tent, where two redlegs were wounded. Then, with mortar rounds still impacting into the five gun-points of the artillery star, two assault waves of North Vietnamese regulars charged out of the predawn grayness toward the startled gun bunnies. One prong of the attack bore down on Gun Number Six, the upper left flank point of the star pattern and the gun nearest the sloping ridge line from which the attack was originating. The second assault column stormed the motor laager of deuce-and-a-half-ton ammo trucks.

Astonished ammo humpers, detailed from other batteries, awoke to find a lava flow of khaki boiling down. Several ammo men attempted to stand their ground against the enemy onrush, but the tide was too strong and most of them quickly fell back to the protection of the howitzer parapets. Two men of the ammo detail stayed with the trucks and died: a private from Alpha Battery was cut off in his foxhole when his comrades fled the truck park and he subsequently caught a face full of grenade shrapnel; a sergeant from Charlie Battery, fleeing in terror from the NVA attackers, jumped beneath a canvas tarpaulin covering one of the ammo trucks, where he was riddled by a crash of AK-47 rounds.

The second North Vietnamese spearhead had in the meantime overrun Gun Six, killing the gunner sergeant with a cluster of grenades as he stirred from his sleep in the gun crew's hex tent and wounding the assistant gunner corporal, who was dragged away by his fleeing comrades, only to be mortally wounded later that tumultuous night. The rest of the gun crew escaped the communists, except for two cannoneers: my friend, Spencer Hartnett, who had attempted to puncture my puffed-up pretensions to glory on the deck of the *Leroy Eltinge*, and Pfc. Willie Smith. They awakened in their pup tent, hidden in the shadows of a gully near their gun, to find dozens of NVA soldiers swarming about in the chaotic industry of battle.

The night was pierced by flashing explosions, commands and cries, and by the snapping whine of bullets, as Hartnett and Smith huddled in their tent waiting for the inevitable moment when they would be discovered and summarily executed. The two had only one rifle with a single ammo magazine; Smith's M-16, as well as the rest of the ammunition, lay stacked outside the tent with the rucksacks. Utterly helpless, completely unable to influence their fate one way or another, the two passed the longest hours of their lives while the battle for Gun Six raged. Bullets from friend and foe alike ripped through the shelter-half walls of their tent and punctured the air mattresses on which Hartnett and Smith lay. A NVA medic slid down into the gully to set up a battlefield aid station a few feet from the cowering troopers' lean-to. As the medic worked to bandage and patched up the wounded, Hartnett and Smith teetered on the edge of an abyss, striving desperately to quiet the bass drum poundings of their hearts and the blacksmith's bellows rush of air from their lungs. They clung to the sheer edge of a cliff; death smiled greedily at the bottom.

Two hours later, the North Vietnamese withdrew in the face of a steady barrage of grenades and rifle fire from the American artillerymen battling to reclaim their lost howitzer. The two refugees at last poked their heads out of their tent, in which they had experienced a dozen times over the lifetime-reviewing sensations of a drowning man, to discover the forms and faces of friends in the midst of yellow flares and flash of bursting grenades. Their own personal ordeal was over; the larger ordeal of their battery was to continue for several more angry hours.

While the redlegs of Bravo Battery were dueling with the North Vietnamese for possession of Gun Six, the two platoons of Alpha Company, 2/502nd, were fighting for their lives against a menacing tide of charging NVA regulars. Their line of outposts resisted for some time but finally caved in under the unrelenting pressure of the North Vietnamese assault. Having lost two of their number killed and thirteen wounded, the infantrymen retired under heavy fire to the parapets of the five guns remaining in American hands.

With the recapture of Gun Six shortly afterward, the 24th Regiment regrouped for a second lunge at the howitzers. When the battle flared violently anew, the flying column of grenade-throwing communist regulars rushed the shell-pocked sandbags around Gun Six and again overwhelmed the defenders.

The attackers splashed gasoline over a jeep parked near the captured gun parapet and laced it with plastic explosive. The jeep went up in an orange globe of flame, followed moments later in the enemy-overrun motor park by the shower of sparks and fire from an exploding ammo truck. Next, the northern soldiers attempted to hoist the M102 howitzer from the ground and haul the gun away. But the task was too much for the dozen NVAs, and the soldiers of Ho Chi Minh had to be satisfied with wrecking the sights of the new model M102 105 mm howitzer, which the battery had recently received to replace the models that had been in use since before World War II.

The battle was finally decided when Gun Five trained its barrel directly on the parapet of Gun Six only forty meters distant and slammed a point blank, high explosive round into the North Vietnamese clustered inside the captured gun pit. That single shell proved decisive; the North Vietnamese abandoned the much fought-over howitzer and retreated to the ridge line. There, as the first flush of dawn rose over the battlefield, the defeated enemy battalion was pounded by the howitzers of the 2/320th, the 155 mm howitzers of B Battery, 1/30th Artillery, and an aerial armada of Huey helicopter gunships and F4C Phantom fighter-bombers.

While the spurs and fingers of Hills 1063 and 1073 were being worked over, a party of cannoneers led by the battery's first sergeant left the shelter of Gun Six's parapet to inspect the thirteen enemy bodies sprawled around the charred ring of sandbags. The souvenir hunters had just emerged from the waist-high wall of sandbags when a blood-splattered corpse sprang suddenly to life to lob a potato masher hand grenade at the Americans. The startled artillerymen raced back to the parapet to dive over the torn and tattered sandbags. The first sergeant and three gun bunnies were lashed with a whip of steel. Fortunately no one was seriously wounded, and the enemy grenadier was quickly dispatched by a volley from the Americans crouched behind Gun Six's fortifications. Except for a few sporadic sniper rounds, these were the last shots of Bravo Battery's long morning.

The redleg paratroopers had suffered surprisingly light casualties considering the close combat. Four artillerymen had died and seventeen had been wounded. Combined with the losses of the Strike Force troopers guarding the fire base perimeter, the American toll was six killed and thirty wounded. The attacking NVA battalion of the 24th Regiment, on the other hand, had lost the core of its strength; eighty-six soldiers of the PAVN (People's Army of Vietnam) lay in bloody heaps around the perimeter or inside the fire base itself. Later, after action reports inflated the number to 192, including a substantial number of enemy soldiers killed by air and artillery bombardment. But even without this usual multiplication — in which pieces of bodies were often counted as whole corpses, with no attempt to fit the dismembered human puzzle parts together into a legitimate tally — it was an impressive victory for the hundred or so cannon cockers of the 2/320th and the thirty-plus grunts from the Five O' Deuce who fought beside them.

One of those victors, Pfc. Willie Smith, did not long survive the victory. Shortly after escaping without a scratch from the ordeal shared with Spencer Hartnett, Smith returned home on leave, only to drown in the deceptive waters of a seemingly peaceful pond in a world 8,000 miles removed from the war.

Bravo Battery's stand along Dak Djram Creek was only the opening volley of the Battle of Toumorong. After the battle furor at the artillery position died down, all three line companies and the Tiger Force of the 1/327th struck northward into the hills from which the enemy had launched their attack and into which they retreated. None of the familiarly long, tiring searches were required to locate the enemy; every company of the battalion rapidly found itself engaged in heated combat. Worst hit of the 1/327th units were the warriors of the Tiger Force, ambushed by a two-company North Vietnamese force as they were hastily marching to relieve one of their hard-pressed sister units. Split into three segments by the enemy ambush, the Tiger Force was nearly overrun and would have been annihilated had not a less heavily engaged unit of the battalion pushed through to its relief. Eight Tigers were killed and nineteen wounded out of a roster strength of forty-two men.

One of the dead was SP/4 Rockford "Rocky" Goddard, a slender, bespectacled, elephant-eared, former clerk of HQ Battery, 2/320th. The nineteen-year-old pencil pusher had not only typed up my extension papers, but had processed a transfer for himself as well, taking him from the paper wars of his clerical duties to the glory and glamour of the Tiger Force. Just two weeks after donning the green and black-striped uniform of the platoon, Rocky was killed as he and a companion sat guarding a stack of rucksacks belonging to the platoon, which had lightened their load for the short recon that ended in ambush.

As the size and intent of the enemy forces arrayed against the 1/327th became more evident, brigade commander General Pearson committed the 2/502nd to the battle on the 8th of June by helilifting the battalion to a blocking position northwest of the maze of jungled ridges and ravines where a series of isolated firefights were raging. From there the companies of the Five O' Deuce, including a reunited Alpha Company already wearied from the early morning minuet of blood and death at Bravo Battery's gun pits, hacked their way through the weavings of dense jungle southward to link up with the pinned-down companies of their sister battalion.

Charlie Company, minus its detached 2nd Platoon, under the command of Captain William S. Carpenter, who had won fame while attending West Point as the "Lonesome End" on the academy's football squad, walked with his seventy-three men into the blazing machine guns and automatic rifles of a NVA battalion dug in along the face of a mountain that the company was attempting to scale. Falling back along an outcropping spur to a second height, the company found itself virtually surrounded and in danger of being overrun. With the weight of the enemy assault threatening to break through the company's thin line, Carpenter radioed his battalion commander, Gunfighter Emerson, to plead for aid, but none could be dispatched. The only immediate help would have to come from Skyraider dive bombers bearing canisters of napalm. At that moment Carpenter was supposed to have uttered his famous phrase, "They're all around us ... let's take them with us ... put it right on top of us!" ... words that for awhile seemed to rank with such stirring cries as: "Don't give up the ship!" "We have not yet even begun to fight!" and the 101st's own contribution, Brigadier General McAuliffe's short, terse, to the point "Nuts!" in answer to the German demand of surrender during the snowy hell of Bastogne.

Although Carpenter himself later admitted that the words attributed to him were the invention of a sensation-seeking journalist, the Charlie Company commander was briefly idolized by the mass media as a hero of a war that produced many brave men but few heroes. The Army manufactured many potential heroes by awarding a proportionally larger number of medals for combat valor than in any past conflict. But heroes require public acceptance and adulation, and an idolizing audience seeking Vietnam era Alvin Yorks and Audie Murphys did not exist in any great number. People do not create heroes from what they hate or are indifferent to. It is a tragic but fitting statement on the war that the only man to win hero status in the minds of many hawkish Americans was Lt. William Calley of My Lai infamy. But in 1966 the war had not polarized the public so badly into Vietnam War haters and those who hated Vietnam War haters. It was still possible for a brave man to become a hero.

Several of the men under Carpenter's command who suffered because of his heroic decision failed to view him in the same valorous light, and there were dissenters in Charlie Company's ranks who claimed their CO had not even intended that the flaming wall of napalm should be dropped over the company's center position. Later I would be told this different side of the story, but at the time I was like the rest of the hero-starved American public, anxious to find a valiant figure with whom to identify in a conflict which had provided little with which to identify or even understand.

Justly praised or not, Carpenter's decision to call for the Skyraiders, made in the heat of battle, did blunt the enemy attack and at least momentarily saved the company. The orange-red sheets of jellied gasoline burst thirty feet overhead and built a fiery wall between his beleaguered company and the enemy machine guns. Unfortunately, burning bricks from this wall of fire fell onto friend as well as foe. One wounded American, unable to crawl away from the tidal wave of red death, was burned to death in the same flames that also consumed many North Vietnamese. Eleven more of Charlie Company's soldiers were burned, including the company's grizzled first sergeant, a Polish-American whose last name everyone shortened to "Sab"—the one top sergeant in the brigade capable of making the growls of our El Cid sound like the meowings of a pussy cat. But the napalm strike did save the company and earned Captain Carpenter a promise from Gunfighter Emerson of "I'm going to put you in for the Medal of Honor for this!" Carpenter was later made Westmoreland's personal aide in recognition of his valor and media attention, but his Medal of Honor was downgraded to the Distinguished Service Cross.

If the company was saved from extinction for the moment, it was not, however, out of harm's way. "Carpenter's Crispy Critters," as they became immortalized in the brigade in honor of their near barbecue in the napalm flames, endured thirty-six anxious hours atop Ncoc Run Ridge surrounded by the rumbling warnings of a yet menacing storm before Alpha Company chopped its way through a nightmare of bamboo and enemy fire on the night of June 10 to bring relief.

Charlie Company, for all the headline-making agony it had endured on Napalm Hill, had lost only seven men killed in the fiery ordeal. The wounded, including those burned by napalm, numbered forty, twenty-six of whom were litter cases.

Desperate for additional manpower to stem the northern communists' attack, the brigade airlifted Bravo Company, 2/327th from the Tuy Hoa screening force left behind during the movement to Phan Thiet in April and organized a provisional company from the rear echelon forces at Phan Rang. This outfit consisted of veteran troopers preparing to rotate home, men recuperating from wounds, soldiers waiting for their R&R flights, an assortment of clerks, cooks and mechanics ... but very few genuine volunteers. But because there was a smattering of real volunteers among the sixty-five men comprising this makeshift unit, the Army saw fit to publicize the company as an all-volunteer formation ... more grist for the 101st's glitter mill. Once recruited, the "volunteers" were hastily flown from the barren boondocks around Phan Rang to the copious green garden around Dak To, where they secured the high ground overlooking the positions held by companies A and C until those units could helilift their dead and wounded.

The necessity to throw back into the hell of combat convalescents and men who had bravely earned their R&R vacations or rotations back to the "Real World" was indicative of the grossly disproportionate ratio of combat to non-combat troops in the U.S. Army in Vietnam. The teeth of the American tiger were sharp, but there were comparatively few of them, while the massive tail was the longest and largest in history.

Although a peak number of 543,000 American military men would be serving in Vietnam in early 1969, the figure is deceptive. According to Col. David Hackworth, 1/327th battalion commander in 1966 and later a regional military adviser (who would resign his commission in 1971 out of disgust at the wasteful way the war was being waged), there were never more than 43,000 U.S. infantrymen, Marine and Army, fighting in Vietnam at any one time. It was this fraction of the huge American military machine that had to carry the main burden of combat and suffer over seventy percent of the casualties. Even including all the combat support troops — cannoneers, tankers, helicopter crews — as well as the non-combat support personnel assigned to the combat units — this total never exceeded 175,000 men in all the formations that made up the equivalent of twelve combat divisions in Vietnam. On average, for every man fighting or directly supporting the men who fought, eight men were feeding, fueling and processing him to and from the battlefield.

It is true that the modern technology and massive firepower of the U.S. military and the need to construct a vast logistical base with roads, bridges, ports, bases and ordnance depots in a country where relatively few had existed before required a gargantuan effort. But still it seemed a strange way to fight a war, when administrative offices in Long Binh were overrun with under-employed clerks (usually Regular Army enlistees), and when support troops sought relief from boredom by drinking, whoring, and later, smoking dope and sniffing smack, while understrength companies of grunts (increasingly either black or drafted or both), were helicoptered into the boonies with little or no rest between operations or were pulled out of convalescent wards to rescue their hard-pressed comrades. Fighting against an enemy whose strength was nearly all infantry and who used the local populace as his logistical force, it was little wonder that the U.S. Army, with infantry divisions in which the actual rifle-carrying grunts were in a minority, failed to win a clear-cut victory.

On June 12 General Pearson decided to break contact with the enemy, withdraw the eight American companies engaged in the battle, and deliver a knock-out blow with the roundhouse swing of a B-52 bomber strike. The next morning twenty-four Stratofortresses struck the mountainsides with an aerial bombardment. Mopping-up companies of Screaming Eagle grunts leaped from hovering helicopters thirty minutes after the strike ended, killing four resisting diehards and capturing fifteen survivors.

The 24th NVA Regiment had suffered an estimated fifty percent casualties in the Battle of Toumorong, including 459 killed by body count — 273 of them to the 2/502nd — and another 485 estimated KIAs (a dubious figure at best). For their victory, the men of the 101st's 1st Brigade paid the price of thirty-nine KIA and 196 WIA. Including ARVN losses the Allied toll was forty-eight KIA and 239 WIA. The victors also captured eighty-eight individual and twenty-four crew-served weapons.

A major share of the credit for victory rested with the howitzers of the 2/320th and 1/30th Artillery battalions and the jets of the U.S. Air Force. The 105 mm howitzers of my battalion had fired 15,250 rounds against the enemy, while the heavies of the 155 mm battery from the 1/30th added the weight of 4,020 shells. The Air Force had flown 473 sorties against the NVA, 160 of which were radar-controlled strikes flying in darkness or monsoon-obscured weather.

Chapter X
Return to Tuy Hoa

A week after the guns around Dak To fell silent, I began the long journey back. My family drove me from the wheatfields of western Kansas to Denver, where I boarded a jet for Travis Air Force Base. After a two-and-a-half day wait at Travis, I boarded a C-141 for Saigon. After a brief fueling layover on the sandspit of Wake Island, where U.S. Marines had fought so courageously against a Japanese invasion force in the dark days of December 1941, we landed at Tan Son Nhut early in the humid evening of June 22. I was back on the green asteroid called Vietnam after briefly orbiting into the by now almost alien cosmos I once called home ... and I strangely felt more secure.

I ate dinner that night at the My Canh floating restaurant — the target of a terrorist bomb in 1965 which had killed forty-two diners — with a Vietnamese girl named Lien I had met during my first trip to Saigon in December 1965. The next morning I hopped aboard a C-130 headed for my base camp. I arrived over two hours later at Phan Rang, after a roundabout flight that included stops at the Montagnard capital of Ban Me Thuot, Pleiku and Quinhon ... where I briefly considered deserting the plane to search for Helen, the bargirl over whom I had made an ass of myself back in October. Max Patterson was there at Phan Rang, having just returned from R&R in Singapore and was now awaiting rotation back to his Missouri Ozark hills. The great terror of HQ Battery, El Cid, had rotated home, as had most of my comrades in Survey Platoon. A few were still awaiting their DEROS (Date of Estimated Return from Overseas) orders which were due before July 8, 1966, the one-year anniversary of our departure from San Francisco aboard the *Leroy Eltinge*.

My stay at Phan Rang was quite brief; simply long enough to gather up my gear and hustle it and myself down to the airstrip, where I heaved the load aboard a waiting Caribou for the leap over the Central Highlands to Dak To. From the dirt airstrip at Dak To, I was carried by jeep to the rolling mounds on which the brigade had cleared a forward area headquarters. The Battalion HQ Battery cantonment was bounded by a long, doglegged network of chest-high trenches that evoked images in my mind of the muddy maze of trenchlines extending along the stagnated Western Front from the North Sea to the Alps during the bloody flood of 1914–18.

The new battery commander, Captain Cardeñal, fearful of a new enemy offensive, had ordered the trench works dug and bunkers erected along their zig-zag route and had constructed a shoulder-high sandbag bunker in the center of the battery's camp a leap and a bound from his own tent. The sandbag fortress was to act as a last line of resistance should an enemy assault break through the trenchline. The builders of Cardeñal's bastion called the redan the "Alamo," in dubious honor of the "Mad Mexican" who commanded us. As expected, Cardeñal was soon knighted as "Santa Ana."

The little martinet quickly institutionalized his unpopularity. Not only did he make us help build his sandbag blockhouse, he also reinstated the spit-and-polish of garrison routine, complete with formations and inspections.

The platoon, except for a few old blemishes, wore a new face. Those who had joined it as part of the 82nd Airborne levy last December still had nearly half their tours left. But just about everyone else was new, and the departure of old comrades with whom I had shared a ration of mud and misery increased my inclination to transfer to the infantry.

After Operation Hawthorne the bleeding enemy chose not to seek an immediate rematch with the 101st. Hoping to intercept NVA reinforcements infiltrating across from the Laotian border, the brigade was dispatched into the mountains west of Dak To on June 24. But Operation Beauregard reaped few rewards; the North Vietnamese had poured enough of their blood into the 101st's brimming cask of victory at Toumorong. Though the enemy inflicted no losses on the Screaming Eagles, again we managed to kill ourselves with our own weapons. During a CA (combat helicopter assault) on the site of an abandoned Special Forces camp, two men from Alpha Company, 2/502nd were wounded by a mine. The wounded were being carried by litter for Medevac (medical evacuation by helicopter) from the LZ when more mines were detonated, killing five Strike Force troopers. Someone had neglected to inform the O'Deuce about the minefield planted around the Green Beret compound.

I took part in few surveys during Beauregard. Usually only one survey team was required to do the job and the new section leader preferred to take the cherries along for training purposes. Most of my time was passed constructing bunkers along Cardeñal's invincible "Little Maginot Line" during the day and manning them at night. It was intolerably boring and reinforced my conviction that only in the infantry would I be able to attain my rightful destiny in consort with glory.

Once I made the decision there was little doubt in my mind as to the company to which I desired reassignment: Bill Carpenter's Charlie Company of the Five O'Deuce; the company that had wallowed in glory and fought their way into history through the napalm of Toumorong and, earlier, had leaped into the guns of a Viet Cong battalion at An Ninh to win the brigade's first victory back in September 1965.

The transfer had to be approved from both ends, so I hitchhiked down to the muddy mire in which the 2/502nd's tents were pitched to ask the approval of "Sab," Charlie Company's first sergeant. The fifty-six-year-old veteran of three wars owned a reputation of being the most ferocious and profane top sergeant in the brigade, if not the Army. But on my first encounter with the lumbering old grizzly bear, with his close-cropped gray hair sprinkled with shafts of white and his wide, sunburned face, he behaved more like a kindly grandfather than a chevroned terror. The reason for his surprising benevolence was that I had hit his soft spot. When I presented my request to him, his hardened old soldier's heart glowed at what he felt was a demonstration of patriotism and American fighting spirit. Sab's bronzed face beamed with a huge grin and he proceeded to praise "his boys" like a proud father, paternalistically patting me on the back all the while.

"I'm proud of you, son. By God, it does my heart good to know that there's still fine young troopers like you who are anxious to fight for their country against those mother fuckin' gook commies. Sometimes, when I hear about all those cocksuckin' draft card burning peaceniks, I begin to wonder if there are any true Americans left with real balls among you young fuckers. But, by God, you've restored this old paratrooper's faith in American youth."

Pushing the transfer through the inevitable tangle of red tape proved considerably more difficult than I had anticipated. I had hoped approval would take no longer than two weeks, but as the weeks inched by it seemed evident that some people with more influence than I owned were reluctant to release my "valuable skills" to the infantry — skills more likely to include building shithouses for the battery and stacking sandbags for Cardeñal's Alamo than those of my survey MOS (Military Occupational Specialty).

The days at Cardeñal's Alamo were anything but stimulating; simply a day-by-day repetition of dreary details and drowsy hours of bunker guard, of gray, humid days and black, rainy nights. A few surveyors tried to break up the boredom by blasting away into the darkness at an imaginary enemy. We were angered by the battery's refusal to take part in the explosive celebration of the Fourth of July. As on New Year's Eve, the brigade perimeter had erupted in a man-made lightning storm of shot and shell to honor the holiday and, just as before, the only sector to remain silent through the fireworks was the line of trenches manned by HQ Battery. Claiming that our constitutional right to observe Independence Day had been infringed upon, we frightened the Mad Mexican and his crew of trench diggers with a fusillade at a make-believe foe.

Consequently, the battery brass found it difficult to accept the validity of an encounter between a member of our platoon and the real enemy a few nights later. Stanley Banks, a Nevadan who had joined us in December from the levy of 82nd Airborne troopers and one of the more dependable and no-nonsense soldiers in the platoon, became Survey's first casualty to enemy action when a grenade burst a few feet from the firing slit of the log and sandbag bunker in which he sat staring into the drizzling black. Shrapnel splattered the log uprights, slashed the sandbags, and nearly tore away a finger on Banks' right hand.

Banks was evacuated to Brigade Clearing and then on to a hospital in Japan, leaving behind an aura of suspicion about what had actually happened. The prevalent feeling among the battery staff was that Banks had suffered his injury while in the process of creating yet another fake fight to relieve the disquieting boredom. To all of us in the platoon who knew Banks, this suspicion was not only groundless but utterly ridiculous, for the man was plainly not the type to invent and engineer excitement. Few craved thrills less than the mild-mannered, taciturn Banks. But the platoon had so often frivolously cried "Wolf" when there existed only empty jungle and undisturbed darkness, that our commanders could not believe the wolf had actually struck.

The brigade resumed its wanderings on July 17, when the men of the 101st loaded themselves and their gear aboard C-130s and watched as the mountains that had framed the scene of their greatest victory disappeared in the wake of the aircrafts' slipstreams. This leg of the 1st Brigade's long odyssey brought us back to familiar ground ... the hills and checkerboard valleys of green rice paddies that were Phu Yen Province, affluent with rice and infested by Viet Cong. The enemy was still determined to conquer the vital province, and in late June had demonstrated renewed strength in a fierce battle with the 2/327th "R&R" Battalion.

Operation Nathan Hale was born amid a flurry of intelligence reports and rumors concerning a major enemy movement west of Tuy Hoa. With Bravo Company detached to the Dak To battleground, the "sun-and-fun" boys of the 2/327th were reduced to two understrength line companies, both of which were helilifted into the Phu Yen foothills to probe in a dual axis advance into the suspected enemy stronghold. The two companies encountered no difficulty in tracking down the North Vietnamese concentration, for an enemy force estimated to number two battalions hit the feeble American columns with a ripping gale of automatic weapons fire, pinning down Charlie Company along a river bank and staggering Alpha Company's advance on the NVA flank in one of a group of four hamlets in the contact area. Instructed to join hands and repel the enemy, the heavily outnumbered companies of airborne infantrymen struggled through the two days and nights of battle to fight through the barriers of North Vietnamese regulars and link with their decimated units.

With the dawn of the battle's third day and no end in sight, Bravo Company was returned from the Central Highlands. The 3rd Brigade of the 1st Cavalry Division was also thrown into the shell storm. Bolstered by these reinforcements, the men of the "No Slack" Battalion broke the back of the enemy assault and added Nathan Hale to the list of 101st victories. More than 400 communist soldiers died in the four days of bloody, bruising battle; of these, 237 fell before the arms of the 2/327th. More than thirty airborne grunts of the 2/327th and about the same number of 1st Cavalrymen died in the hills northwest of Tuy Hoa. The battle had floored the enemy but had still not knocked him out of the ring. It was to swing the KO punch that the rest of the brigade was redeployed into the Tuy Hoa arena.

Survey Platoon was included in the advance guard. Our surveying mission was completed in the first two days in the great sandtrap around South Field, and we were generally free to pass the time riding the South China Sea surf on our air mattresses and were even allowed passes into Tuy Hoa.

The city had been kept fairly clean of terrorists, but Viet Cong agents occasionally contrived some nasty tricks. The extra ingredient of glass slivers was added to bottles of Coca-Cola peddled by barefoot urchins; gunpowder and iron scraps were inserted into the wax and tallow of red candles sold to Americans; and even cucumbers and melons were hollowed out and booby-trapped. After a red candle blew up in the face of a 2/327th trooper, the order was given that only white candles, which could not conceal black grains of gunpowder or iron filings, could be purchased from the Vietnamese peddlers.

Once the brigade had completed its movement to Phu Yen Province, we were helicoptered out into the sticks to support the infantry companies beating the brush for the enemy in Operation John Paul Jones. One mission took us on a three-day circuit of three Special Forces compounds, sitting like frontier forts in the savage heart of Indian country. We returned to find our base camp very nearly blown away. A typhoon had brushed the South China Sea coast, ripping many of our tents to shreds, overturning latrines and shower stalls, and seeding the air with stinging sand and flying sump garbage. The worst of the tempest had expended itself before our return to base, but for several days we had to contend with its stormy afterbirth. It was a constant battle to keep our patched, tattered tent from swooping off on a carpet of agitated air. An atmosphere of sand lacerated our faces, stung our eyes, and mixed with our chow. Again, belligerent nature seemed a more determined enemy than the Viet Cong.

On July 29 we observed the first anniversary of the brigade's landing in Vietnam at Cam Ranh Bay, with cans of Budweiser and bottles of 33 Beer LaRue. During the first year of the 101st's turbulent marriage to the Vietnam War, the brigade had carried out operations in ten different AOs in the country, ranging from the coastal lowlands of Phan Thiet and Phan Rang to the mountains of An Khe and Dak To. We had endured more days in the boondocks domain of the enemy in the past year than any other unit of comparative size in the Allied command — long days of sweat and death in which 1,814 North Vietnamese and Viet Cong soldiers were killed by small arms and artillery fire, with another 327 dying under the napalm flame or the burst of bombs dropped from fighter-bombers flying tac air missions for the brigade. The 101st had exacted this toll at a cost of 193 KIAs, giving the brigade a kill ratio of almost 10:1, one of the highest friendly-to-enemy kill ratios of any U.S. unit, although well short of the ROK Tiger Division's 16:1 ratio.

Overall, the brigade's record was one to warm the hearts of its brass-bearing commanders, the only men to profit from the bloody ledger of war's debits and credits. But the cold, hard statistics of the brigade's body-counting bookkeepers could not express the full meaning and significance of our accomplishment ... the cooperative slaughter, absolved by honor and cleansed by ideology, of more than 2,000 human beings, whether they wore khakis, black pajamas, or olive drab jungle fatigues.

Part II
Grunt

Chapter XI

First Mission

Captain Cardeñal notified me on the morning of August 9 that orders had finally come down approving my transfer and directing me to report to Charlie Company, 2/502nd Airborne Infantry. I packed my duffle bag and rucksack, wished the men of Survey Platoon a brief farewell, endured a host of "crazy fucker" and "ignorant bastard" comments thrown my way, and lugged the gear across the sandy perimeter to the rows of GP tents erected in the Five O' Deuce battalion camp. I was finally an infantryman.

That overburdened walk through the sand dunes of Tuy Hoa beach to my new unit was to carry me closer to the edge and essence of life than I had ever ventured or would ever do so again. Though the days and nights of my year in the artillery in 'Nam had been unmatched by any previous season of my life, they could not compare with the intensity, comradeship, and strange and sad fulfillment those five months as an infantryman would provide. I doubt if that sense of fulfillment can be explained or illuminated. It certainly did not spring from the chauvinistic pride of a superpatriot, swollen with self-esteem for service rendered to flag and country — although that was in great part what I originally thought I was searching for. Even then, before I could observe the conflict with any degree of detachment or objectivity, I was unsure of the reasons for which we fought and killed. Though fighting for a noble cause had been part of my boyhood dreams — and for me, like most of my contemporaries then, noble causes in the Cold War era were usually anti-communist — I found it difficult to consider myself a crusader fighting to eliminate communism. I never felt I was defending my home and freedom from the yellow hordes of Oriental Bolsheviks, nor did I ever glow with the pride of upholding the honor of the "Red, White and Blue." I wanted to feel all those things; I wanted it to be like John Wayne in *The Sands of Iwo Jima* and Gregory Peck in *Pork Chop Hill*. But it would never be that way. Except for the unknowing and unthinking, the war held too many horrors and too much hopelessness to cling to its cause.

90

My sense of fulfillment came from none of the sources for which pompous politicians commonly cover up their abuses of power which result in the bloody catastrophe of war. Patriotism and anti-communism had nothing to do with whatever fulfillment the 'Nam brought me in the end. It came instead from the profound comradeship of men facing side by side the severest physical and emotional hardships and the ever present threat of death or mutilation, drawing strength, patience and perseverance from their collective spirit, and contributing to one another the sanity-saving moments of grim humor, compassion and concern. And, of course, another part of that fulfillment was born from the sense of being part of a great historical happening; if not grand, noble and inspiring, certainly momentous, though in a darkly tragic sense.

Of glory I would find little, other than a few ribbons awarded me more as a morale booster than out of any real recognition for feats of valor. Glory, after all, would prove an elusive and ultimately disappointing prize. Neither glory nor patriotism in the end sustained or inspired me and my comrades in combat and in the harsh search for combat; it was the need to earn and retain self-respect and the respect of our brothers-in-arms. The fear of losing that respect was to prove stronger than any hunger for glory or natural inclination to flee at the first crack of bullets. We would learn to recognize that it was this, more than discipline, regimentation, patriotism or glory that keeps men in battle, prevents them from wholesale flight in response to all instinctual calls for self-preservation, and enables them to endure the unendurable; that without it armies could not exist, wars could not be fought, regiments would melt at the first shot ... that it eventually assumes an importance for most soldiers more precious than life. And I was to discover that the men who chased the brief meteor flash of glory, though they might win a fleeting notoriety, would often become the objects of scorn. Men would give their loyalty and respect not to the glory hounds but to the strong, steady, solid men who shrugged off glory's temptations, held up their end in a firefight, carried their share of the load on the march, served their time as point man at the head of the column, resisted the temptation of pretended illness to desert their comrades in the bush. These were the kind of men you respected and were determined to become, even at the risk of death.

On the day of my renaissance as an infantryman (for all soldiers begin military life as infantrymen in basic training), I was assigned to the 1st Platoon's 2nd Squad. Platoon Sergeant Peron, my new "platoon daddy," took charge of me and acquainted me with his platoon and its squad leaders. The 1st Squad leader was a stout, extroverted, black buck sergeant by the name of Tower. The 3rd Squad was led by a swarthy three-striper named Blanco. My

2nd Squad commander, Sgt. E-5 Heywood Welch, was a short, muscled, sandy-haired professional soldier, not yet twenty-two but having already served nearly six years in the armed forces, including a one-year stint in the Navy before being discharged when his true age of sixteen was discovered. A bond of almost instant rapport was fixed between us at our first meeting; the beginning of a close friendship that would eventually be wrecked on the shoals of disagreement over the war and the degree of murderous intensity with which it should be waged.

Sergeant Welch introduced me to the men of his "Hard Core Squad," as he had boastfully named it, borrowing the term from military jargon used to describe the regulars of the National Liberation Front — as distinct from their regional and local guerrillas. The Hard Core Squad was supposed to number eleven men — a staff sergeant E-6 squad leader in command of two fire teams, each with a fire team leader sergeant E-5 leading an M-79 grenadier and three M-16 riflemen. An airborne infantry rifle platoon in 1966 had an authorized strength of forty-seven — three eleven-man rifle squads, a nine-man weapons squad consisting of the squad leader and two four-man M-60 machine gun teams, and the platoon headquarters, made up of the 2nd lieutenant platoon leader, the platoon sergeant E-7, two RTOs, and a medic. But like practically every other squad and platoon in the rifle companies of U.S. brigades and divisions, the Hard Core Squad and 1st Platoon were undermanned.

Besides Welch and me, the Hard Core Squad numbered six: Pfc. Wendell Rose, a lantern-jawed, willowy Appalachian from tough, coal-mining Wolfe County, Kentucky; Pfc. Foxx, black, stocky and stoic; Pfc. Bresnahan, tall, solid and solemn in his blackness; a yellow-haired, studious-looking fellow by the name of Douglas Detwahler; a blank-faced, hefty Wisconsonian and unicycle rider named Barry Burghart; and a slender fire team leader with a face peppered with freckles, Angel DeJesus, a Chicano from Wickenburg, Arizona. Though Welch, Rose and Acting Sergeant DeJesus would quickly impress me as men, more janissaries than G.I.s, capable of holding their own against any enemy, the others would appear far less imposing, regardless of what was to become a very familiar trumpeting of his men's lionlike courage by the persistently praising Welch. For better or worse, though, I was now locked to these men in a bond of peril and adversity.

After the ritual of introduction Welch took me aside for a strong dose of Hard Core philosophy.

"I'm really proud of my Hard Core Squad, Mike. We've demonstrated beaucoup balls in the past, and we've used our heads too ... balls without brains will do nothing but get you blown away. Our object is to waste Charlie, not get wasted ourselves.

"We're heroes ... fuckin' A right we're heroes. But not those phony pop-corn heroes in the movies who go down fighting to the end. I'm the best fuckin' squad leader in the 'Nam, and none of my men are going to get zapped by Charlie for no fuckin' hero horseshit. But we're heroes, still ... real heroes, the kind who kill the enemy and kill him with flair and boldness and balls, and the kind who stay alive to get those medals pinned over a beating heart ... none of this posthumous crap for us. A lot of jerk-offs who don't know shit about it scoff at the idea of heroes, but I tell you there are such critters. I've got a whole squad of heroes ... men who take pride in their strength and daring and professionalism.

"You're a member now of what is gonna be the best squad in the U.S. Army, and I want you to take pride in that. Forget about that other shit ... about fighting for South Vietnamese self-determination and halting communist aggression. We're soldiers and this is the only war the politicians gave us, so we've got to make the most of it. Your loyalty lies number one with the Hard Core Squad, then with the platoon, then Charlie Company, the O'Deuce, and finally, with the 101st. You take pride in your outfit and the men who fight beside you, not in your country or your cause. That's all bull-shit. It's not going to be the cause of democracy or self-determination depending on you to keep your cool in a firefight, or helping you by carrying part of your load when you get immersion foot or jungle rot out in the boonies. It's going to be your squadmates, who care almost as much about their reputations and your reputation as they do about their lives and your life. We haven't got any luxuries out in the bush; the only luxuries we can afford are our pride, our prestige, and our reputation. Just remember now, Mike, you're fighting for the Hard Core Squad, not for some slopehead pimp politician in Saigon."

I had hoped for a few days to adapt to my new environment, but the company was, at the moment of my reporting, on reaction force alert, waiting for the scouts of the Recondo Platoon to bump into the enemy. Consequently, my first duties as an infantryman were those of preparation for the impending CA. This involved the packing of three days' worth of C-rats (six boxes) into my rucksack, along with the poncho and poncho liner that would be my bed. Then in went extra 5. 56 mm ammo magazines, the standard ammo ration taken by each grunt into the field being twenty 20-round magazines, for a total of 400 rounds — though most riflemen actually carried somewhat less because they inserted only eighteen rounds into each magazine to prevent the spring from weakening, which, in turn, might cause the rounds to be seated improperly in the chamber and jam. Of the ammo magazines, four could be snugly fitted into each of the two ammo pouches (a few men carried three pouches); five, if one was crammed into the covering flap of the pouch — one was inserted into the weapon itself, and the remainder was tucked inside the rucksack.

Also packed or attached to the LBE were an entrenching tool, four grenades — two fragmentation and two either colored smoke or white phosphorous — and either a green plastic-cased Claymore mine with fuse, detonating cord and detonator, or a use-one-time-and-discard LAW (Light Anti-tank Weapon), a sort of compact bazooka or rocket launcher. Finally were added the various odds and ends of a groundpounder's load: mosquito repellent, blue heating tablets, water purification tablets, first aid packets, and, for the squad and fire team leaders, maps, flashlights, compasses and anti-malaria pills. For all the mechanization of modern warfare, the foot soldier in Vietnam still bore an average load of sixty pounds on his straining shoulders and back.

I had hardly completed stuffing my rucksack with my livelihood when word was shouted throughout the company area, "It's a go! Saddle up!" Unsure of exactly what to do, I watched as my new comrades donned steel pots and LBE, from which hung ammo pouches, E-tools, and three or four canteens. Heaving bulging packs on overburdened shoulders, they tucked the black stocks of their M-16s and M-60s under their armpits and tromped through the sand toward the battalion's helipad. Lining ourselves in six-man chalks, we awaited the Hueys. They were not long in appearing. With sand stinging our faces, we heaved ourselves aboard the choppers. Moments later we were heliborne, looking down on the sandy sweep of beach bordering the blue-green sea and crowded with the olive drab-colored rows of U.S. Army tents we had occupied moments before. I was finally on my way to battle and ultimate glory.

Our LZ was a lofty hill covered by elephant grass. The helicopters circled the designated landing zone for several long minutes while the accompanying escort of rocket-firing gunships blasted the surrounding hills. Then, one by one, the slicks (troop-carrying helicopters) descended to hover a few feet over wind-whipped stalks of elephant grass as their cargoes of infantrymen jumped awkwardly onto the LZ.

With a hundred doubts and uncertainties winging through my mind, I threw myself out of the chopper to tumble into clumps of rippling grass. Then I followed two men from my chopper chalk as they moved to the edge of the hilltop landing zone to provide security for more incoming flights of slicks. After the last Huey had dropped its load of armed men onto the hill, I tagged along behind my squadmates across the LZ to a predesignated assembly area for the 1st Platoon. It was not until then, as the platoon gathered its squads on the eastern side of the hilltop, that I saw the platoon leader, 2nd Lt. David Novak. He was tall, confident-looking and confidence-inspiring, and bore a marked resemblance to Gregory Peck. He reminded me of Peck in the role of a company commander in the Korean War motion picture *Pork Chop Hill*— my favorite war movie. He spoke with a slow, steady assurance that commanded respect and trust. The man obviously "had his shit together."

Prior to moving out, Sgt. Blanco became violently ill and had to be Medevacced. His 3rd Squad was placed under the charge of "Acting Jack" DeJesus. Then, in tune with Gunfighter Emerson's checkerboarding tactics, the company started threading its way down the hillside, each platoon pointed for a designated quarter of the checkerboard which it would reconnoiter in a fan-shaped pattern of individual squads. Once that collection of grid squares on the map had been scoured for traces of the enemy, the company would move on to another sector, with platoons still separated to repeat the process until either the "old man" (the battalion commander) was satisfied that Charlie had deserted these stomping grounds or we tripped into an enemy force and ignited a firefight.

Taking one of the platoon's two RTOs along, Welch's 2nd Squad trampled down from the LZ headed for its initial objective, a nearby dome-shaped hill, found nothing there but boulders and bugs, and then slid down to follow a winding stream for 1,000 meters to link up with the rest of the platoon. That night we lay in our NDP (night defensive position) astride the rush of a mountain stream in three-man guardposts, in which a man could sleep for two hours before being awakened to sit and stare into the darkness for a long, ominous hour. Each hour of guard seemed endless; sixty minutes stretched into a timelessness of fighting back the beckoning fingers of sleep pulling at eyelids, shaking a snoring companion from his nasal symphony, waiting for the agonizingly slow hands of the watch to signify the passage of an hour and a chance to snatch a few more hours' precious sleep before taking another turn at peering in half-awakened consciousness into the impenetrable night.

My first night as an infantryman passed without incident. By 0630, we had gagged down our C-rat breakfast heated on the blue flames of heating tablets, pulled in our Claymore mines and trip flares, and were moving out in detached squads to scout a series of ravines which radiated in tiny tributaries from the main stream. In one we discovered a herd of twenty cattle and two ponies. We slaughtered Charlie's beef on the hoof with M-16 bursts and made the ponies our prisoners, loading our heavier gear on their spindly swaybacks. Our butchering completed, we were summoned by the CO's excited commands over the PRC-25 radio to hasten to a nearby ridge line, where we were to locate and destroy the remnants of an enemy force being pounded that very moment by an air strike of Navy Skyhawks. Dropping our packs in a collective pile with the platoon sergeant and another grunt to guard them, we rushed to the scene of the air strike and divided to envelop the enemy in a double pincer attack. The Skyhawks had just broken off their attack and were banking skyward for the return flight to their aircraft carrier as my squad pushed its way through the thorny mesh of undergrowth to hit the enemy's flank.

My heart was pounding with expectation; fear and fascination gripped me in a simultaneous embrace as I followed the single file of six soldiers, a couple of whom had served with the company only a few weeks, but all of them veterans compared to me. I was sure any second that a blast from AK-47s would tear into us and anoint me in a baptism of fire; that my earning of the coveted CIB (Combat Infantryman Badge), with its silver Kentucky rifle enclosed by a silver wreath on a blue infantry background, was near at hand. But I was to be denied initiation into infantry combat, for the enemy had escaped our envelopment by melting into the leafy jungle enigma. Later an AO (air observer) pilot in an Army L-19 Bird Dog observation plane spotted two Viet Cong fleeing down the stream bed and reported the sighting to the lieutenant. Once again we were put to the task of beating the bushes along the stream bank, and once more my heart fluttered anxiously, expecting any moment to part the green strands of elephant grass and discover the deadly end of an automatic rifle pointed at my face. But, as before, we found nothing ... a result which I would learn was far more common in this dangerous but drudgerous occupation than was making contact with the enemy.

At twilight, after an afternoon of more fruitless checkerboarding, the platoon leader divided us up. He dispatched 3rd Squad and Acting Sergeant DeJesus into the ravine, where we had destroyed the V.C.'s cattle herd, to arrange an ambush position around the stinking carcasses in case the Viet Cong attempted to retrieve them. Welch's 2nd Squad was placed on a small hillock overlooking another possible infiltration route on the opposite side of the stream. The 1st Squad remained with Lt. Novak and platoon HQ in a position alongside the stream itself, midway between the two ambush patrols.

Shortly after nightfall it began to rain and continued to do so most of the night. Now I was without even the scant shelter of a pup tent, under which I had endured rainy nights as an artilleryman. My only protection from the rain was my poncho, which rapidly soaked through. I found that misery was really quite relevant, and no matter how terrible one's living conditions in this country and in this war might appear, there were worse conditions existing to be experienced. It was a lesson I was to learn over and over again in my five months with men upon whom the worst miseries were heaped.

But the rain was quickly forgotten when around 0100 the echo of an exploding Claymore mine resounded from one of the two friendly positions across the stream. A rattle of machine gun fire ripped through the rain, followed seconds later by a heavy volley of rifle fire. We waited for the drilling rat-tat-tat of the firefight to reach us with its cracking of bullets and whine of shrapnel splintering the curtains of rain. Both radios were with the other two squads and the short range walkie-talkie we had was useless in the downpour. We were forced to lie on our bellies on that muddy mound, not knowing what was happening at DeJesus' and the lieutenant's positions. The commotion of arguing weapons continued unabated for several minutes and then abruptly stopped.

Morbid thoughts of a massacred platoon stabbed like mental daggers through the flesh of my imagination. My fears projected a horde of blood-crazed communists rushing up the streambed to complete the annihilation by wiping out our tiny team. My mind flashed to memories of Rocky Goddard, of his excitement at the prospect of becoming a Tiger Force trooper, and of his death under the fire of an overwhelming rush of North Vietnamese while conducting his first and last mission as an infantryman during the Battle of Toumorong. I wondered if I was now to suffer the same fate. Glory now seemed far less important in the rainy perdition of this terrifying night than simply staying alive.

My dark deliberation was interrupted as the lull in the firing ended and the popping of small arms fire resumed. I identified the gunfire as the barking of American-wielded M-16s and the virago's scream of M-60 machine guns. A sunburst of relief warmed my body. The spurts of firing finally dwindled away after about an hour, and we were allowed a few hours' calm before the sun rose on a new day and another hump through the jungle.

Marching to the scene of the night's action at the first pink hint of dawn, we spotted DeJesus seated on a boulder, nursing a wound that had left his right eye swollen nearly out of its socket. Pfc. Comiskey, the platoon medic, was applying a field dressing to the acting squad leader's head, while the lieutenant was inspecting the bodies of two NVA regulars attired in blood-stained khakis and "Ho Chi Minh" rubber tire sandals.

A trooper stood nearby holding a mud- and blood-splattered AK-47 assault rifle as a trophy of the firefight. I hobbled my way across the ravine bed of boulders to stare at the lifeless forms heaped snugly together in a muddy crevice between two rocks. Both victims of war's riot looked quite young, probably no older than seventeen or eighteen. Each had been shot in the head and riddled across the body. One of the dead had his left eye torn away, the whole left side of his forehead split open to expose the gray and pink curls of brain matter.

Their deaths and DeJesus' injury had come about when seven members of a North Vietnamese patrol filtered down into the ravine, evidently bent on reclaiming the herd of cattle we had slaughtered. The two point men of the enemy squad had received warning of the American ambush position by discovering the detonating cord of a Claymore mine. Rather than planting the curved screen of the mine on the same side of the gully along which the ambushers waited — thus averting the giveaway stretch of cord snaking across the ravine floor — Pfc. Glen Whitehall had carelessly placed the Claymore on the opposite side. The pair of NVA scouts picked up the cord and followed it to what they must have hoped would be the end to which the Claymore was attached, undoubtedly intending to turn it about so that the fan of steel pellets would strike the hidden Americans when it was detonated. Unfortunately for them, they went the wrong way. A U.S. soldier, Pfc. James Burgess, himself on his first operation, waited on the detonator end of the cord.

Unaware of the two NVA soldiers following the Claymore's cord in the ravine, Burgess was staring into the black, carcass-filled gully, fairly certain by now that the odorous bait had failed to attract enemy attention. Suddenly, his complacency was shattered when a hand reached out of the darkness to grasp hold of a bush beside his foot. A fraction of a second later, a head popped up over the rock slab on which the stunned paratrooper sat. Startled into reaction, Burgess jerked back on the trigger of his upraised M-16, shearing off the side of the climbing gook's head and wounding his companion crawling up the side of the ravine behind him. Burgess' deadly blast touched off a chain reaction as flashing darts of yellow flame spurted from the muzzles of a dozen rifles; glowing green and red tracer bullets zipped in criss-crossing patterns across the dark ravine. Someone squeezed the detonator of the Claymore mine and it ignited with a deafening roar, spraying hundreds of iron pellets against the rock walls of the hollow. Grenades danced back and forth, blasting back the darkness in their split-second flash. One of the enemy grenades plopped into snagging brush a few feet below the position of DeJesus and his RTO, Pfc. Monday. The blast inflicted DeJesus' eye wound and laced a tattoo of iron ink across Monday's buttocks.

After a few minutes, the only weapons still firing were those of the G.I.s. With some effort, the wounded squad leader succeeded in quieting his trigger-happy ambushers. Then, nearly blinded, DeJesus continued to direct his men with the help of Pfc. DeWitt, who acted as his eyes. Refusing the suggestion that he leave his post to seek medical attention at the lieutenant's position, DeJesus remained as alert as possible throughout the drizzling night. He could not, however, keep his men from nervously discharging their weapons frequently as they detected strange sounds or distinguished shadows that inevitably, in their battle-charged imaginations, took on the forms of crawling men.

At least once, though, that sporadic firing was directed at a real rather than imaginary enemy. The wounded enemy point man cut down in the burst of fire from Burgess' M-16 that had slain his comrade, stirred and attempted to crawl out of his deathbed. A swath of fire from Pfc. Whitehall, the man whose carelessness with the Claymore could have caused disaster, snuffed out what little life remained in the communist soldier.

After the details of the night's action had been recounted to the platoon leader and Comiskey had patched up DeJesus and Monday, the two wounded men were escorted to a small clearing where a Medevac "Dust-Off" helicopter landed to evacuate them amid swirls of purple puffing from a signaling smoke grenade. DeJesus departed in pain but also in pride, having added by his actions in the preceding night's combat two more ribbons to his rapidly growing garden of military decorations. Now he was able to add the oak leaf cluster to his Purple Heart, the cluster signifying the attainment of a second award to the original. His injured eye was his third wound, the other two being pungi stake injuries, one of which was so minor that DeJesus had refused to accept a Purple Heart for it. He had also earned the Bronze Star with V device for valor, the Army Commendation Medal with a V, and was now recommended by the lieutenant for the nation's third highest military decoration for bravery in battle, the Silver Star.

As the Medevac helicopter flew overhead bound for the brigade aid station, the pilot sighted two more enemy scouts threading their way through the underbrush. Alerted by radio, Lt. Novak fanned his men out through the thick vegetation for another futile, frustrating hunt for an amorphous enemy. Giving up the search, the lieutenant marched his platoon along a narrow jungle path to a round-top hill, where a "Firefly" resupply helicopter dropped its load of rations, ammo and "Pony Express" mail. Detwahler, the scholarly-looking fellow with the blond curls, was evacuated with the Firefly helicopter, having been bitten by the malaria-carrying anopheles mosquito. He was the first of many men in the platoon to fall victim to the fever during my months with Charlie Company. Malaria would hospitalize more men from the company than would the enemy.

That night our squad was again placed in an ambush position along a lazily flowing creek. Nothing occurred, except in my mind, which concocted dozens of stealthily sneaking foes creeping up on me under the forest canopy. Somehow I survived the night and all its terrors. With each new dawn safely attained, I would become less a captive of my fear of the night and what it held in its black fog.

The following day, my fourth as a grunt, was uneventful, as I would discover, with considerable wonder, were most days for most infantrymen in this strange war. Unlike conventional conflicts, where active front lines existed along which a man knew he would find almost constant action of varying intensity and rear areas where he could feel reasonably safe, a soldier in the counter-insurgency war of Vietnam could never know when violence would run amok and peace would interpose its fragile reign. Vietnam was the unexpected war, an alien world ruled by its lack of rules, totally at the mercy of its unexpectedness. A soldier could hump the boonies of Vietnam for weeks without encountering the slightest hint of enemy activity, and then, just as he was beginning to feel secure, a howling hurricane of screaming steel winds might blow. It would be as if some cosmic boot had kicked away all the celestial beams holding up the heavens, so that the skies collapsed inwardly on a moment which had just registered serenity. Few soldiers could anticipate or predict when that awful moment would occur, when war's fateful factory would begin to mass produce blood, death and savagery.

The fifth day of our boondocks tour did, on the other hand, offer more to snap the wearisome sameness of marches by day and unproductive ambushes at night. Early in the morning, we discovered a series of log bunkers dug into the side of a stream bed. All apparently were abandoned, but to insure that no V.C. lurked inside, Foxx, the squad grenadier, began plunking buckshot rounds from his squat-barreled M-79 grenade launcher into the openings of the bunker complex. On about the sixth shell, one of the round iron balls of buckshot struck a boulder and ricocheted into the grenadier's leg. We were operating in terrain devoid of any clearing which could serve as a Medevac LZ, and the wound was not serious enough to warrant the hazards of helicopter extraction by winch and cable. Therefore Foxx had to hobble painfully along at the "drag" (the tail end) of the platoon column, as it humped over and across boulders, up and down cliffs, and through a rushing stream that seemed to wind and twist back through millenniums of time to prehistoric harshness.

It was during this passage, that the day's bloody thrills were experienced. The action riveted around the point man, Pfc. Rose. Although this son of a Kentucky coal miner had been with the company for less than two months, he had already established a reputation as a first rate point man. The job of marching point at the head of the usually single file columns of American platoons and companies was one of the most hazardous duties a groundpounder could perform. The point man had to be not only acutely alert to signs of enemy ambush or booby traps, but also had to be able to locate and continue on course along the often nearly invisible jungle footpaths or, when trails did not exist, he had to find the best avenue to follow while maintaining the march along the compass azimuth set by his squad or platoon leader. In densely overgrown jungle, the point man's job became especially difficult and exhausting, for then he also had to chop a path through the tangled clutter of thorny brush and bamboo for the platoon behind to follow.

Rose, with a born woodsman's keen sense of direction, sharp hearing and vision, a sixth sense which alerted him to the presence of the enemy, and speedy reactions and steadiness of aim — all seemingly part of his mountain heritage — was the perfect choice for point man. Though the duty of walking point for the platoon was supposed to be distributed equally among the platoon's riflemen, Rose was awarded the honor most frequently, particularly when the enemy's presence was suspected. He often claimed he felt uncomfortable in any place along the platoon file other than point. I envied the man for all his Daniel Boone senses and skills, particularly when I compared them to my pitifully poor sense of direction and my slow, often fumbling reactions in the firestorm of crisis. On this day of August 13, a few hours after Foxx had suffered his self-inflicted leg wound, Rose demonstrated just how sharply honed his reactions were.

Scaling the side of a canyon wall, Rose spied a gook peering around a shelf of jutting rock. Firing from the hip, Rose slugged ten rounds of automatic fire into the man's exposed head and chest ... this being the shoot-first-and-ask-questions-later territory of a free fire zone. The man toppled without a groan, dead testimony to Rose's sharpshooting. He had not missed the victim with a single round, even though he had fired on full automatic at a target nearly fifty yards distant and largely concealed behind the protection of a giant rock slab. It was a hell of a demonstration of marksmanship and, in our manly art of combat, a sure prestige winner.

Rose raced up to where his victim had fallen to discover a shallow cave chipped out of the cliff's walls. Inside he found two cowering figures: an emaciated man with a stomach bloated by disease, and a young woman cradling in her arms an infant with skin the color of cocoa. In a mixture of Pidgin English and Vietnamese, the couple claimed they had been loyal peasants abducted by the Viet Cong and forced to slave as laborers and coolies. They asserted that a company-sized enemy force had fled this area only a short time before, leaving behind a few scouts such as the man just slain by Rose. We placed the pair under our custody, adding them to the sure-footed ponies in our collection of contraband.

Though the Army Commendation Medal with V for valor later awarded Rose for his sharpshooting stated that the man cut down by his burst of fire was aimed and about to deliver a volley into the American column, no weapons were found on either the dead man's body or in the cave. The citation attached to Rose's medal was, nonetheless, only typical of the Army's embellishment of reality in their decoration distribution ... colorful baubles of cloth and bronze doled out like sweetmeats to the egos of men upon whose manipulated morale and esprit de corps depended the careers of the tycoons of the sword.

We continued our march down the hellish canyon, considerably slowed by the crippled Foxx, the sickly Vietnamese coolie, and the confiscated ponies. A short time after resuming the trek, 1st Squad, which had been detached from the platoon to scout a parallel running gorge, reported that its point man, a fierce, fearless Mexican-American named Tommy Morales, had matched Rose's feat by bowling over a fleeing V.C. scout, also unarmed, with a single well-placed shot from fifty yards. The 1st Squad RTO announced the kill with the enthusiasm of a home team sports broadcaster proclaiming a touchdown by his team and an evened score against a longtime rival. Like athletic teams competing for points and prestige in this most violent sport, the platoon squads carried on an intense body count rivalry upon which their reputations depended.

Later, 1st Squad linked up with the rest of the platoon, emerging from the winding canyon to follow a prominent trail right into an abandoned Charlie encampment. A thorough search of the dozen or so log and bamboo huts in the camp turned up a few medical supplies, clothing and rice. We then marched on to join with the company headquarters section, led by a new CO. It was the first time we had seen any other part of the company in the last five days. An LZ was secured and Foxx and the ragged family of suspects were lifted out by Huey.

Orders for the following day included welcome news. Each platoon was to make its separate way to a common landing zone, from which the company was to be withdrawn from this leafy forum of battle by chopper on the morning of the 15th. Second Squad, with its dependable point man, Wendell Rose, was selected to precede the rest of the platoon and the CO's party by several hundred meters. We had marched about 1,000 meters toward our objective when the squad came under fire from an M-1 carbine in the hands of a sniper. He was hidden in an arc of steep, green hills about 300 meters from the grassy clearing onto which we had just walked. Three rounds snapped the air above our heads and plowed into the ground directly behind me and just inches from Burghart, following, as was his habit, too close behind me. We dived off the trail into a small wash-out running alongside the footpath, anxiously scanning the foliage covering the hills from which the sniper had hurled his leaden insult. Ordering us to stay low and study the hills for a glimpse of the sniper, Welch jumped up and down in a vain attempt to draw the sharp-shooter's fire. Moments later the lagging remainder of the platoon, with company HQ in tow, reached us. While everyone else sought cover, the first sergeant walked openly onto the trail, totally indifferent to the danger as he demanded to be told from where the sniper's shots had come.

It was said of the first sergeant — who, though fifty-six years old, prided himself on his ability to outhump the youngest and strongest straplings in the company — that he lacked any emotion even faintly resembling fear, his emotional vault being stuffed with too much overblown pride. It was evident that the present threat failed to stir the slightest sign of apprehension in the old gray-haired gorilla's profane composure. Had he seen one of "his boys" prancing back and forth in utter defiance and disregard for the enemy rifleman as he was doing, 1st Sgt. Sab would have thumped the reckless soldier over the head with his rifle butt. But the Polish grizzly must have believed himself invulnerable to the puny bullets of the foe. He probably had good cause to feel so confident, having survived three wars, in all of which he had behaved in a similarly lackadaisical manner in the face of enemy fire.

The sniper did not accept Sab's invitation to take another pot shot. To insure that the sniper would cause no further interruption in our progress toward the LZ, Lt. Novak directed grenadier Glen Whitehall to plunk a half dozen high explosive 40 mm grenade shells from his M-79 along the rising slope of the jungle. Then we picked ourselves up out of the shallow ditch into which we had leaped and headed on toward our objective, 2nd Squad again assuming the lead position several hundred meters ahead of the platoon's main body. Within minutes the lieutenant radioed the RTO attached to Welch's point squad to inform us that the elusive sniper had struck again, firing several rounds at the 1st Squad marching at drag position along the platoon file, but with no effect other than further frightening the troopers.

The trail we followed soon broadened as we humped out of the green enclosure of the bamboo forest onto a rolling plateau of ankle-high grass and few trees. We were faced with a proliferation of trails splintering off from the main path, and it required all of the navigational skills of both Welch and Rose to find their way through the maze to the LZ. The piloting of the lieutenant following behind was not as sure, and by nightfall he found he had led the rest of the platoon several klicks in the wrong direction.

I for one was grateful for the little halts during which Welch and Rose consulted the crystal ball of map and compass to see the future their steps would bring them along the diverging trails. I was fighting a bout of diarrhea, and at each halt I would jump frantically into the bushes to squat and shit. The intervals between my quick trips to the bushes became progressively shorter and shorter. I rapidly expended my own and everyone else's supply of tiny C-ration rolls of asswipe and was reduced to wiping my nasty behind with leaves. Every twenty minutes or so I had to leave my place at the end of the squad file to leap into the trees. There I would wiggle out of my LBE and rucksack, pull down my fatigue pants just in time for the gushing tide, and then rush in a fumbling furor to replace my gear and stumble in a clumsy gallop to catch up with the marching squad. Finally, I despaired of continuing the losing race against time to ready myself before the dam broke and the brown torrent rushed out, so I just continued marching as my pants slowly filled up with the noxious liquid flooding from my bowels.

Upon reaching the LZ at nightfall, we discovered that the rest of the company was still short of its goal. Thus our little squad of nine men found itself alone and unsupported that night, but my sense of vulnerability — of being like a tiny island isolated in the center of an ocean of Viet Cong — was overawed by the misery of my nasty condition. It began to rain early in the evening and continued for most of the night. Thankful for once for the downpour, I squirmed out of my foul fatigue trousers, wiped them off on the grass, and laid them out in hopes that the rain would wash them off enough so I could at least stomach crawling back into them at sunrise. The trots continued through the night. Unable to leave the small circle of trees in which the squad was concealed, I was forced to drop my malodorous load in the center of the ring of troopers, each time whispering urgent warnings to the guards on duty so that they would not mistake me for an enemy intruder and blast my ass off, and then returning to my post where I would wrap myself in my rain-soaked, mud-splattered, shit-stained poncho liner to seek a few moments of fitful sleep before either guard duty or diarrhea called.

At dawn of the day of our extraction back to the canvas tents and blessed wooden latrines of the rear, the flow from my bowels abated considerably. One by one the four platoons of the company plodded onto the LZ. Late in the morning, helicopters choppered onto the landing zone to swallow up waiting sticks of men and flutter off into the clean, clear, uncontested sky bound for South Field. The helicopter ride back to camp was then and would remain one of the more pleasant experiences in the harsh life of the American infantryman in Vietnam. High over the steaming, insect-infested jungle, with the cool air whipping over worn and exhausted bodies, and without the pressing, heart-thumping realization all too imminent in the tense helicopter flights bound for the other direction — for the jungle and the enemy — those rides often seemed to have more to offer than the destination itself— the HQ camp, where Army regimentation would prevail.

This first return to South Field from an infantry mission gave me an indication of the typical bullshit that would make our brief stays in the camp anything but relaxing and rejuvenating. I had naively assumed that because the grunts spent so little time in the rear area there would be comparatively little of the harassment which was so common in the 2/320th Artillery. Now, as we were herded in and out of formations, inspections and work details, I discovered there was little difference between units. All the brass, whether wearing the crossed rifles of the infantry or the crossed cannons of the artillery on their lapels, had to play their Mickey Mouse games and the Army would forever remain the Army.

Our first duty upon returning to the brigade camp was to clean our weapons. While thus engaged, the new company commander, Captain William Silvasy, toured the company area to introduce himself to the men under his command. The man bearing the two silver bars of a captain was husky, in his early thirties, and a blend of strident nationalism and passionate ambition.

I tolerated the ritual of saluting, shaking hands, and receiving words that were supposed to arouse my fighting spirit and sense of patriotism from the brisk, square-shouldered captain. He had just passed on to the next trooper when a volley of shots broke up the CO's receiving line in a flurry of grunts diving behind sandbags for cover.

The swath of rifle fire had not come from a V.C. attack force, however, but from the M-16 of a runtish-looking black trooper called "Lightning" by his sardonic comrades. Pointing the black muzzle of his rifle at the tarpaulin roof of his 3rd Platoon tent, Lightning had emptied a twenty-round magazine into the canvas and had threatened his hoochmates with a second burst of fire. Taking the situation in hand, Sgt. Welch scooted on hands and knees into the tent, determined to save the day. Several minutes later, the young sergeant emerged, triumphantly hoisting the G.I.'s weapon above his head. Welch had won another feather in his warbonnet, although this one was gained by counting coup on one of our own braves. He was later awarded the Soldiers Medal for disarming the trooper, equivalent to a Silver Star and the highest decoration for valor in a non-combat situation given by the U.S. Army.

Later that afternoon, we had to dismantle our large GP tents and erect pup tents in their place. This demotion in our sleeping accommodations was because General Pearson, the brigade CO, had become upset with Gunfighter Emerson for bringing the battalion's GP tents up from Phan Rang to Tuy Hoa for his men's comfort and shelter, while the other line battalions, with less considerate COs, had to remain content within their leaky two-men pup tents. Appalled at this flagrant disregard for the camp's uniform appearance,

Pearson ordered the Five O' Deuce to pull down their canvas palaces and return to the miserable little hooches under which the rest of the brigade's low ranking foot soldiers slept. I'm sure General Pearson rested contentedly in his spacious French villa headquarters, knowing that all his brave grunts were now uniformly miserable.

Chapter XII

Vung Ro Bay

While still engaged in erecting the sandbag keeps around our shelter-half castles, we received the not altogether unwelcome news that our "rest" at South Field would end the day after tomorrow. At that time we would depart by truck convoy for the new mission of providing security for an Army engineer company laying a fuel pipeline through a mile-long tunnel down to the beach of Vung Ro Bay, south of Tuy Hoa. The next day brought more formations, more harassment, more bullshit. We were all ready to begin the security job when the morning of the 17th dawned. The company piled into the trucks that would transport us to Vung Ro Bay, convinced that guarding a bunch of leg engineers could not possibly be any less restful than the rear area camp.

Vung Ro Bay, nestled in an azure blue cove surrounded by a ring of verdant mountains, which edged in descending levels to a narrow stretch of white beach, was a spectacular scene and provided us welcome relief. The three rifle squads of the platoon were positioned at strategic spots near the tunnel to provide security for the engineer crew.

With little enemy activity reported in the area, our sentry duty was executed in a very relaxed style, our time being spent in writing letters, reading paperback novels, inventing new C-ration recipes, and swimming in the shimmering blue-green waters of the bay. Our only opponent was regiments of rats that sometimes at night rattled our nerves as they rattled discarded C-ration cans in search of chow. One night they nearly scared Burghart senseless when a particularly bold member of their ranks hurled himself from the dark depths of the tunnel directly onto the sleeping trooper's chest.

Though it was a hard, hot hump up the steep mountain trail to the highway where we were resupplied with C-rations, the grit and grime of the climb could always be washed away by the cooling silver spool of a waterfall cascading off the rocky spine of the mountain or in the coral-gardened bay. It was as close to paradise as the 1st Platoon, Charlie Company, 2/502nd ever ventured.

The Army could not allow its armed servants to suffer such pleasures for long however. Someone in brigade staff learned how terribly inactive we were. Aghast that America's finest should be wasting in idleness, this brass-buttoned bastard concocted a project to keep us in fighting trim. Picking out a suitably rugged peak, he assigned Lt. Novak the mission of leading a patrol up to the summit to scan the mountaintop for signs of the enemy.

Taking a seven-man patrol, of which I was a member, the lieutenant scaled the treacherous face of the mountain after a climb of several excruciating hours. Often we were forced to sling our weapons and use hands, feet and fingernails to lift ourselves up the razorback heights. Thankfully, we did not have to bear the weight of rucksacks or a machine gun; the only heavy piece of gear we carried was the twenty-four-pound PRC-25 radio set, which we kept shifting from man to man so that the burden was shared.

The mountain's pinnacle for so long seemed an impossible goal, never coming closer regardless of all the climbing and crawling, the scraped knuckles and bruised shins. And once the peak was somehow attained, we faced the only slightly less daunting prospect of the descent. As for the presence of Charlie, all was forgotten. No one believed the Viet Cong would use this high hell as a sanctuary. Our only enemy was the mountain itself. Our mission had been conceived to put the anxious minds of our leaders at ease, lest they concern themselves unduly that the mortal tools of their trade might rust from inaction. But, halfway up, our cursing contempt had trailed off; the absurdity of the climb had become a challenge. The mountain had threatened to defeat us, to sneer at our feeble efforts to reach its contemptuous summit. There would be no rewards for its conquest; no praise, no cases of beer or passes into town ... we would receive only an indifferent acknowledgment over the radio that we had completed our mission and a sigh of disappointment from the brigade staff that we had added nothing to the body count. But, somehow, conquering the mountain took on an importance to us, added new strength to muscles that had seemed drained, and drove us with determination to succeed.

By twilight's haze, we had won our struggle with the mountain, tripping down the last rocky ramp to a swamp hugging the rising angle of the mountain. There had occurred only one mishap in a setting that had so strongly suggested broken bones and fractured skulls. Lt. Novak had slipped off a boulder to plummet ten feet onto a stony ledge and suffered a deep gash above his temple and a dizzying headache. Other than that one injury, we survived the patrol in remarkably good shape, with only minor cuts and bruises. But the victory that had seemed so important to us halfway up the mountain, so important to our pride, to our manliness — whatever it was that pulled our weak bodies up that severe incline — now took on the shape of a grotesque joke we had played on ourselves. We could have taken the option which many other patrols on similarly imbecilic missions had chosen. We could have settled in some leafy grove for the afternoon and called in on the radio, at the appropriate time, the coordinates that would place us (in the minds of the brigade staff) on the top of our objective. The lieutenant was not an unreasonable man. Once we had begun the climb and it had become obvious that there would be no enemy to find and that scaling the mountain would demand an excessive outpouring of sweat and exertion for no good purpose, he might easily have been amenable to the suggestion of a fake report of mission accomplished. But no one suggested that; after awhile I doubted if anyone had even considered it. Getting to the top of the mountain had become the only thing that mattered. Our pride, the same pride that made us continue marching and fighting in a war for which we had no passion or purpose, had played a cruel joke on us. The mountain was a metaphor for the war ... a war whose black humor employed us to practice and perpetuate even greater frauds; a war that brought us victories even more shallow and hollow than this triumph over the mountain; a war that would use us as objects of the cruelest joke of all.

Our leaders quickly dreamed up other projects to keep us busy. First, we were forced to run through a squad reaction course, followed a few days later by a platoon reaction course. One 1st Platoon grunt was wounded when a piece of shrapnel from a grenade thrown by one of the trainees lodged in his leg. He was our only casualty while the company was engaged in its Vung Ro Bay security mission.

Two new replacements joined the platoon while we were languishing at the position near the black mouth of the tunnel. One, a New Jersey boy named Lee Miksis, had been a clerk in HQ Battery, 2/320th Artillery. Catching the same fever that his colleague, Rocky Goddard, had fallen victim to, the symptoms of which were powerful cravings for glory, excitement and prestige, Miksis had joined the growing list of artillerymen converted voluntarily to ground-pounding infantrymen. Like most of the cannon-cocker-to-grunt converts, the short, burly ex-clerk would prove himself a brave and ballsy infantryman.

The platoon's second recruit was a man of vastly different caliber. Pfc. Walt Johansen was a tall, lanky Minnesotan, with an almost foppish attitude and arrogance. He quickly made an impression on his new platoonmates, but it was an impression compounded of resentment and derision that would only increase with time and was to make Johansen's months with the company seem even longer than they already were. Not only would he have to face the enemy and the elements, but the blusterer would also have to confront the contempt of his comrades. Johansen would prove unable to endure either the hardships of war or the isolation from his peers. A strong man needed the crutch of his comrades' friendship and respect to bear the war's awful burden; Walt Johansen showed himself to be anything but a strong man.

Far more confident of my abilities than I was myself, Sgt. Welch had appointed me to be one of his two fire team leaders and was promising me a promotion. I could not possibly envision myself as a sergeant. This was not only because of the heretofore low opinion I had held of NCOs. I was beginning to look upon the NCO caste as a necessary evil, in which there were a few well meaning and even capable individuals like my squad leader. No, the main reason for my inability to see myself in the role of a noncom was my lack of confidence in my capacity to lead. I simply did not feel qualified enough to command soldiers who had been humping and fighting over half the mountains in Vietnam while I was still an untried, unbloodied novice with only a week-long operation under my web belt. I attempted to make it evident to the sergeant that I was not now, and probably never would be, ready to lead a fire team. Nevertheless, Welch continued to insist that I had what it took to make a good leader and promised that he would see to it that I would soon wear the three chevrons of a buck sergeant.

A few days later, as our stay at the turquoise bay neared its end, Angel DeJesus returned from two weeks' recuperation in the Quinhon hospital, his face still puffy and swollen. He brought with him a chubby, silver-gray-haired black sergeant named Hagan. The lieutenant gave the new sergeant command of the Weapons Squad, which was really no command at all, for the two machine gun crews making up the squad were nearly always separated and attached to the rifle squads under the command of the rifle squad leaders, leaving the Weapons Squad leader free to serve as a flunky for the platoon sergeant.

On August 29 we loaded ourselves back aboard deuce-and-a-half-ton trucks for the return to South Field. Except for the tactical reaction courses we had run and the horrible hump up the mountain, Vung Ro Bay had been restful, refreshing, almost like a vacation. Our next mission was to be totally different.

Again we were granted only a day and a half in the rear area before being ordered back into the boonies to chase Charlie in those constant search-and-destroy missions that were collectively labeled Operation John Paul Jones and accounted for thirty-three NVA KIAs by the O'Deuce, at a cost to the Strike Force of six killed and thirteen wounded. Most of our brief visit to the rear was taken up by the usual Army bullshit. I did succeed in sneaking away from the parade of formations and work details long enough to visit my former comrades in Survey Platoon and recount the unparalleled excitement and glory of butchering cattle, of humping the heights and wading swamps, of waiting in ambush through a rainy night for an enemy who never came.

Chapter XIII
Operation Seward

On the last day of the month we were lifted from the brigade sandbox by UH-1B helicopters into the mountainous area west of Tuy Hoa called the "Hub" to resume the never ending search for Charlie. With rockets from helicopter gunships slamming into the surrounding heights and our own Hueys spitting a stream of red tracers from the hammering pair of M-60 machine guns mounted on each helicopter, we jumped into the tall clumps of elephant grass cloaking a rectangular clearing.

We shouldered our loads and walked through the woods until sunset. The following day we resumed the march, moving a great distance but getting nowhere, aware only of the soreness of backs and shoulders suffering under the weight of rucksacks and of the agony of jungle-booted feet constantly wet and tripping over kilometers of tormenting terrain. Everywhere there was a maddening profusion of trees and insects, of hills to climb and slide back down, and of yet more insects ... but nowhere was there Charlie. Sometimes he seemed as make-believe as the play enemy we had fought in the war games back at Fort Campbell ... at least until the crack of his AK-47 would once again reaffirm his reality.

In late afternoon, a call came from the CO directing us to retrace our steps back to our LZ starting point, which we were to secure until the rest of the company reached the location. From there we would be helilifted from this unproductive region to an area further north that promised a more plentiful supply of game to the hunters. The platoon backtracked its way to the landing zone, where the lieutenant positioned us in a half-moon perimeter around its northwest corner.

Several hours before daybreak the thunder of artillery shells smashed the silence of the jungle night. In rapid succession, three 105 mm high explosive shells crashed into the damp forest floor. The first two mauled the earth some fifty meters to the front and between the post shared by Welch, Rose and me and the machine gun crew's foxhole. This was occupied by machine gunner

111

Steven Herman, a second generation Screaming Eagle, his father having served with the 101st in Normandy and at Bastogne; by SP/4 James Henk from Chicago, who, with a tuft of sandy hair shading his forehead like the bill of a baseball cap, his sly homespun grin, and easy, soft-as-velvet voice, reminded me of a latter-day Will Rogers; and, finally, by the slender, meek-looking James Burgess, who had blasted the life from the NVA soldiers in DeJesus' ambush the month before.

The last round exploded less than ten meters from the startled machine gun team. A dirty rainfall of mud and brush showered us with each shell burst. Two trip flares popped in a sizzling solar glow, ignited by the explosions. The 2/320th Artillery very nearly killed me and my comrades that night. I thought to myself how ironic my death would have been at the hands of the very people who had so adamantly warned me against transferring to the infantry, where they were certain I would be killed within a matter of weeks and now seemed intent on fulfilling their prophecy.

We passed a second night ringing the LZ, and although no more friendly artillery shells rained down on the platoon, I did experience another harrowing event. The rain came down in a steady shower that night, and when my hours of guard duty did not require maintaining an at least half-conscious alertness, I would nestle myself, weapon and rucksack underneath the stingy protection of my outstretched poncho. During one of those all too brief periods of sleep a pungent, musky odor assaulted my nostrils.

Welch and I scanned the dark ground for the intruder and lit matches beneath the concealment of our ponchos but failed to locate the source of the smell. But what our eyes failed to find, Welch's sensitive sniffer tracked down. Pointing to my rucksack, Welch commanded, "Open the flap on your ruck and I'll guarantee that you'll find more than C-rats and ammo."

I did as the sergeant directed and, true to his prediction, a long, plump snake of the same dark colors as the forest slithered out, almost rubbing against my arm, and slid through the grass looking for a new haven.

"What the hell was it doing in there?" I asked. "I suppose it was after a free meal on my Cs. I would have been happy to give it my ham and lima beans. Of course, then it probably would have slithered back here and sunk its fangs into me for trying to poison it."

Welch smiled at my inhospitable attitude and went on to explain that not all snakes would have been so gracious about being rudely evicted from a warm bed. He cited as an example a 3rd Platoon squad leader who was awakened one morning by a heavy, slimy weight pressing down on his chest. Noticing a long, thickly rounded bulge extending from his Adam's apple to his groin, the paratrooper frantically unbuttoned his fatigue jacket to discover the slumbering rope of an obese, gray snake, with its serpent head resting on the man's penis and testicles. Terror-stricken, the sergeant nearly jumped out of his pants to free himself from the snake's cold embrace, but not before the sinuous slumberer had sunk its fangs into the howling soldier's balls. Though the snake-bitten victim was not seriously injured by the monstrous, but fortunately not poisonous, snake, it was no longer Charlie against whom he guarded so fearfully for the duration of his Vietnam tour.

My squad leader then related his own snake story. He had, some months before, been leading a patrol in the wilderness around Nhon Co when he decided to call a break. The sergeant moved off the trail to sit down on a green and brown banyan log. Preparing to light up, Welch felt a slight movement underneath him and turned his head toward the end of the log, which suddenly reared up to reveal the triangular head and evil, yellow eyes of an immense cobra. The cigarette dropped from Welch's open mouth and his eyes bugged nearly out of their sockets. But, though his heart may have frozen in the middle of a beat, his reflexes still functioned, as he jammed back the trigger of his M-16, geared on full automatic, and did not release it until the magazine was empty. The riddled "log" was measured to be an astounding sixteen feet long.

We lingered around the landing zone for most of the following day, receiving a host of contradictory orders from Captain Silvasy, who kept changing the time for our helicopter extraction in confusing consort with the ebb and flow of the fluid tactical situation. Finally, as evening spread its shadow across the land, we were lifted out to a new LZ. As we approached the landing zone, the two machine gunners on my Huey added their fire to the rockets, grenades and 7.62 mm bullets lashing out from the escorting gunships. Both "shotgun guards" held back on the triggers of their rapping M-60s almost without pause from the beginning of the approach until a second before we flung ourselves out of the hovering helicraft. Other choppers, thundering in behind my chalk, spewed forth a stream of machine gun shells over our heads into the forested hillsides snuggling the LZ. It was a crashing concert of American martial music ... another flexing of the overpowering American military muscle that was inexplicably not overpowering enough to crush a rebellion of barefoot peasants with no helicopter gunships, no jet fighter-bombers, no tanks, and little artillery. The only thing Charlie had on that LZ was a forest of sharply pointed bamboo punji stakes. It was against these primitive weapons that all this firepower was expended.

The day had been locked in the black dungeon of the night by the time we assembled and started what was to be my first night march with the platoon. Unlike other American units at that time, the 101st thrilled in demonstrating its daring and prowess by undertaking night movements against an enemy highly skilled in the art of nocturnal ambush. Tradition told us that we were the best unit in Vietnam, so tradition's claims had to be put to the test. We were delegated by the division's history to equal or even surpass the proud legend carved out by our predecessors in World War II. That "Puking Buzzard" patch sewn onto our uniform shoulders not only painted us with prestige, but weighted us as well with an obligation to lacquer the divisional image with new coats of glory. And stumbling through the jungle night, where a platoon could easily stray in harm's direction, was — at least in our leaders' judgment — one way to brighten that image of superiority.

I personally did not feel superior to any man that night — though it was for young, impressionable minds like mine that such myths were created — as I stumbled and groped clumsily along the rock and brush-littered lane, reaching out now and then to touch the consoling backpack of the man in front to insure I was still following the thin thread of the platoon file that was my only security against the night's dark demons. With Sgt. Welch consulting his compass and his point man — Rose, of course — following the sergeant's azimuth and somehow uncovering the almost indistinguishable trail that would end in a thorny orchard of bamboo and bramble and resume a dozen meters to the left front, right rear or wherever, we eventually reached our objective, where we set up a NDP and settled down for fitful spurts of sleep and drowsy ages of guard.

The new region seemed at first as devoid of the enemy as had the hilly district from which we had been helilifted. Two days passed without contact, the only sign that Charlie might be roaming the woods around us being several sorties of swooping fighter-bombers lacerating an adjacent ridge line with a ruby corolla of napalm and the sulphur-colored hammer blows of 500- and 750-pound bombs. Otherwise, it was monotonous marches and recon patrols, quick halts beside the trail to force down C-rats and catch our breath, merciless mountains, and a throbbingly bright, azure-glazed sky.

The morning of September 6 at last brought a flurry of action. As we were moving through an abandoned V.C. bunker complex terraced upon the gently rising slope of a flat-topped hill, two yellow men in black peasant trousers and shirts suddenly popped out of the bushes to point man Rose's right. They scampered off into a hedgerow of tangled bramble as Rose let loose an automatic burst. Most of the platoon broke file formation and charged over the crest of the nearest terrace in a wild fox hunt without horses, hounds and red hunting jackets, and with a fox of a different breed and color. The two hunted prey thrashed through the brush and scurried across a narrow, open stretch to dive into another thorny hedgerow. DeJesus and Rose both ripped automatic blasts and DeJesus exclaimed, "I got me a dink. By God, I wasted me one!"

We raced down the slope to ram our way through the green chaos. A splotch of blood reddened the brown earth next to a cowboy hat dropped by one of the fleeing Charlies. Pursuit was resumed for some distance, but when the lieutenant realized his men were becoming dangerously strung out in the undergrowth, he called off the chase and ordered us to reassemble.

I had, however, flamboyantly charged through the thickets, fired with the fantasy of leading a charge under flapping battle flags through gray gunpowder smoke to close with flashing bayonets against the enemy line. My imagination, alternately picturing me as one of Alexander the Great's pike-wielding phalanx, as a blue-coated grenadier of Napoleon's Young Guard, or as a Rough Rider following Teddy Roosevelt up San Juan Hill, carried me far from the platoon in a blaze of glory. When the plumed hordes of Persian charioteers, the Thin Red Line of British Redcoats, and the tropical white uniforms of the Spanish defenders of Santiago de Cuba faded into a knitted barrier of prickly vegetation, and I perceived through the adrenaline rush that my gallant "bayonet charge" was nothing but a futile chase through the brush after two unarmed, barefoot fugitives who had lost themselves in the overgrown labyrinth by now, I turned back to relocate my platoon.

Once the platoon had reassembled, Sgt. Welch rebuked us for our disorderly charge in pursuit of the two escaping Charlies.

"Now you men are all supposed to be members of the Hard Core Platoon, but you all acted like a bunch of low-life legs, dashing off like that to chase down two ragged slopes, as if catching them would force Uncle Ho to surrender tomorrow.

"You've all read stories or watched movies where a handful of Indian decoys taunt and tease a cavalry patrol into chasing them right into a box canyon where there's no escape except back the same direction they came, and that's plugged up by a war party of painted braves ready to swoop down on them all and take beaucoup scalps.

"Now, Charlie's a lot like those red Indians, using many of the same old tricks that Geronimo used. Charlie is just following in the tradition of the Apache, some of the finest guerrilla fighters in history. The only real difference between the Cong and Cochise's warriors is that Charlie's got a hell of a lot better weapons than bows and arrows, so that makes him twice as dangerous. They could have been trying the same old trick today ... and let me tell ya ... the way you were all bunched together it could have been Custer at the Little Bighorn all over again!"

Lt. Novak decided to remain on the fortified hill for the rest of the day and night in hopes of bagging some V.C. stragglers that intelligence reported were wandering the area in search of their unit, from which they had become separated during the explosive confusion of an air strike. The platoon leader set up two ambush sites, dispatching 2nd Squad and Herman's M-60 team to a grove of trees on the crest of the hill and stationing his platoon CP with Sgt. Tower's 1st Squad at a Stonehenge-like collection of boulders at the bottom. The men of 3rd Squad were again distributed between the other two rifle squads, Sgt. Blanco again being absent, this time detached to our Phan Rang base camp to attend the newly organized Squad Leader's School.

The night passed without incident. Sgt. Welch entertained us with outlandishly high-blown, tall tales and claims of preposterously exaggerated talents. According to his own reckoning, Welch was invincible, irresistible, and indefatigable. He was a royal bullshitter without compare, but it was testament to his charm and charisma that many of the men gathered in that ambush grove, chewing the cold turkey loaf and beans-and-franks of C-rats and sipping Kool-Aid mixed in Halozone tablet-purified water in green plastic canteens, actually believed at least part of the blustering sergeant's grandiloquent claims.

Midway through the next morning, RTO Mancuso, a Roman-nosed, whimsical Italian-American, was sent with his radio set and several armed escorts to climb a nearby mound rising from the green inland sea of elephant grass, with its terraced triangle shaped like a Mayan pyramid. There they were to scan the surrounding terrain for signs of the enemy. The sun was pulsating claws of heat which seemed to reach down inside a man's lungs to burn out every hard gasp of breath. The observation party left their fatigue shirts behind and several who had T-shirts knotted them around their foreheads as sweatbands.

Halfway to the hill, an L-19 Bird Dog artillery spotter plane flew low over the file of barebacked soldiers and then returned to swoop back and forth like a hungry hawk surveying a field for prairie chicken. The aerial observer in the circling prop plane — a throwback it seemed from this supersonic air war of jet fighters and eight-engine Stratofortresses to an earlier conflict of cloth and wood biplanes, of Lewis machine guns and Flying Circuses, of bescarfed, begoggled baron aces of the sky — must have been so hung over from last night's beer bust that both his vision and judgment were impaired. Though he glided over the paratroopers at almost treetop level — where he could plainly observe Mancuso and his guards wildly waving their black M-16s to confirm their identity, the AO could see only a chain of Viet Cong rambling across an open plain inviting destruction.

Within minutes, two 105 mm shells crashed into the plateau's hard-baked earth fifty meters from the column of G.I.s-turned V.C. by the faulty judgment of the blundering Bird Dog pilot. Fortunately, only dirt clods pelted the frightened soldiers, but the two rounds had been but bracketing adjusting fire; the next adjustment would be the final "Fire for effect" volley of six guns. The lieutenant, watching from a Sphinx-shaped boulder at 1st Squad's position, urgently radioed the FO attached to the Charlie "Six" ("Six" being the radio code for the company commander) to demand a cease-fire. This time, the commo network between units worked with lifesaving speed, preventing the cannoneers, who were one pull on the howitzers' lanyards away from wiping out an American patrol, from firing. Though Charlie had yet to present a serious threat to the platoon since I had joined it, we had twice narrowly escaped death or injury from the guns of my old comrades in the artillery. Though it was the infantrymen who did most of the dying, it was the men who fired the big guns of the artillery — those howitzers dubbed by their crews as "Cong Killer," "Charlie Zapper," or "Dink Downer," — who did most of the killing, without ever seeing the faces of their victims ... and far too often their shells failed to discriminate between friend and foe.

Chapter XIV

Firefight

Phu Tuan was an obscure little hamlet of mud and bamboo huts twenty miles from Tuy Hoa. It meant nothing to the world, but it would have real significance to a tired and understrength platoon of paratroopers and an equally ragged and undermanned company of North Vietnamese and Viet Cong regulars. For seven hours inhabited by hell, Phu Tuan became the shell-shocked center of the universe for 100-odd men sharing similar dreams and desires, but now intent on killing one another because the opposing men's faces were masked with the stamp of the "enemy."

This, then, was to be my ritual passage into the organized, often glamorized mass violence called combat, which I had sought with knowing zeal since my first day in Vietnam. Sniper rounds and mortar shells aside, this was to be the site of my first real bloodying in battle; where I would share in an experience so intimately close to death and yet one in which I was never so intensely aware of life; where that enigmatic creature of my dreams — the glory to be found only in war — was to show its true face to begin the long sobering process that would awaken me to the painful realities that my glory-fueled fantasies had so long concealed ... awaken me to the realities, but still not completely dispel war's allure.

September 8, 1966, dawned on 1st Platoon's weary troopers. While cutting into OD-painted tins of C-rations with our P-38 can openers, the voice of Charlie "One-Six" (the radio code for the 1st Platoon commander) crackled over the radio set for us to link up with platoon HQ for a new helilift several klicks north. While 2nd Squad was sent out on patrol to locate Alpha Company, to which we would be attached, the rest of the platoon remained on the terraces of the fortified hill, scanning the countryside for prey, like hunters poised for the kill in a duck blind. Morales soon spotted a Vietnamese from his crow's nest atop the Sphinx rock and, escorted by Doc Comiskey, who sometimes seemed as anxious to take lives as to save them, the fleet-footed trooper raced downhill to overtake the gook and slay him with a steel-jacketed spray of 5.56 mm bullets. The victim was a wrinkled old man who, had he been a communist guerrilla, must have retired from the terrorist trade a quarter of a century ago. But he was a gook, he was in V.C. territory, and now he was dead ... so, by the logic of the body count, he was Viet Cong.

The Recondos had crossed Charlie's path early that morning near Phu Tuan. Alpha Company and 1st Platoon were to assault onto several small landing zones and checkerboard the village complex, flushing out the enemy.

It was raining lightly as the three Hueys of the first wave touched down on our LZ of dry rice paddies intersected by crumbling dikes, surrounded on three sides by jungle and on the remaining side by a shallow stream meandering its lethargic way between ten-foot-high banks. All went well at first. My 2nd Squad fire team jumped off awkwardly with heavy rucksacks on our backs and rushed to the edge of the woods. Lt. Novak with platoon headquarters and the other fire team of 2nd Squad scooted to the stream bank on the opposite side. Then, dropping our rucksacks, we sat down in the drizzling rain to await the second wave. Welch, who had just been notified of his promotion to Staff Sergeant E-6, was on the stream side bent over a map with the lieutenant. Sgt. DeJesus, with Pfc. Johansen and Pfc. Burghart, lay in position nearby.

The light sprinkle had just ended as the last three choppers bearing the platoon sergeant and Sgt. Tower's 1st Squad made their approach. It was 1100. The two lead helicopters had dropped their loads of grunts and the last was hovering four feet over the paddy floor when the crack of AK-47 assault rifles shrieked above the thunder of the helicopters' blades. Then came the chorus ... a semi-circle of withering fire from the northern and northwestern edges of the LZ.

Machine gun fire ripped across the Huey's tail. The right door gunner slumped over in his seat and was silent. The startled troopers aboard leaped from the injured bird even as the craft began to rise to beat a hurried retreat into more friendly sky. The noise of chopper rotaries subsided but was replaced by the greater racket of heated combat. Somehow, none of the men were hit as they sought cover from the murderous stream of fire. All rushed to the safety of the stream bed, except for SP/4 Terry, who ran a few paces toward the opposite side facing the jungle before spreading out flat with his M-60 machine gun behind the doubtful cover of a foot-and-a-half-high intersecting paddy dike. He was immediately pinned down by an overhead hail of fire.

I was lying in position at the southwest corner of the LZ, with Pfc.s Rose and Whitehall of my fire team further up along the wood's edge. At first I thought the outburst of firing had been the nervous reactions of one of our cherry replacements fresh up from repo-depo (the Cam Ranh Bay replacement depot). My first realization that we had made contact with the enemy was the sight of a steady stream of green tracer bullets streaking from the jungle on the northern face of the LZ. In this, my first real taste of all-out battle, I found myself more confused than frightened; my nerves pulsating with excitement, my mind staggering under the sounds of combat. I sat momentarily frozen by indecision, stunned by the roaring voice of battle, far louder than I had ever imagined, even after all the training of live fire exercises, and far more terrifying.

From this vantage point, I could view the firefight without being overly exposed to our opponents' fire. I spotted the darting figure of a Viet Cong, the first time I had seen a live, armed communist soldier in fourteen months in Vietnam, but my reactions were still too dulled by combat's confusion to get off a round. Several other enemy soldiers attempted to flee from the northern curve of the woods, where they had become subjected to heavy fire from G.I.s in the stream bed. Two Charlies, attempting to join their comrades on the northwest corner of the LZ, were cut down almost instantaneously by M-16 bullets fired by Sgt. DeJesus and Sgt. Cuyler, a gung-ho fire team leader in 1st Squad. They sprawled lifelessly, side by side, not twenty meters from Pfc. Herman's crew of machine gunners, pinned down on the jungle side of the embattled field.

The platoon was returning fire in deadly earnest. The troopers staggered in position along the stream bank could only fire high across the LZ for fear of hitting their comrades pinned down on the opposite side ... for by now all the North Vietnamese had fled from the woods to the north of the rice paddy battlefield. A few men lay cowering in fear. Sgt. DeJesus became a one-man fire team, as Johansen and Burghart lay behind the cover of stream walls, offering no assistance. An even more frightened Weapons Squad leader, Sgt. Hagan, huddled beside them, his eyes bugged in mortal terror. Bresnihan lay near me with fear burned into his dark face.

I had by now recovered from my initial state of inertia and was anxious to join Herman's sorely pressed crew some forty meters away, behind the dike separating rice paddy from jungle. But I feared an attack from the quarter my fire team was to guard, so I held my position with Rose and Bresnahan. Pfc. Morales was with us also, having become separated from the 1st Squad. I could not restrain him from heading for where the storm's fury was hottest and heaviest. My first moments of shock shaken off, I too, like Morales, felt the tingling excitement, the chaotic call of combat. Several times I started to inch my way toward the eye of the hurricane. But always the nagging fear of an attack on the flank I was supposed to be defending and my new responsibility as fire team leader held me back. I was so close to battle's breath, feeling the heat of its exhalation, closer than I had ever been before ... but still, still its grand, seething thrill remained elusive.

Our two machine guns was blazing back at the hidden enemy. Only the fire-swept space of ten meters and a tangle of brush separated the hammering RPD machine gun of the enemy from Herman's gun. Neither gun could see its opponent, but each waged a blind, determined duel. Terry, some fifteen meters behind Herman, could see the Charlie machine gunners when he dared raise his head above the scant protection of the paddy dike to face a 7.62 mm hailstorm. His M-60 was spitting lead almost without pause, but it was all wild and high, as the weapon, without the brace of Terry's shoulder, jerked about in the convulsions of unrestrained recoil. Terry must have felt like all the fires in hell were leaping at him as two RPD machine guns vented their fury. Herman, almost within hand's reach of Charlie but far less exposed than Terry, was periodically up on one knee with his M-60 cradled in his arms and blazing away.

Both gunners were rapidly burning up their ready ammo. Terry, separated from his ammo bearer, Pfc. DeWitt, yelled for ammunition and Pfc. Burgess responded, leaping from Herman's side with 200 rounds. He rushed for Terry's position, dropped the ammo bandoliers, and returned to Herman's M-60 as bullets screamed over his crouched body.

Morales, rushing up from the rear with another 100-round belt, stopped short of Herman's gun, stood up, and hurled the belt across to Terry. SSgt. Welch, fighting behind the stream bank, also heard the machine gunner's cries for ammo. Throwing four 100-round bandoliers across his shoulders, Welch zig-zagged at a dead run across the longest fifty meters of his life. Most of the enemy fire was high, but that hardly lessened the terror of running toward two hammering NVA machine guns. Diving down beside Terry, Welch left two bandoliers and then bounded across the fire-purged ground to the second M-60.

But Welch was denied a chance to catch his breath there. I watched horrified as a smoking potato masher hand grenade came arcing over the brush to land almost in the laps of the four men clustered around the machine gun. I mumbled a low cry to myself, "Oh, God, those are dead men!"

Three men stared frozen in the face of imminent death, but one sprang into action. SSgt. Welch, diving on the grenade, scooped it up with his right hand, rolled over on his back, screamed at Terry to hug the ground, and hurled the smoldering death several feet into the paddy between Herman's team and Terry. The burst of yellow smoke and gray earth followed immediately but harmed no one. I let the air go that I had inhaled and held in expectation of seeing my comrades killed, and said to myself in admiration of the sergeant's brave deed, "Damn, I just saw John Wayne in action!"

The battle continued. The troopers who, seconds before, had narrowly escaped death seemed determined to allow the enemy no second chance. Blasting away and lobbing grenades, they were going all out to end the stalemate. With Terry screaming out range and deflection from his vantage point, Welch and Burgess were hurling grenades over the thicket. Whitehall, his short, stocky form hugging the ground, joined this focal point and began hurling blunt-nosed missiles from his M-79 grenade launcher. Unfortunately, most of the six-ounce rounds, which had to fly twelve feet before they were armed and which exploded into 300 fragments slicing the air at 5,000 feet per second, were bursting among the vines and limbs overhead, because they were point-detonating, unlike the time-fused M-26 hand grenades. The battling G.I.s were also plagued by many duds among the grenades thrown. Nonetheless, the screaming wounded were evidence that some damage was being inflicted on the hidden Charlies. Gradually, the returning fire slackened. A few more minutes of sporadic firing passed before we realized that the screams of the AKs and harsh crescendo of RPDs no longer intermingled with the racking thunder of our own weapons. Our crippled opponents were breaking contact and fleeing into the jungle.

The more lionhearted NCOs of the platoon followed the bloody trail of the retreating North Vietnamese west from the LZ into the forest. Fifty meters into the trees the trail led to a collection of thatch huts with air raid shelters and spider holes dug into the damp earth. Here, the battered NVA lashed back like wound-crazed animals striking back viciously at the hunters. Then those who were able fled, leaving behind two of the most seriously wounded. Both limped into the underground havens, but one foolishly raised his head up and felt the crashing impact of M-16 bullets. Three NCOs laid down a wall of protective fire as Morales crept up to the second enemy's shelter, grenade in hand. He heaved the grenade, striking the injured Charlie full on the face and hurling him violently skyward as it exploded into a thousand steel fragments.

Coming up the trail with the rest of the platoon, I saw first the two slain Charlies who had fallen early in the battle near where the LZ merged with the forest. Both wore ironic expressions of contentment on their young faces. Though caking, crimson pocks of bullet wounds and vacantly staring eyes were the only indications that these men were dead instead of dreaming, they already seemed somehow less than human to me. I could not allow myself the awareness then that I could have easily been lying there in my death posture; my life's experiences, hopes, memories, all suddenly terminated, as were those of the young men whom I could not now grace with the quality of humanity for fear of its implications of my own mortality.

I then saw the horrible effectiveness of Morales' grenade. The face was gone except for one charred, dangling eyeball. The pinkish-gray matter of his brain hung from tree limbs or mingled with blood, torn flesh and intestines on the jungle floor. His body was ripped and gouged, as if some blood-bloated beast had been feasting for days. I passed the mutilated form to post my fire team in a defensive circle around this former enemy haven.

I was disappointed with myself for taking no part in the firefight. It was over and I had done nothing but watch for an enemy on my flank who never appeared. I had not fired a single shot. I tried to console myself with the knowledge that I had acted responsibly by remaining at my post, when every nerve in my body was beckoning my brain to hasten me toward the hysteria at the focal point of the battle. But nagging doubt ambushed my thoughts. Maybe not all the tempest saturating my senses was the opiate rush of excitement, but possibly in part the deadening Novocain of fear. Was it possible that I had used the need to provide security for the platoon's exposed flank as an excuse to flinch from the flames of combat? Did glory, honor and valor weigh like feathers when measured on combat's demanding scale against a heavy, immobile block of fear?

I had no answers to such questions. The test of my courage, the moment I would win the glory I had sought, the event I had anxiously anticipated for so many months, had once again been denied me. The questions about myself, about my courage or the lack of it, which I felt more than anything else made a boy into a man, went unanswered again. I had once again been only an observer, a spectator, closer than I had ever been before but still not a part of the beating heart of the action. The chance to prove something so profoundly important to myself had passed. It had been only a little firefight, one that would not have even merited mention in the pages of the military histories with which I had shared my boyhood, and now it was all over. I could not have been more wrong.

Everyone felt reasonably sure that Charlie had been hurt too badly to demand an early rematch. The battle's tally was one-sided ... four dead gooks, several others wounded. Other than the wounded Huey door gunner, no one in the U.S. force had suffered a scratch. It seemed almost a miracle, considering the fiery cascade that had descended on us. The firefight was typical of a war in which both sides expended a great amount of ammo, much of it blindly into the brush, to kill but a few men. In terms of lives lost, numbers engaged, property destroyed, and political, social and economic costs to the populations directly and indirectly involved, Vietnam was a great war. But it was a great war with remarkably few great battles. Even the battles of the Ia Drang, Khe

Sanh and Dak To paled in stature when compared to the gigantic armed clashes of past conventional wars. Only the 1968 Tet Offensive and the 1972 North Vietnamese Spring Offensive — when taken as a whole instead of a series of interrelated battles, which they really were — will be considered by military historians as truly great clashes. Our firefight was the typical combat action of the war ... a war of skirmishes in which only a handful of men died, but a war in which thousands of such skirmishes were waged each year of an interminably long conflict to accumulate a final toll surpassing almost all wars.

Proud victors, their triumph unsullied by casualties of their own, the men of the platoon glowed over this violent challenge met and overcome and agreed that they had earned their combat pay on this one day. But our battle was not yet ended; several more lives were to be sacrificed to add bloody weight to its relative importance ... one based entirely on the number of dead it contributed to the volcanically rising mountain of corpses.

To make sure no Charlies remained in the area, Lt. Novak sent out recon patrols. I led one for a short distance west along an abandoned path, encountering nothing. Sgt. DeJesus was to take his fire team across the now quiet battlefield of the LZ to check out the stream bed.

DeJesus had just started to break out of the jungle at the very spot where the battle had burned brightest, when a blast occurred in the middle of his fire team file. It was one of the many dud grenades thrown by both sides during the LZ firefight, now tardily bursting out. Miraculously, Johansen, standing only five yards in front of the exploding grenade, was unharmed. Shrapnel ripped a piece from a canteen on his hip and tore through his baggy jungle fatigue trousers near his thigh, but none of the hot metal touched him. Not so lucky were DeJesus and Whitehall, both of whom were much further from the grenade than Johansen. Shrapnel chunks imbedded themselves in Whitehall's buttocks and a single sliver struck DeJesus in the spine, making him eligible for a third Purple Heart and providing him the option, because of the injury, of rotating home early, though it was doubtful the pugnacious paratrooper would take it.

While the medic tended the wounded, our platoon leader detached another patrol. Sgt. Tower's squad moved cautiously south along the ridgeline and crossed the stream, which curved east down a rugged ravine clogged with boulders. Moving up the wooded slopes of the hill opposite the stream, Sgt. Cuyler and Pfc. Morales at the point sighted several gooks, some limping, others being half carried by their comrades. Almost simultaneously, the enemy soldier covering the fugitives' rear whirled around, his AK screaming death. Cuyler dropped behind a tree; those behind him immediately hit the ground. Only the indomitable Morales remained on his feet. Attempting to dart across to Cuyler's side, Morales ran into a burst of 7.62 mm bullets. He crumpled, blood gushing from a gaping hole in the left side of his chest. Cuyler returned the volley with effect, but the wounded communist soldier managed to stagger away. Tower placed his men in a protective ring around the fallen trooper, as Cuyler vainly tried to hold back the flood of life streaming from the wound.

We at the NVA camp heard the clamor of renewed battle. Within a few minutes, Pfc. Shelby, a man existing in a state of perpetual bewilderment but now seemingly lost and confused more than ever, ran breathlessly toward our perimeter. He stuttered excitedly for the medic and, with him groping for the way, the two moved out. I accompanied them, hoping finally to join the fray.

Terry was hammering away with his M-60, while Pfc. Box's M-79 coughed grenades as we splashed across the stream. I joined the defensive circle of men, as Comiskey sought to save our comrade's life. Tower threw together a litter of bamboo poles and a poncho on which we laid Morales. With SP/4 Henk pressing hard on the gushing chest wound and on the exit hole in the back, we moved toward the LZ, I on one end of the litter, Bresnahan on the other.

My arms ached under the heavy load of the dying man. Henk was having difficulty holding back the surge of blood and several times we had to halt momentarily to allow Morales a chance to regain his failing breath. A deathly pallor was settled over his face and his voice was weak and fading. Reaching the LZ clearing, we placed Morales as gently as possible on the hard ground of the dry paddy as the lieutenant radioed for "emergency evac" the top Medevac priority (the lesser ones were "routine" and "urgent"). Morales began choking and then started vomiting blood. We uttered hopeless words of encouragement to him and made feeble, painful jokes about his great good fortune in getting out of the boonies and into a nice clean hospital bed with round-eyed nurses to pet and pamper him, but he seemed unable to hear us.

The gasping and vomiting continued until his face was covered with a bloody sheen and his head rested in a pool of red vomit. "My God, he is actually dying," I thought; a real man of flesh and blood, of emotions and memories ... not one of those little yellow moving targets whose humanity I had denuded so as to make the slaughter easier. For the platoon, which moments before had walked tall with pride over its easy victory but was now slumped disconsolately like sad olive drab apparitions, the heady thrill of the battle was dying with Morales. The enemy had scored a big goal in this deadly game, knocking out a bold and fearless man, a trooper who had often flaunted his invulnerability to enemy fire. We all seemed more vulnerable now; we all could die as easily as the slight, black-pajama-clad men lying in bloody pools at the edge of the LZ.

The platoon sergeant popped smoke and a purple cloud arose. The Dust-Off chopper approached, whipping the smoke into a violet vortex. Comiskey hoisted himself onto the Huey with Morales, leaving the twenty-one men remaining in the field without a medic. But the lieutenant knew how close Comiskey was to Morales and must have felt fairly certain that Charlie would be reluctant to test our mettle again this day. The action was ended; the fighting had ceased. The loss of Morales was a tragic epilogue to an otherwise triumphant day for the 1st Platoon, the lieutenant probably (and wrongly) reasoned.

We moved out immediately, with SSgt. Welch's squad leading. Rose, as usual on point when danger threatened, looked somewhat out of place in the Vietnam jungle. One could more easily imagine him attired in buckskin trousers and coonskin cap, a long-barreled Kentucky rifle cradled in his arms as he stalked the trail of the savage Shawnee in the tall pine forests of the Appalachians. But he was at home in any type of woods and wilderness, even the alien boonies of Vietnam.

Moving southeast down the opposite slope of the hill on which Morales had fallen, Rose spotted a prominent, recently traveled path. It led along the edge of more dried rice paddies and then skirted back west onto a low wooded ridge. Rose was just about to step out of the brush line into the open rice fields when he heard voices. He turned around to inform SSgt. Welch, but the squad leader was already aware of the danger, and in fact had been frantically whispering to his point man to halt. We sank to the ground as silently as possible on a forest floor matted with brush that crackled spitefully with each step we took. We detected what must have been officers and noncoms barking orders and heard the groans and cries of wounded men. The lieutenant assumed this must be the straggling enemy remnant from the LZ battle preparing to make a last-ditch stand.

With other platoons (and particularly in later years), the situation would have dictated the calling down of an artillery fire mission on the enemy concentration. The infantry would increasingly become just a tool to locate the enemy and then withdraw, or at most fix the NVA and V.C. in a vulnerable position while the air and artillery accomplished their execution. To find the enemy and later count the bodies once the last bomb had burst and the last shell exploded, but rarely to engage the enemy directly in sustained combat unless it was unavoidable, would become dogma and doctrine. But in the early years of the American ground combat war in Vietnam, before drugs, dissent, and the draft had sapped the infantry's fighting spirit, and before American commanders had acknowledged that the North Vietnamese and Viet Cong regular was at least the equal of the U.S. infantryman, American platoons, companies and battalions were often willing to close with the enemy in the deadly personal duel of pure infantry combat. That was the creed of our platoon and our platoon leader. Lt. Novak felt it was the duty of the American infantry to fight the NVA and V.C. infantry and to employ the arty and tac air only as an equalizer or in situations of desperation. Thus did the lieutenant decide to pick up the mailed glove thrown down in challenge by the enemy. With Herman's gun attached and accompanied by himself and his RTO, Pfc. Mancuso, he dispatched 2nd Squad to move behind the covering screen of brush to the ridge onto which the trail eventually curved and to strike the enemy unit in flank and rear.

Dropping my rucksack with 1st Squad, which was remaining behind in the brush for fire support, I crept on hands and knees toward the ridge, third man in line behind Rose and Welch. Lifting ourselves onto the higher terrain of the ridge, we crawled along an unused trail snaking along the four-foot height separating ridge from paddy. I moved slowly and deliberately, straining for silence in my approach but mocked for my efforts by the cracking contempt of the brush. I felt that the NVA soldiers not far ahead must surely hear what sounded to my mind like a colossal racket.

The voices could be heard clearly now and a few more steps brought us so close that we feared stepping on some dink crouched in his spider hole. Rose very nearly did so.

Creeping cautiously forward, Rose suddenly heard a shuffling noise in the clump of kunai grass only a hand's reach ahead. He spotted the flash suppressor on the black barrel of an M-16, probably taken off the body of a slain American soldier, then the black-clad back of an enemy soldier huddled in his freshly dug hole. At that moment, the gook heard a whispered command from Welch and whirled around. Rose, startled, fell straight back, accidentally pulling the trigger of his M-16, whose barrel was scarcely a foot from the surprised gook's face. Nearly twenty rounds lashed into the NVA soldier, and, while his body was still being buffeted, Welch pumped more lead into the Charlie.

The commands of leaders on both sides rang out and were followed seconds later by a barrage of enemy fire. We soon realized we had run into far more than a few crippled survivors from the first fight. As we were to discover at the end of this, our longest day, only our overhearing of the enemy's hurried preparations had prevented the platoon from following a path of destruction to where a company-sized ambush lay waiting.

Above the din of battle, Lt. Novak shouted instructions to Herman and Welch. The machine gunner slid down a slight incline into a dry rice field and placed the bipod of his M-60 on the two-foot-high paddy dike bridging the distance between the ridge and the small hill to the east. Again only a few yards of jungle separated dueling machine guns. Once more Herman found himself pinned down behind the meager cover of a dike, his M-60 blazing furiously. At least three NVA machine guns were belching lead in accompaniment to at least a score of automatic rifles popping caps, as Charlie faced about from his expected ambush site on the main trail to contend with our sudden appearance on this unexpected side. I jumped from the curve of the ridge into the paddy and assumed a kneeling position behind the dike and to the right of the M-60 team. Johansen momentarily inched down into the rice paddy, but decided the place was too hot and crawled back to the trail where he was less exposed. Rose and Welch lay in the same prone firing positions from which they had initiated the fray. Behind them and on the trail in an old spider hole quivered a pale-faced Burghart, then the less than gallant Johansen, followed by the lieutenant and his RTO. Ten men faced the firepower of an NVA company.

We were now more or less positioned in the shape of an inverted L. Rose and Welch lay at the point where the two legs of the L met, the legs being the intersecting dike and the ridge trail. Along the dike were the three men of the machine gun crew: Herman, Henk and Burgess. I knelt beside the M-60 team, and the rest of the squad lay along the trail. The RPD machine gun hammering at us along the dike was the North Vietnamese rear security. Most of the enemy positions were some fifty meters behind this gun and staggered to the left along the main trail crossing the width of the ridge. Unsure of our exact location and having to fire at odd angles to avoid hitting their own men protecting their rear, most of the North Vietnamese were firing high. Only the machine gun within spitting distance of us was causing any serious concern.

This time there was none of the hesitation that had immobilized me before. I immediately opened fire, though no enemy came within my sights. The firing on both sides was all blind, the thick kunai grass blocking out all vision. I rose from behind the dike on my knees, where I could place grazing fire on the unseen enemy, firing alternately short automatic bursts of three or four rounds and more carefully aimed semi-automatic volleys. Charlie's rounds streaked high over my head and churned up the dirt in the rice paddy several meters behind me.

Platoon Sergeant Peron and Sgt. Tower rushed the remaining eleven men to our aid, but in so doing hurled them straight across the open paddies. Fortunately, the dinks were too hotly engaged with Novak's patrol to turn their weapons on these easy targets. The platoon leader ordered Tower to flank the enemy, while Welch's men laid down heavy supporting fire. But the dink line extended much further to the left than Lt. Novak had calculated, and a steely shout from a NVA machine gun quickly convinced Tower that this maneuver was hopeless.

Welch had by now joined Herman and Burgess beside the machine gun and was demonstrating the best throwing arm in the platoon. Collecting grenades from the others, he was hurling the olive-colored steel eggs in a high arc to clear the kunai grass screening the gooks. A stricken communist soldier began the wailing of a wounded man. Welch hurled spears of profanity with his fragmenting rocks, as he stoned the enemy relentlessly.

"Here, you slopehead bastards. Take this trophy home to Uncle Ho!"

Zeroing in on the moans of the wounded North Vietnamese, Welch urged, "Come on, crybaby Charlie. Cry over this!" Again his arm jerked upward, catapulting death toward the enemy. The sergeant appeared to be having the time of his life. He was in his element, playing with deadly earnest the role for which he had seemingly been created. Welch was a true warrior ... one who loved war for war's sake alone, unencumbered with any pretensions to patriotism or idealism; a man who would be lost in a world which had eliminated the red test of war.

More orders were shouted in the excited monkey voices of the Vietnamese, and Charlie slowly started pulling back. His farewell to us came in the form of a hand grenade making a long, smoking arc over the grass to thud onto the hard earth not a foot from my right leg. In a moment of pure terror, I imagined my mutilated leg ripped from my body, leaving only a bloody stump and the twitching ganglia of severed nerves. I screamed "Grenade!" and hurled myself over the dike into a muddy puddle. But on that side of the dike I found myself exposed to RPD fire. Hardly before the grenade's blast had cleared, I once again flung my body, propelled by the force of fear, over the small bridge of earth that had offered death in two variations on its opposite sides.

I was unharmed ... but what of those who had crouched alongside me behind the dike? I was afraid to look where they had been clustered ... terrified I might see an abattoir of bloody corpses that had once been my comrades. Why hadn't I valiantly scooped up the grenade and thrown it back at the enemy as SSgt. Welch had done earlier? Why had self-preservation ruled, rather than heroism and courageous concern for the fate of my friends? Medals were not handed out to those who let their buddies die to save themselves. The call of glory had proven less compelling in the white-hot core of combat than the instinct for survival.

But my fears were unjustified, if the disappointment in myself was not, for the M-60 team had escaped the shrapnel storm unscathed. Henk, lying next to me, had heard my warning as I was springing over the dike. Glancing over his shoulder, he had asked, "Where? " But I had not lingered to inform him. The blast provided a violent answer to Henk's inquiry. The hundreds of iron splinters were blown upward and outward, over the prone bodies of the men stretched out behind the paddy dike. The steel spray of the grenade's deadly sneeze spent itself in the turbulent air already heavy with streaking lead.

The battle continued. Henk and I moved further right along the bank to throw an enfilading fire at what we supposed were Charlie's fighting holes. Here the dike crumbled away to nothing, our only protection being a shallow, muddy depression. The enemy fire continued high and was causing us no particular worry. We were making little attempt to use what cover there was and were pumping shells along the length of the enemy-held ridge. I was exposing myself far more than was necessary, anxious to convince myself, at least, of my courage, after failing to do the heroic thing when the grenade had put me to the test. Daring came easy now and presented little danger, with the NVA seeming to break contact and withdraw. It seemed like the enemy was admitting defeat again.

But the lull was merely a prelude to far worse action than we had yet experienced during this never-ending day. I heard the first crumping explosions far to our rear and assumed they were from our own artillery shelling the village complex. But then came the unmistakable coughing of mortar rounds streaking from their tubes.

I yelled, "It's a mortar ... we've got incoming!" ... as if everyone else were deaf to the reverberations of the bursting rounds.

The NVA mortarmen were rapidly narrowing the range. The roar grew louder as rounds fell on the other side of our dike-bordered paddy. I rose up on one knee to spray a hundred meters back on the ridge line to my left. Others commenced firing, all hoping that a few of the hundreds of rounds tearing at the jungle would find the mortar crew and silence them. Now the thunderous din of explosions almost seemed to engulf us. The cracked earth underneath us shuddered as shells came screaming into the tiny square of rice paddy where we lay. Lt. Novak pleaded into the black handset of the PRC-25 for artillery fire to rescue us, but it would be several endless minutes before the 105 mm shells would be on their way.

As I fired again in desperation toward the ridge, I heard Herman scream, "Holy Christ! I can see it coming!" and then, with rising terror cracking his voice, "It's gonna land right on top of us ... let's get the hell out of here!"

I glanced up to see the lethal black projectile come spiraling down on us like a ghastly iron football. Herman flung the M-60 into his arms, the powder-hot barrel burning red brands into his flesh. I lay in the shallow scoop of dirt beside Henk, trying to thrust my whole body up underneath my steel helmet, hugging the earth, feeling every crack in the hard soil beneath me, every little dirt clod ... as if this speck of the planet that I was embracing so passionately would be the last thing I would ever feel before eternity's black curtain came crashing down. As death — 82 millimeters wide, its silver warhead and orange fins blurring black in high-arcing flight — dived greedily down on us, I dug my fingernails into the barred gates of the ground which callously refused me asylum, pushed my face into the dirt until I tasted its gritty flavor, thrust my body into the unyielding sod, wanting to mold myself into it, to melt into it. But the earth was indifferent, implacable ... leaving me alone and isolated, helplessly exposed to the savagery of that horrible black shell screaming down on me. I sucked in a burning gasp of breath — hot, dry and stale, and tasting of panic, but possibly the last I would ever take — closed tightly my eyes, and endured the long vigil of endless seconds for the shell to impact. Finally, came the crash of climaxing earth and metal and then the fire of shrapnel against my back.

To Henk I muttered, with a mixture of relief and pride in my survival, "Well, I just earned my first Purple Heart." But Henk showed little interest in my wound; he was busily searching for sanctuary from a more painfully earned Purple Heart of his own.

I lifted my head to witness another shell soaring in and again panic possessed me. "Oh God, this is the one. This one is going to cream us for sure," I thought to myself. I had never felt closer to the eternal bondage of death than at that moment, as I watched the foreboding trajectory of the mortar round, slow enough to see but too deathly fast to avoid. We seemed helpless, condemned men in the electric chair waiting for the sudden, searing bolts. Nothing at that infinite moment could have convinced me that the onrushing shell would land anywhere else but squarely in the center of my spine, smashing me into a violent nirvana.

The earth heaved and quaked; a barrage of rock and rubble pelted me. But Odin was not yet ready to receive me through the gates of Valhalla; Ares had provided me with a shield; Osiris had raised me from the dead. As if by divine intervention, I had survived the annihilating shell. Once again the armor of invulnerability had protected my body, mind and spirit from the demons of death. My headlong fall into the black chasm had been broken by the net of life reclaimed, of survival. I had stared into the face of oblivion, but turned away at the last moment from its awful visage; I had seen the Stygian shore, but stepped back from the edge of the dark river. I had wrestled with Thanatos and won. Now nothing could kill me.

The dull, almost pleasant pop of a dud round followed. A volley of shouts were directed at Henk and me. Looking around, I discovered we were the only soldiers remaining in the erupting paddy. The platoon was retreating up the trail. I yelled at Henk to follow the retreating column and, firing my last, hopeless bursts at the triumphant enemy, I too abandoned the paddy square, almost tripping over the twisted tails of two exploded 82 "Mike Mike" (millimeter) mortar rounds that lay in the craters they had molded along the trail. The platoon was rushing away from this gunpowder purgatory. So very close had we come to beating Charlie at his own art of the ambush, and now we were surrendering the contested ground ... we were running away. I was sorely disappointed that my first full-fledged battle would be labeled an American defeat, but at the same time relieved that we might soon run far enough to win respite from the relentless mortar shells.

I was wrong; Lt. Novak had no intention of admitting defeat. He was pulling back a short distance and leading his men off the trail that had become a gauntlet through which his platoon had been forced to run, flailed by the explosive clubs wielded by the NVA mortar. We were deployed further up the ridge, the lieutenant hoping once again to strike around the North Vietnamese flank. We were back in the battle, though out of the maw of death that would have consumed us had we remained along the trail. I joined Rose covering the trail, as the platoon climbed through the thorns to its new rallying point. Then we too struggled uphill.

Platoon Sergeant Peron, who had been little more than a spectator throughout the fighting, was exhorting the men to hasten to where the platoon was reforming. "Let's go, come on men. Charlie plays a rough game but we can beat him. The only thing we can do against mortars is crawl toward 'em. Charlie can always increase his range if you run from him, but he sure as hell can't lob 'em in on top of you if you've got him by the balls." As far as I know, that speech was the platoon sergeant's only contribution to the battle that day.

PSgt. Peron was certainly no hero, but his actions were glorious when compared to those of Weapons Squad leader SSgt. Hagan. The grizzled lifer had been completely immobilized with fear all day. Now he was burrowed into the hollow of a huge tree, huddled up as if in devout prayer, his eyes like two white cue balls almost ready to pop from his head.

Next came the long awaited and greatly welcomed locomotive hiss of artillery shells. First two adjusting rounds rumbled. Then resounded a roaring chorus of HE shells tearing into the ridge in a bursting chain of steel, earth and jungle. A second, then a third volley from the howitzers of the 2/320th Artillery collided against the ridge. The mortars ceased their coughing. Everyone felt a close kinship to the gun bunnies of the 2/320th at that moment, and the two incidents of the accident-plagued week before were forgotten in a surge of gratitude.

I paused briefly to check the seriousness of my shrapnel wound. There was a small throbbing in the back of my shoulder. I could probe the wound with my fingers, and a quick investigation indicated it was little more than a scratch. I had fantasized about a wound that would leave an honorable and admirable scar to be proudly displayed as my sacrifice in torn flesh and lost blood for my flag and country. But the flecks of metal had barely penetrated the skin. I easily dug the largest piece out. Wait-a-Minute bushes, with their carnivorous claws of thorns, had inflicted more painful injuries on me. I decided the wound wasn't worthy of a Purple Heart, though others had won it for even less significant scars, and I did not bother to report the wound to the medic after the battle. What honor was there in a scratch, when so many other men's Purple Hearts were pinned to a body bag?

The cry now rang out for 2nd Squad to lead the attack, and Rose and I wove our way up to the side of SSgt. Welch. The word "attack" had always made me envision a colorful, bugles blaring, banners flapping rush of cheering soldiers with fixed bayonets into an erupting horizon. But the imagery failed in the green madhouse of Vietnam. Ours was like most attacks there ... a slow, torturous crawl that allowed a man plenty of time to think about what he was heading into. The color, the dash, the grandeur was absent. There was only the fear and a tense, black thrill.

Once again came the rush of mortar shells. Lt. Novak was immediately on the radio requesting more salvos of artillery fire. As 2nd Squad on the left had advanced closest to the enemy, it was 1st Squad on the right flank that bore the brunt of this second shelling. Fragments from the same round hit both Sgt. Tower and Pfc. Shelby. The platoon leader yelled over the din of battle to inquire about the seriousness of the wounds. But Shelby, being who he was, was puzzled, unsure whether his leg had been blown off, or if the skin had even been broken. He was still pondering his wound, when Miksis crawled over and diagnosed Shelby's injury as little more than a scratch. The bewildered private was greatly relieved and ready to fight again. In a constant state of shock, he blundered on, somehow in the confusion inflicting not a single casualty on the platoon and even claiming credit for one of the NVA dead that lay scattered among the leafy ruins following the firefight. Tower, whose leg wound was more severe than the platoon dunce's but not crippling, continued dragging himself toward the North Vietnamese.

In the distance we heard the rumble of a battery volley. The last mortar shell plunked, a dud, into the soft jungle floor as our howitzer rounds plowed into the enemy-held ground. The NVA mortarmen hastily withdrew, but no one else followed. It would be left to us to defeat the gook riflemen. Several North Vietnamese began pulling back to the main trail, giving us glimpses of their darting figures as they abandoned their forward positions. Rose loosened a long burst into a fleeing group of six. The only answering return was a wounded gook's cry.

The communists' fire dwindled as they regrouped with the main force in the fighting holes overlooking the trail. SSgt. Welch, seeing this withdrawal, interpreted it as the panicky flight of the entire force opposing us. He decided to move his squad rapidly around the left flank, gain the enemy's rear, and trap those who had not yet fled the battlefield. We rose to our feet and struggled as fast as possible through the jungle's entwining growth. The enemy remained silent ... ominously so. We waited for the shattering impact of concentrated automatic rifle fire. The image kept flashing into my mind of some Charlie hidden among the trees waiting for the right moment when I would be so close it would be impossible to miss and then thrusting his blazing AK-47 into my face. Was I now, at this very second, the target aligned in the v-sights of a rifle held by another nineteen-year-old boy, as frightened, confused and excited as I was? It was like walking into a primeval tiger's open jaws, his saber teeth the blue-black barrels of Kalashnikov automatic rifles.

I glanced over my shoulder to see Johansen, Burghart and the M-60 crew rush forward a few steps, then dive behind cover to anxiously scan the forest ahead. The squad was supposed to be advancing on line, but only Welch, Rose and I were so deployed. The rest were straggling, advancing hesitantly to our right rear and screwing up Welch's encirclement maneuver. I stopped to yell at the stragglers to move up on line, while Welch and Rose moved on ahead, unaware they were charging the foe unsupported. A flurry of firing popped and both men hit the ground. Noticing his "invincible" squad cowering to his rear, Welch turned to exhort us forward. I ran, feeling horribly exposed, to where the squad leader and his point man lay firing at the concealed foe. The rest of the squad still hung back, finding it much more difficult to force reluctant limbs forward toward an entrenched enemy than to fight him off in a defensive battle, as they had at the LZ.

Welch tried his best to convince his hesitant heroes to form up on his right, but to no avail. Finally, the sergeant dashed back to the stragglers and angrily ordered them forward on line. He did everything but bodily drag them by their collars. He could not have been too proud of his "Hard Core" troopers at that moment. He was utterly incapable of comprehending men who placed their lives before his lust for battle and their asses before honor.

Another lull descended over the battlefield, giving Lt. Novak the chance to bring up the rest of his platoon on line. Sgt. Cuyler and SP/4 Miksis moved up on the extreme left, the rest of 1st Squad forming up on the right of Welch's men. Sergeants Peron and Hagan valiantly covered the non-combatant rear. Once again we moved out toward the waiting enemy.

Nothing was more frightening that protracted day than the long walk into a smothering silence, rife with the expectation of fire and death. Heat and fear allied to stream sweat from my pores; my heart pounded in terror; waiting, waiting for the maddening moment when violence would come, unleashed like a rabid dog. The sudden storm came as almost a relief. Less than twenty meters had been covered — though it seemed like twenty leagues — when the heart-stopping eruption of enemy fire shattered the counterfeit silence.

The North Vietnamese fire crashed into us more heavily than ever. Like a giant scythe, it ripped apart tree limbs and branches, splintering small trees and scissoring loose a downpour of falling leaves. A young sapling beside me was sawed in half and toppled over my back. Bark and wood splinters whipped me across the face. Our own ragged return volleys were like lady fingers set off in the midst of a thunderstorm. Gratefully, the Charlie gunners were mostly firing high, inflicting incredible damage to the jungle foliage above our prone bodies but causing no harm to the platoon.

We continued to inch forward, pressing closer to Charlie's spider holes, AKs and RPDs. A concealed machine gun halted our progress on the left. It was practically in our faces, but the denseness of the jungle prevented our spotting its exact location. We returned heavy fire, but to no avail. Then Welch rose up into the maelstrom of streaking lead, trying to spot the RPD that was bogging down our assault. Flat on my stomach, I marveled at how the sergeant could survive what seemed like a tidal wave of machine gun fire. He continued bobbing up and down trying to locate the menacing RPD until, finally, machine gun bullets savagely stitched an ugly pattern across a tree trunk beside which he was crouching.

"Damn, I guess Charlie is serious about this shit!" he exclaimed with insouciant calm, though apparently convinced there was an outside chance that he was not totally invulnerable to Charlie's bullets.

SP/4 Maranville of 1st Squad slithered up on my right and decided that the RPD was behind a small mound less than ten meters to my front. "I'll lob a grenade into it," he shouted above the battle racket.

Both Welch and I tried to convince Maranville that the brush was much too thick there. A grenade could never find a path through the tangle that entrapped us and would probably rebound right back into our faces. But Maranville persisted and, crawling to a rotted tree trunk a few meters closer to the enemy gun, he tossed the grenade. It sailed a couple of feet before running into a net of vines which bounced it back toward Maranville's horror-stricken face. Frantically, he burrowed his body into the thick moss surrounding the tree and somehow sustained not a scratch. The concussion of the exploding grenade lifted me off the ground, shrapnel and dirt clods bouncing off my helmet.

Welch, bounding up on his knees again, caught sight of the NVA machine gun — not in the dug-out position Maranville had aimed at, but in a second hole some ten meters behind. We crawled to the first mound and laid down a blistering bullet barrage on the dink machine gunners. The foliage being less dense here, Welch lobbed a grenade, but it too was swallowed by the brush and exploded harmlessly between our mound and the enemy's position. Charlie had taken his limit however. One by one, the enemy squirmed away from the ambush position and fled down the trail. Automatic bursts from Cuyler and Miksis tore into the fleeing foe.

The bullet storm abated until only our weapons fire was heard. Finally, the platoon leader passed the word for cease-fire, as we occupied Charlie's surrendered fighting holes. They had left behind some booty for the souvenir hunters among us, though making sure they had escaped with the RPDs and other automatic weapons they had lugged over so many torturous, B-52 bomb-blasted kilometers down the Ho Chi Minh Trail. I gathered up a potato masher hand grenade and a North Vietnamese entrenching tool. The rest of the loot, other than the captured AKs and SKS carbines taken from the enemy dead, consisted of several hundred rounds of ammunition, several grenades, two canisters for transporting mortar rounds, and the belt and belt buckle bearing the engraved star of a North Vietnamese infantry officer ... always a top prize among the scavengers policing a 'Nam battlefield.

We staggered back in shifts to the slope where our rucksacks had been dropped to replenish our empty ammo pouches with the reserve magazines still in our packs. Meanwhile, the lieutenant radioed in an urgent request for ammo resupply. We had seeded the air with a prolific planting, seeking out its harvest of death. After firing not a single shot in the opening scene of this combat drama, I had overacted in the second violent act, firing seven magazines (nearly 140 rounds) at an enemy I rarely saw. But I had demonstrated temperance in my shooting compared with others, who had trimmed the jungle's green tresses with as many as 300 rounds, while the two machine gunners had all but defoliated the forest with over a thousand rounds each.

Certain studies by military researchers, including S.L.A. Marshall, have claimed that as few as one in seven U.S. infantrymen actually fired their weapons when they had the opportunity to do so in combat situations in the

Second World War, while the ratio for the Korean War improved considerably to one out of every two. Judging on the evidence of my own company and the claims of other veterans I have questioned, I would estimate that at least two out of every three foot soldiers in Vietnam fired their weapons whenever they were given a chance to do so ... at least in the early years of the war.

Certainly we had men like Johansen and Hagan and Peron whose weapons remained silent through every firefight, but their abstinence was more than compensated by a surplus of gunmen whose trigger fingers grew calloused from constant use. I suppose part of the reason we expended far more ammo per grunt than did our World War II and Korean War predecessors was simply because our light automatic M-16s were more fun to shoot than the heavy semi-automatic M-1 Garands of 1941–45 and 1950–53. In those earlier conflicts, only two men out of an eleven-man squad carried automatic weapons and they were the twenty-pound BARs (Browning Automatic Rifles). Our M-16s had selector switches that could be flipped on either automatic or semi-automatic fire, and our leaders cautioned us against flagrant automatic firing, both because of its inaccuracy and its incredibly rapid expenditure of ammunition. But all too often grunts ignored this advice and the instruction to fire automatically in three-round bursts to improve accuracy and conserve ammunition, so that they could experience the thrill of twenty rounds spurting from smoking muzzles in a few seconds.

Everyone was exhausted and still shaken, but relieved that it really did seem over this time. The vanity of our victory rose as we surveyed the battlefield to discover that the North Vietnamese 95th Regiment had occupied 30 two- or three-man fighting holes, indicating that we had battled and beaten a force at least three times our strength. That was, of course, part of my fantasies ... that in my heroic battle we would be a valiant handful overcoming vast hordes of the enemy — like the thirty-two bluecoats against 1,500 Sioux and Cheyenne at the Wagon Box Fight in 1867, or like the 100 redcoats of Her Majesty's 24th Infantry Regiment fighting off 4,000 assegai-armed Zulu warriors at Rorke's Drift in 1879.

I was spent. A rudderless raft with sails powered by the adrenaline rush of combat had sailed through my system. But the fireship had now burned itself out, and the first heavily laden frigates of fatigue were beginning to ply their way downstream.

But if the surface was returning to a calm flow, beneath surged a strong, euphoric current. For awhile at least, it outraced the tide of weariness breaking over me from nearly seven hours of combat. That current sent a glow of elation through my tired body. I had survived my first battle, only a firefight of platoons, but for me, the eager novitiate to the gladiator's ring, a great, decisive Waterloo.

I had felt fairly certain that when my moment of glory or infamy came I would not be relegated to the dishonored regiments of history's cowards. Should those temples exalting glory collapse from the Samson's wrench of terror, the apprehension that I might disgrace myself in the eyes of my comrades-in-arms would surely, I felt, protect me from the temptation to flee from a place of death.

If I had little fear of bringing dishonor on myself by cowardly acts, I was apprehensive that a self-defensive inertia in the heat of battle would prevent my undergoing the full test of courage. Indeed, that was what initially appeared to be the outcome of my first firefight. A paralysis of uncertainty and confusion had made me an invalid, tormented by contradicting voices pointing my passion toward the eye of the hurricane and at the same time commanding me to stay in the harbor and secure the boats. After waiting so long for my valor to be tested, hoping for a score requisite for entry into the great academy of glory, where degrees were awarded not in rolled diplomas but in ribboned medals, I, because of halting indecision, was not even allowed admittance into the testing hall ... though I could peer through its windows to watch the test being administered to others.

But a rekindling of the battle's ashes into a second fire saved me from the ignominy of my static role in the first blaze and enabled me to glimpse the general shape of my courage. I had not won the right to cloak myself in the scarlet robe of glory, had not performed heroic deeds as had my Assyrian squad leader, but I felt I had conducted myself with determined dignity ... not spectacular, not heroic, but with a steadiness that would permit me entrance into the barracks of Valhalla should that display of steadiness under fire be amended by death. My courage, thus far at least, was the shared, quiet, cooperative courage of the Roman Legionnaire, not the flashy, fiercely individualistic Viking courage characteristic of Welch. I had demonstrated a sometimes dismaying urgency to preserve the integrity of my ass from enemy fire. I had exposed my life to sudden, violent termination only when the fortunes of battle necessitated it and had kept my ass down when it wasn't required that it be exposed, while Welch had tempted fate constantly with an indifference born of invincibility. I was unsure whether I lacked his kind of courage or the certainty of his own immortality.

Though pleased that I had unearthed with the spade of battle the treasure chest containing my courage, I was still disappointed that it did not bear more glittering gems of glory. But I was consoled by the certainty that the desert isle that represented my months in the war must surely conceal more buried treasure beneath its wastes. Today's firefight was only a beginning; I would march on to greater battles and greater glories.

Little did I suspect that there would be no more battles ... that this firefight, that had seemed like a carney barker's sneak preview enticing crowds into the big top for the main show, was to be the only show. The carnival would prove to be cheap, dirty and bloody, presenting acts with no glamour or glory, featuring snipers, booby traps and fearful, frustrated men who became murderers. There was to be no great circus of sacrifice with grand, three-ring acts of battles, sieges and campaigns. This one insignificant skirmish was to be my Zama, my Shiloh, my Verdun. I would see many men die and watch their blood flow, but not into any honorable sea of heroes as I would have imagined; I would witness it dripping instead into a vast, red, rising swamp.

Twilight was settling in and the tall jungle canopy was already creating its own premature darkness. A platoon from Alpha Company moved to link up with us. The artillery came crashing in its DTs (Defensive Targets), first with Willie Peter airbursts, then with marking HE rounds. Some of the rounds splintered the jungle perilously close to our NDP, but it remained a greatly reassuring thought throughout the long night that our artillery was close at hand. It was a hot, largely sleepless night with the fear of renewed battle haunting us. No one pulled out his poncho to sleep on for fear that the slightest rustle might attract enemy fire; no one dared to smoke or even slap at the butterfly-sized mosquitoes dive bombing us.

With the new dawn, there would be more fighting and a few more men would die, but the worst was over. It would be three days before we would hear that Morales had died on the way to the hospital in Nhatrang. Other than this tragic loss, we had escaped with miraculously light casualties. Who knows why one man dies while others escape unscathed? Only circumstances and uncompromising fate had allowed us to come through the ordeal so lightly scarred while another platoon at some other time and place, but under similar fire storms, would have been all but annihilated. We could find no explanation for fate's capricious quirks; we could only, in our incomprehension, label ourselves lucky and be thankful for whatever or whoever had directed the bullets away from our bodies.

I rarely reflected on death while in Vietnam, except for those chaotic moments when battle's metamorphosis transformed it from a shadowed thought into the heavy form and substance of a dark presence. Death was an unseen but constant companion. It was impossible to ignore its omnipresence, but it was almost as difficult to stop and confront the ultimate coldness of this comrade marching darkly at our side. To stare boldly into the black abyss of its countenance demanded greater courage than was required to march into the guns of the enemy. And so we wore the psychic armor of invulnerability, each man carrying a certainty that though others might die, he himself was destined to survive. At times, such as during the mortar bombardment at Phu Tuan, deep cracks appeared in that armor. But with each fiery ordeal we came safely through, our sense of invulnerability grew stronger.

Eventually, survival itself became a badge of honor; we developed a sense of superiority and eliteness in the mere fact of our survival. Often we were torn by conflicting feelings of relief and guilt; relief that others had been struck down while we had somehow survived, and a guilt that our lives had been purchased by their deaths. We needed that sense of invulnerability though; it was essential to our spirit and morale. But it had its cost, for once Vietnam was left behind and the armor of invincibility was discarded into the dust along with the rest of our 'Nam legacy, we were left feeling naked and defenseless against our ruthless mortality. Life would seem but a moment's usurpation in death's eternal reign; a quickly burnt out comet streaking through an infinite blackness called death. My immortality in Vietnam would be followed back in the real world by a powerful sense of vulnerability. Though only in my early twenties in my first years back from Vietnam, I was like an old man fearful of the passing years that seemed to gather in dark alliance to wait in murderous ambush.

Nineteen bodies were found posed in expressions of death in their vast green sarcophagus. The only acknowledgment of our execution of those men would be an entry in the neat, fine print of official battle reports, the military's book of record that neither bled nor carried the stench of death.

In the gray mist of the morning after the battle, as I stared at the debris of human beings reposing in bloody somnolence, conflicting emotions parried their swordblows within. A conscience, wounded long before the catharsis of this battle, but still hobbling alongside, whispered a hope into my soul that no man who bore the brand of "the enemy" had exchanged his blood for my bullets. But another part of me, my conscience's dark reflection, thrust with a rapier of disappointment at my failure to outline in enemy blood the boundaries of my courage.

The battlefields on which fought the armies mobilized by my boyhood imagination had been decorated with red wreaths of the fallen, but they had been only bloody ornaments on my glory tree. In those fantasy battles, I had killed enemy soldiers and then rushed on to greater glories, never pausing to study the grim sculptures my steel-jacketed fingers had molded out of the human clay of my victims, all of whom fell before my blasting weapon in the easy, bloodless, instant slumber of John Wayne war movie deaths. But with my eyes now riveted to the humanless, dead forms, the appalling significance of what I may have done struck me for the first time. Though I had seen no enemy fall in worship to the war god of my weapon — and thus could not nick with my bayonet a notch into the black stock of my M-16 as many in the company did, like ace fighter pilots painting growing rows of downed enemy planes onto their aircrafts' fuselages — still I could not be certain that none of the 140 steel sperm that I had ejaculated into the jungle's wet womb had not flagellated their way to the soft egg of human flesh. Only half of the enemy corpses could be the verifiably claimed bounty of individual hunters, because so much of the firing had been blindly directed. The rest of the dead represented the commonly killed bag of every man in the platoon who had fired a single shot in the blind melee. No one could be certain whose squeezing trigger finger had catapulted the few bullets which had ravaged human flesh and bone. It was a profoundly unsettling feeling, not knowing for sure whether I had taken a life.

Some of us in the platoon would be rewarded for our actions in the firefight. Most were greatly deserving of the medals — colored ribbons and bronze medallions, reminders of an interminable day of sweat, death, and a sweet, dark thrill as close to heaven as hell — a few less so, but receiving them nonetheless as the Army's compensation for pain and horror endured. SSgt. Welch would win the Distinguished Service Cross, the nation's second highest award for combat valor. One should also have gone to his guardian angel who was vastly overworked that day. To a very brave and very dead Morales went a Silver Star. Lt. Novak was also pinned with a Silver Star. A Bronze Star with V went to Herman, who had performed valuable service with his M-60 "pig." Rose and I were awarded Army Commendation Medals with V.

Chapter XV

Night March

September 9 dawned over the battlefield and a long sleepless vigil came to an end. Soon after the sun had popped its orange stare over the horizon, Sgt. Tower's squad was dispatched to guide another platoon from Alpha Company into position astride the path which was to have become our place of execution. An AK opened up on the squad as it crossed the paddies, but as the squad deployed the lingering NVA rifleman fled. It was a weak encore to the crashing concert of arms the day before. One platoon of Alpha Company did bump into the rear guard of the retreating foe half a klick away, killing one and putting the rest to flight, but otherwise Charlie avoided any further contact with the Five O' Deuce.

That afternoon we hiked back to the NVA camp near the LZ where Lt. Novak greeted the new battalion commander, Lt. Col. Frank Dietrich. Not to be forever in the shadow of the departed Gunfighter Emerson, the new CO had assumed the title "Gunslinger," intent on molding a legend of his own. Dietrich dropped his heavy arrogance and huge frame out of his command copter to pump the lieutenant's hand and express appreciation to us for procuring for his body count keepers all those career enhancing corpses. Then he turned to gallop confidently back to the waiting chopper. We had just received our reward for the previous day's work of slaughter. Somehow, it did not seem to compensate fully for those blazing hours when bullets ruled the wind.

The night provided us a few hours' sleep between stints of guard duty, the stench of rotting flesh clinging like a vile mist to the captured enemy camp. The new morning brought orders for the platoon to link up with the rest of the company for extraction to another jungled estate of Phu Yen Province. Shortly after moving out, Herman, one of the platoon's rallying points during the stiff fighting two days before, nearly canceled out his heroics by a careless discharge of his M-60 pig. It coughed a staccato burst of bullets inches from the scalp of a startled Lt. Novak. Herman paled with a sick look, but the lieutenant was unharmed.

The march to the company link-up site was over grueling terrain, which we were to cover in ASAP time. Johansen was no more able to face this challenge of nature than he had been able to show courage before the mortal enemies that had confronted us in the firefight of September 8. Almost in tears, the delicate dandy pleaded with a disgusted Welch to distribute the contents of his pack among the other men of the squad, claiming the back-breaking load was conspiring with the horrid moonscape we were marching across to grind his weak spine to dust. He finally crumpled in a moaning heap, begging for rest and wailing about his snapping spine. Reluctantly, Lt. Novak left Doc Comiskey, who had rejoined us, to nurse or kick the malingerer back into shape while the platoon continued toward the company assembly point. The disease afflicting Johansen was not contagious; the other men of the platoon were aware that what was needed now was the perseverance of the suffering soldier, not the evasions of the "ghost" or goldbrick. In the boonies, where each man was expected to carry his share of the burden, to do his part in and out of battle, to absorb an equal part of the allotment of adversity dealt out to us all, a ghost was intolerable to those who were forced to lug the additional physical and emotional load cast off the coward's weak shoulders. Johansen's status in the platoon hit rock bottom. From now on he would be exiled from the platoon's respect and concern.

United with the company, the platoon was reinforced by two cherries, both black draftees: Pfcs. Meadows and Rhodes. Meadows was grumpy, grouchy and loathed everything military. He swore to retain the roll of blubber around his waist as his symbol of a civilian forced into uniform, regardless of the claims of his new comrades that the wedges of fat would soon dissolve in the Army's weight-reducing program of starvation rations and jungle humping. Rhodes was a gangling, coal-black giraffe, whose most prominent features were monster-sized feet that spread across the ground like lumpy black batter, the sagging ankles drooping almost to the ground. He looked the epitome of clumsiness and events would prove appearances correct. Meadows mockingly called Rhodes "Captain Tugboat," but the sluggish Watusi took his and others' ridicule in easy stride and carried himself with a kind of improbable dignity.

The man's amorphous snowshoe feet were the worst I had seen and represented a major handicap for an infantryman. I had known several men who failed the Army's physical test for induction because of flat feet that, in comparison to the fourteen triple X monstrosities attached to Rhodes' skinny black stilts, were like the sturdy hoofs of a mountain goat. Rhodes' feet seemed to spread wider and flatter with each agonizing step. When stumbling across a rocky streambed, his feet appeared to melt to liquid, streaming over the surfaces of each boulder. Propelling his feet up a steep incline was like trying to force water uphill without a pump. For Rhodes, marching was often the painful process of a few steps forward followed by a crashing collapse to the ground.

The company waited for its weapons platoon to join up. That platoon finally filed into the company NDP as evening approached, having killed two fleeing Viet Cong encountered along the way. The next day our rotary-bladed pack mules cantered cumbersomely down from a sun-emblazoned sky and carried us back to the rear for a three-hour interval between missions.

Intelligence reports indicated a Viet Cong battalion was preparing to strike a village south of Tuy Hoa, with the aim of confiscating 300 tons of recently harvested rice. Our battalion's battle plan called for a night airmobile assault on landing zones ringing the village and then deployment into ambush positions to catch the withdrawing enemy battalion. We were granted time enough to gulp down a hot meal at the South Field mess tent, restock our rucksacks with C-rats and ammo, and gather up four more cherries: Pfc.s Booth, Burke, Jefferson and Landon. Then at sunset we shouldered our packs and gear and loaded ourselves into helicopters. Johansen was left behind in the rear area among the greasy pots and pans of the company mess to doctor his ailing back. This was, of course, exactly what he wanted, KP or no KP, but nobody wanted his gutlessness out where little mattered except guts.

This was my first night heliborne combat assault. The night seemed almost surrealistic ... the chopping thunder of helicopter blades swiping away at the lavender sky; the shadow-world landscape of paddies, mountains and forest all rushing beneath our heliborne feet with a mystery born of madness. The air was cool, as rotary-whipped currents flapped my grimy fatigues and filtered through my second skin of two weeks' accumulated filth. Nevertheless, beads of perspiration teardropped on my brow as our choppers switched off their flying lights and began the blacked-out descent to a dark LZ dimly out-lined by flares and the red-lensed flashlights of the advance Recondo element. A LZ assault now held for me a deep-seated dread — not the trembling terror of pure panic, but a weighty sense of menace — a result of the fiery reception we had met on the landing zone near Phu Tuan. Anxiety's embrace gripped tighter as I struggled against a sinister-looking night that might hide an engulfing violence. My stomach muscles tightened as though in self-defensive effort to forge armor from flesh; a choking lump swelled in my desert-dry throat as the ground loomed closer and my expectations of mad battle sky-rocketed.

The chopper settled to the floor of the landing zone and men scrambled ungainly, backpacks wobbling and canteens and grenades flopping against LBEs, to the edge of the LZ where they would provide security for the incoming chalks of Hueys of the second wave. Noise and nervousness ruled this kingdom of shadows. How hellish things might have been had a single sniper added his violent offering to the reign of confusion. Fortunately, all the danger remained in men's minds. Men located their comrades, who in turn found their companies, and order slowly succeeded disorder. The anxiety heightened by our night landing slid back down to its normal percolating level. The night heliborne assault had brought only black bewilderment; it was the night march ahead that was to bring us hell.

The distance we were to cover to reach the platoon's objective was not great according to its map definition, but the map was an accomplished deceiver. There would never be another hump, day or night, to compare with its tortuous route. There was never a darker night nor more treacherous terrain to negotiate than that which tested the quality of our endurance during those hours ironed forever in my memory.

Once again Rose and Welch led the stumbling procession. The route led through a streambed abundant with boulders and other booby traps erected by a malicious nature, all of which we tumbled over or into as our night-blinded eyes easily led us astray. Long hours passed ... of shins scraped and knees knocked by boulders; of faces slashed by thorny limbs, flailing like cat-o'-nine-tails out of the darkness; of dropping off into stagnant, water-filled holes and sliding down muddy banks. Men strayed away from the staggering column to wander in the jungle labyrinth, whispering desperately for their comrades. Orders were relayed down the tottering platoon file to pass the count up from the last man in the column periodically to reassure the platoon leader there were still the same number of men following him as there had been at the beginning of the night's agony, and for each man to grasp ahold of the rucksack straps carried by the man in front of him. But still we strayed and staggered.

Even the indomitable point team became lost in the undercurrent of this stumbling stream, their usually razor-sharp senses smothered in the welter of topographical confusion that led us in circles, caused the platoon to retrace its own excruciating steps, and forced us to ramble aimlessly through a twisted torment of rock-clogged streams. A dozen delays impeded our progress as we waited for the straggling tail-end of the column to catch up, or as the count suddenly registered one or two men short, causing other men to wander off in search of those who had strayed and become lost themselves in the spongy, black amoeba of forest that seemed to absorb men into its opaque entrails ... just as Vietnam seemed to be absorbing America's purpose and innocence into a grinding gut of confusion.

We seemed to be walking through an eternally black tunnel with no reflection of light visible at either end ... in fact there seemed to be no end, and the beginning was so far lost in the consuming darkness that there appeared no possibility of regaining its enlightenment. We tumbled through a cave locked in an endless midnight and populated by a cruel host, inanimate, but nonetheless mocking and deriding us for our futile efforts to navigate a passage through its stony complexity.

It was the first night in the 'Nam boonies for several of the men. Of course, the cherry who suffered most was Captain Tugboat. The misfit infantryman would have experienced difficulty maintaining his balance on a sidewalk in his windy city of Chicago, let alone on a rugged jungle trail in Vietnam. But piloting a passage through a blind channel choked with the challenges of a malevolent nature was almost an impossibility for poor Rhodes. The flat-footed soldier was careening directly behind me as if in a drunken stupor. Able to distinguish Rhodes' attenuated frame only by his huge white eyeballs, I struggled to guide him along the obstacle course. Again and again I was forced to whisper for the platoon file ahead to halt while I turned back to aid the lagging Rhodes in his unsteady scaling of a slippery incline, pull his bony body out of a mudhole, or search for him as he roamed off into the bowels of confusion. Finally, I took his massive, coal-colored hand in mine to lead him along the path and try to keep pace with the platoon.

We kept going, on and on, groping through the darkness, almost in a state of numbness, searching for a pinpoint on the map that was our objective. At last, three hours before the sun rose, the lieutenant gave up and nestled his footsore platoon in a rocky scar on the earth's rugged face for a few hours' rest. Few of the sentries were able to fight off the overpowering temptation of sleep. An enterprising Viet Cong patrol could have strolled unimpeded through our cluster of sleeping soldiers and cut everyone's throats. That night, exhaustion assumed a more overpowering presence than fear.

Rhodes did not immediately fall asleep like the rest of the platoon. He first groaned out of his huge jungle boots to massage his surfboard-sized feet. Then he too collapsed, his battered feet sticking up like two dark tombstones.

As it turned out, the scraped shins, turned ankles, holes we had fallen into and ravines we had tumbled down, the sweat and shit we had endured — all were for nothing. Not a single enemy soldier was encountered during the night by any unit of the battalion, nor during the patrolling of the following two days. The torment of the night march made us thirst for bodies and blood to make our agonies seem worthwhile. But we found nothing and no one to wreak our vengeance on; nothing but the same rocks and thorns that had caused our suffering, and they were impervious to our weapons.

We began to suspect our leaders had known all along that we would encounter no human enemy; that they had dispatched us out here to suffer, and through the frustrating, losing battle with the land and jungle to perversely motivate us to seek revenge against the people who inhabited the land. If we could not draw blood from the jungle, we could from the human foe who haunted it. We speculated that the mission had been nothing but a scheme by our depraved commanders to respark our dark passions, inciting us, their killing machines, into a pogrom against this hateful land and its alien inhabitants.

Though the area was barren of the enemy, one would have thought we had penetrated into a major V.C. bastion by the sound of the calls radioed to the platoon leader by the company CP on the mission's second night. For hours, the captain insisted he was surrounded by enemy hordes creeping through the undergrowth toward his position. The company's ultra-violet Starlight scopes failed to pick out and identify the adversary, and Captain Silvasy's fear of pinpointing his men's positions for the enemy amid the glow of artillery flares prevented him from calling in illumination rounds. Consequently, his men had to sweat out a sleepless night until daylight could reveal the enemy assault wave ... a tribe of playful spider monkeys scampering through the treetops. They had given the company its only anxious moments during the operation.

I experienced my own moment of fear, though, when Welch dispatched me and a five man fire team on my first independent patrol as patrol leader. Certain that I would get my patrol hopelessly lost, I set out with a bespectacled, beanpole recruit named Jerry Booth blundering along as my point man, who had no more idea of what he was doing than I did. My patrol also included Rhodes, tumbling into the creek that everyone else easily skipped across on a natural bridge of water-polished rocks, falling into holes everyone else avoided, entangling himself in a prickly welter of serpentine vines which the rest of the patrol threaded its way through without trouble, and bumping his kinky-haired cranium into low-hanging limbs safely ducked by his comrades.

I attempted a show of confidence and competence, but as I plodded along with nose glued to the map and eyes fixed on the compass, it was obvious to all that I had a long way to go as a pathfinder. Fortunately, the route was fairly easy and I did succeed, without too much brain damage, in finding my way back to the platoon. Our mission was to scour the area for signs of the enemy, but I was too deeply immersed in trying to save face with my comrades to keep in mind that we were in enemy country, subject to ambush at any moment. I looked for neither ambush nor enemy ... only for the way back. The fear of being ridiculed for my incompetence outweighed all other concerns.

Upon the patrol's return to the platoon, I was greeted with Welch's praise and his announcement that he was to be extracted back to South Field to straighten out a bureaucratic foul-up in his records, leaving me in command of the Hard Core Squad. I was momentarily panic-stricken. I had wanted glory and derring-do in the infantry, not leadership and responsibility. My ego needed to be fueled by medals, not by command. The fates of ten men were thrown into my weak hands and all I could do was tightly interlace my fingers and pray that no lives slipped through.

To my vast relief, nothing arose in the next few days to test my command competence. We linked up with the company for extraction to the rear, but that was delayed when Lt. Strong of the 3rd Platoon lost his men in the jungle derangement. A Huey brought in the Pony Express and a "Brown Derby" (a hot meal flown in from the South Field mess tent) and carried back Burghart, sick with malaria. The following afternoon, September 15, the lost sheep of Lt. Strong's 3rd Platoon returned to the company fold, and Charlie Company was removed from the scene of its latest wild goose chase.

Almost immediately upon arriving back at brigade camp, I was confronted by the company ogre, Moses Atticus Tate, a human fester from the hills of West Virginia. The platinum, burr-headed, flushed-faced mountaineer, with features as sharp and harsh as the raw, red walls of his state's open pit mines and slag heaps, had suffered a broken leg late in July. Thus I had seen little of the man. But from the stories told of the "Wild Man from West Virginny," I had tagged him a psychopath. He was alien to any of the more gentle qualities that make humanity tolerable as a species; his heart had atrophied into a hard, flat stone and at the center of his soul lay only a cold, black vacuum.

Tate delighted in testing the mettle of each new cherry or transfer. If the new man failed to withstand Tate's torments, he would be subsequently terrorized by the madman at every opportunity. But should the object of the wild mountain man's harassment show an unwillingness to turn the other cheek, then the lunatic would grudgingly give him his respect. I was expecting the Appalachian lycanthrope to put me to the test at any time, so it was no great shock when an empty beer can sailed from his swinging hand and bounced with a metallic clang off the side of my head.

"Sorry about that shit, hero!" Tate snarled belligerently. "You are a fuckin' hero, aren't you? Mr. Acting Jack Squad Leader!"

Too weary from our just-finished operation to put up with his shit, and realizing that I would have to confront Tate eventually anyway, I stomped angrily over to the grinning, wild-eyed bully. Ushering forth all the fury I could muster, I growled with Hard Core fierceness, "Don't ever do anything like that again, Tate.

"I've seen you throwing the weight of your tongue around here.... Well, it doesn't impress me, Tate. The only way you're going to impress me is with your conduct out in the boonies. I haven't seen you out there yet, so as far as I know you ain't shit!"

With this blow to his pride, Tate's eyes took on an even wilder glare. "Look here, Acting Jack.... Nobody calls Moses Atticus Tate a ball-less wonder. I ain't afraid of no man alive, including all the slopehead bastards in Southeast Asia. I can outhump, outfight, outdrink and outfuck any man in the O' Deuce ... shit, any man in the whole fuckin' One O' Worst. You might also ought to know that I'm the craziest fucker in olive drab. I'd cut the balls off any man for a piastre and fuck a water buffalo if I get too horny. And I'm a gook gobbler.... I just love gook meat, man. Ain't nothing better than ripping out a gook's heart with my bare hands and consumin' every bloody bit of it!" Tate culminated his fit by bursting out in maniacal laughter.

"You don't belong on a battlefield, Tate. You should be locked up in a loony bin," I said in disgust.

"You're wrong there, Acting Jack. I'm just the right man for this war. Those mother fuckers in Washington have got to be crazy themselves to send us over here and I'm sure they want crazy fuckers like me to do their killing for 'em. Shit, man, you've got to have crazy men to fight a war like this. You see, some of these nervous Nellies around here might be a little squeamish about blowing away some slopehead brat and his mama-san who smile at you during the day and plant punji stakes at night. They're expecting a regular war with regular soldiers to fight. They want their glory all clean-cut and cuddly. Well, I don't give a shit about who I waste; I just want gook blood. And it's the same color coming out of a baby-san as it is coming out of Mr. Hard Core Charlie!"

"That's all bullshit," I said. "You're just spitting out trash. War may not always be justified, but it's not always just bloody butchery either. There have been a hell of a lot of honorable men fight wars and fight like men, not like beasts."

Tate stared for some time with a look of scornful disbelief; then he ridiculed my idealism with a hyena laugh.

"Holy turds! You wear that honor shit around your neck like a fuckin' crucifix, Acting Jack! Your fuckin' honorable men fight wars for the same reason us murdering bastards do ... to spill blood and not get your ass fried for it ... get medals for it instead of the electric chair. They just try to fool the world and themselves with all their talk about noble causes and all their gentlemanly ways of waging war. We in the Hard Core Platoon got honor ... the honor of zapping more gooks than any other platoon. We've got balls too ... that's courage, to your way of thinking, Mr. Knighthood-in-Flower ... and pride too ... pride in our unmatched record for terminating dink lives, not some silly-assed pride in any of your goddamn causes. We're not defending anybody's democracy, we're lightin' up slopeheads and doing it better than anyone else. You're Hard Core material, trooper, but you're going to have to forget your kind of horseshit pride and adopt the Hard Core kind of pride ... pride in murdering better and bolder than all them other pussy platoons put together."

"I don't believe that shit, Tate. I believe there can be honor in war. I think that brave men facing death for a cause they believe in is just about as honorable as you can get. I don't know about motivations; I'm no shrink. But whatever it is that makes a man put his head in the cannon's mouth without flinching, it's an honorable act ... hell, a heroic act, as long as it's a free choice of his own, regardless of what motivated him, and not one dictated by a bay-onet up his ass."

"Oh fuck it! I'm tired of puking out philosophy with an 'Honorable Man.' Let's go see how much honor we can squeeze out of a beer can," said Tate.

I was, indeed, a creature of the nineteenth century, with concepts of honor, sacrifice and nobility, confronting a madman, but one who possessed within the scope of his madness the twentieth century's profane view of reality. I resented the modern age's questioning and doubts about the glorious abstrac-tions I held dear, its ceaseless investigations into the motivations for a hero's act. I needed an age in which such abstractions were accepted without ques-tion, instead of being regarded, as they were by the twentieth century, as papering to be peeled back to reveal the psychological worms.

I remained irreconcilable toward Tate. "You just go right ahead and be as utterly crazy as you want. But you'd better try to regain a scrap of your sanity before you try communicating with me again!"

Suddenly turning defensive, Tate reacted as if he had been unjustly wronged. "Well God in heaven, man. I was just fuckin' around. That damn little beer can didn't cause any brain damage, now did it? Shit, that was just my way of saying welcome to the Hard Core Platoon!"

The wild gleam never entirely fading from his icy blue eyes, Tate then became grossly amicable. "Now let's forget that stupid beer can. Come on over here and gulp down some of this boiling brew they ration us. You like your suds hot don't you? Hell yes, you're in the Hard Core Platoon and that's the only way we drink it ... warm as Tiger's piss. Hell, I think I'm gonna get along with you just fine. We're gonna cut a few slopehead throats together, me and you. You've got blood damn near dripping out of your eyes."

We did not heave ourselves aboard the Hueys for another three days. It hardly seemed longer than a furtive breath of fresh air. There were the almost habitual work details and the never-ending job of stacking sandbags around tents, bunkers, ammo dumps, latrines and shower stalls. But during the evenings we were free to gather around the platoon's two balladeers and guitar strummers, Rose and Whitehall, to rattle off in discordant choruses, gulp down our two-cans-a-day allotment of beer, and listen to the outrageously exaggerated exploits performed by Welch and the accounts of blood and madness claimed by Tate.

Meanwhile, the West Virginia madman had turned his aggression against the perfect target of Walt Johansen. He was no more able to stand and face Tate's madness than he was enemy fire or malicious nature. Tate assaulted Johansen's courage, his masculinity, even his basic right to live while courageous men like Tommy Morales died. Johansen was shoved, kicked and slapped by Tate, who seemed to gather new strength in his aggression as his victim became progressively more intimidated. Finally, after Tate had slapped Johansen down in a whining heap in the sand, I and several others intervened and convinced the platoon psycho to lighten up. The crowd of onlookers then dispersed, leaving Johansen sprawled pathetically in his shame.

Those three days at South Field were the first extended period in which I could observe our ursine first sergeant, and I began to understand better why he was universally feared. The top sergeant had spent twenty-six years in the Army screaming at ignorant privates blundering around "with their heads up their asses," and it was widely suspected that all the vituperatively abrasive language he had belched forth had also helped loosen his brain bolts. Sab's flammable schizophrenia was particularly unnerving when, for reasons known only to himself, he would suddenly transform, as if by some vile sorcerer's black magic, from a kindly grandfather-like figure into a fiery-eyed foul mouth, all granite face and volcanic soul, spouting profane oratory. His verbal typhoon of obscenity included compounds and combinations that demonstrated a unique talent. It was the first sergeant's unique burst of creativity, weaving the profanity of English, German, Korean and Vietnamese into a mind-blowing opera of filth. Though I never witnessed Sab bodily lifting some unfortunate soldier off the ground and shaking him silly, as El Cid had frequently done, Sab's slashing claws of lewd language and dynamite, decibel screams were as demoralizing to a chastened trooper as the artillery sergeant's brain-scrambling shakings.

Chapter XVI

Snipers

On September 19 the company once again jumped into helicopters, once more tumbled from the hovering craft to dash to the edge of another LZ, once again divided into platoons for the checkerboarding search for the Viet Cong. And once again Johansen contracted a severe battlefield allergy, this time the virus afflicting his yellow belly instead of his backbone. In Oscar-winning style, Johansen wailed in agony that his guts were about to burst. He and his bright yellow entrails were unceremoniously dumped into the helicopter, leaving the platoon smaller in number but improved in quality.

Our route led us down a deep gash in the earth in which a glacier of rock obstructed progress and challenged that master of agility, Captain Tugboat Rhodes. The black rafts that were his feet were pulverized and, by day's end, cracked and bleeding badly. Somehow next morning he struggled to his feet and went on just like the rest of the men in the snaking platoon file, constantly moaning but never failing or quitting. He seemed to be of a species entirely removed from that of men like Johansen.

Early that morning, we approached a large village shaded beneath a green parasol of banyan and tamarind trees. The platoon conducted a house-to-house search for men of military age, fifteen to fifty, whom we could tag as V.C. suspects and manhandle over several forested miles to an LZ, where they would be hustled into waiting helicopters to be flown to the ARVN interrogation center in Tuy Hoa. But the village produced only crippled veterans with missing limbs or men old enough to have bounced a toddling Ho Chi Minh on their knees. There were many women and small children, dressed or half-dressed in drab peasant garb, wearing wearied expressions on their ocher faces and smelling of poverty. The young men were gone ... all of them. Some were fighting with units of the National Liberation Front; others were serving with ARVN battalions; still others had already joined their ancestors.

The platoon lingered at the village for some time, waiting for a chopper to evacuate four of our men: Herman, shaking in hot and cold spasms with malaria; new meat Burke, stricken with Vietnam flu — gonorrhea; Rhodes, sent back to nurse his feet and wait until supply could requisition another pair of canoes for those monstrosities; and Welch, returning to base to sign extension papers. I was again left in charge of the squad, which consisted now of only three men besides myself: Rose, Whitehall and Pfc. Joe Jefferson, another of the new men, a cocksure, bebopping Cajun cat from Louisiana.

Our sick and red tape cases dispatched to the rear, we moved out along a winding trail that led to a hamlet which we scoured for suspects. One paddy farmer who appeared to be well past his fighting prime, a teenage boy who looked hardly hefty enough to lift a rifle, and a moldy old-timer who may have fought the French when they first conquered Vietnam in the 1880s but certainly had not taken to war in recent times, were apprehended and flung into a beckoned Huey for interrogation sessions in Tuy Hoa. I sat on a huge bag of peanuts, munching a handful and watching the chopper lift off. Suddenly, the crack of a rifle interrupted my goober feast and startled the platoon into a scurrying rush for cover. Seconds later another shot sang its shrill tune over our ducking heads as we anxiously scanned the surrounding terrain for signs of the sniper. A third bullet cracked the air over Terry's machine gun team, which replied with a sputtering volley of M-60 fire. One man, RTO Monday, finally spotted the assailant dashing through the undergrowth of a ravine.

"There's the gook bastard!" Monday proclaimed. "I'll go zap his ass!"

But the lieutenant restrained his headstrong radioman and grabbed the handset of the PRC-25 to request the fire of Weapons Platoon's two 60 mm mortars (they were carrying the lighter, smaller mortars because the regulation 81 mm mortars were not humpable in this terrain). The mortarmen plopped several rounds, all either too long or too short and way off target, into the absorbing green profundity. Novak then released his glory hounds. Sgt. Blanco, Monday and I scrambled down into the ravine, my heart drumming with a pounding rhythm, part dread and part thrill.

The wait, the moments endured between thunderclaps of rifle fire, was of gratifyingly short duration. The three manhunters had been stalking their prey only a few minutes before the RTO yelled that he had spotted the sniper. A cacophony of automatic rifle fire rebounded down the narrow ravine almost simultaneously with a triumphant shout from Monday, "I hit the dink. He's limping away with half a leg left to him."

Blanco, cautiously treading the ground to my right, caught a glimpse of the wounded V.C. and raked the undergrowth into which he had disappeared with a burst of automatic fire. The three of us converged but found neither the enemy sharpshooter nor any bloody evidence of a wound inflicted. Monday was disgusted that a confirmed body count for his record had narrowly escaped.

The lamed foe having been chased away, we again piled rucksacks on our beast of burden backs and resumed the march. Blanco's 3rd Squad, with the attached machine gun team of slump-shouldered, straw-shocked Pfc. Harvey Hickman, recently returned from his convalescence from malaria; blubbery, bellyaching Meadows; and stodgy, scruffy DeWitt, led the platoon on point. The platoon was winding its way along a rice paddy dike bisecting a short open area surrounded by trees, when the popping of an automatic M-2 carbine snapped our raw-edged nerves taut. My squad, trudging along in the center of the platoon file, had not yet emerged from the tree line onto the exposed length of paddy dike. Consequently, we heard the burst of fire but did not immediately see its effect. Positioning the three men under my command on opposing sides of the trail, I scurried in a half-crouch up the platoon line to survey the scene and get the lieutenant's instructions.

I tried to gulp down a bitter taste of apprehension, but before I had made my way through the obscuring line of trees, I knew that the enemy marksman had not wasted his bullets. The groans of a wounded soldier, the cries for the medic, the lieutenant's anxious inquiries, all quickly combined to tell me that at least one of the men with whom I marched and shared hardship and danger had been felled. The faces of those walking at the front of the platoon file flashed through my mind. I picked from among that gallery the ones I wished most strongly to have escaped unscathed. I was attempting to usurp fate, to deny destiny its awful, inexorable will.

Thus I felt a sense of relief, mixed with a rush of grief, at the sight of the two men stricken by enemy fire; two men for whom I felt no great attachment, but for whom I did feel the common compassion one soldier feels for a comrade fallen in battle. Although I had served in Vietnam for over a year now, the sight of dead or gravely wounded Americans was still not so familiar to me that it could evoke only a resigned acceptance of fate. Two men with whom I had shared the rigors and rewards of our precarious Spartan existence lay in bloody poses. Sgt. Blanco lay with death tracing its irrevocable pattern across his dully staring eyes. Pfc. Meadows sprawled moaning, as much from the sight of the wound as from the pain, as a crimson geyser erupted from an ugly hole in his left leg.

The gushing blood terrorized the once impassive Meadows. "Oh fuck! My leg! My fucking leg! I'm gonna bleed to death for this mother fuckin' country!"

Meadows was flopped like a wind-blown shock of grain atop the tiny, exposed ridge of the paddy dike. His comrades, clinging to the scant cover available, were all too distant to aid the wounded man without risking another thunderbolt of enemy steel. Following the lieutenant's admonishments, Meadows, calming somewhat as the flow of blood diminished, slid down behind the dike to await the medic's attention. Returning to his normally taciturn self, Meadows sarcastically exclaimed, "Man, I wasn't even gonna lose none of my blubber in this war. Now it looks like I might lose my whole fuckin' leg!"

Meadows was hurt badly, but he and his leg were going to survive, regardless of his own pessimistic diagnosis. But Blanco was hit far worse. His eyes bore the ghastly vacuousness of impending death; foamy rivulets of bloody saliva drooled from his lips; his face bleached to a ghostly white shroud. A single, dime-sized bullet hole punctured his stomach; the exit wound was a fist-sized red cavern. Novak radioed for a Medevac Dust-Off, Urgent Priority. But no helicopter in the world would have been fast enough to save Blanco's life. While part of the platoon maneuvered against the sniper, my squad remained with the lieutenant to guide the copter into a swirl of yellow smoke and carry the wounded men to the open bay of the hovering ambulance. I helped carry Blanco, wrapped in a bloody poncho. I glanced into his face as we placed him onto a stretcher aboard the Medevac chopper. His once olive-colored features were now the color of a forbidding fall of snow; the tiny rushes of air from his lungs seemed to have stopped. Not even inches separated him now from the brink of a dark descent.

I turned to the medic and asked, "Has he got any chance at all, Doc?"

Comiskey winced his freckled face and replied, "Blanco won't be alive when that chopper lands. The sarge will be sleeping in a body bag tonight."

Ours was not the only platoon to suffer a fatal casualty on September 20. In 2nd Platoon, a grunt tripped over a leafy leg thrown out by the bullying jungle and discharged his rifle into the spine of the soldier humping in front of him as he fell to the ground. Another fatal accident, but one that would not have happened had not 750, 000 Americans and South Vietnamese and 250,000 Viet Cong and North Vietnamese been carrying weapons of war. How many men had I known who had died at the hands of their own comrades? It was becoming a very old but still very sad story.

My brooding on Blanco's death was interrupted by the day's third blast of sniper fire slashing a splintery swath across the trees above our heads. This time the bullets found no fragile flesh in which to bury their steel-jacketed heads. The platoon flattened itself on the ground and returned heavy fire. In the rush for cover, machine gunner SP/4 Chance was separated from his ammo bearer, DeWitt, who refused to budge from his cover. Seeing my chance to emulate the heroic feats of Welch during the Phu Tuan firefight, I leaped to my feet, grabbed the ammo belts from DeWitt, and rushed the few yards to Chance's side. But no enemy fire accompanied my rush to valor; the bright feather of glory I was to have won for my warbonnet swirled away out of reach.

This third attack was the last of the day. We linked up with the mortar-men of the Weapons Platoon to camp overnight on a knoll overlooking a dismal collection of gray peasant shacks. We agreed that someone should be punished for the sniping attacks. Since the tiny ville below our position was easily available and, by the logic of our anger, was undoubtedly guilty of harboring the gunman who had slain Blanco, we cheered our platoon leader's decision to bombard the hamlet with Weapons Platoon's 60 mm stovepipes. Our platoon had been hit, had suffered casualties, all without being able to strike back. We felt vulnerable now, almost defenseless against the crafty corps of snipers who seemed able to strike whenever and wherever they chose with little risk of retaliation. We desired some form of revenge, some method or manner to demonstrate — as much to ourselves as to the enemy — that we were not simply targets and could return as much as we received. We wanted to restore the confidence in ourselves that we had possessed after the triumph of the September 8 firefight.

We roared our approval as mortar teams executed the commands of "Hang a round!" "Round hung!" to cough a dozen shells from the two mortar tubes toward the hooches of a hamlet targeted for our vengeance for violent acts committed by men probably miles distant by now. Evening's lavender haze soon gave way to the brighter burgundy glow of burning peasant huts. Beyond the flames' flower, the stars were saddened dull with our primal shame, looking now more like slivers of bone thrown to the sky than the suspended diamonds of other nights. We never discovered if anyone died in this act of retribution, for the next morning we moved down the hill in the opposite direction, without bothering to inspect the results.

Early the next morning, the enemy riflemen struck again. First Squad had been assigned point. With Morales dead, the dubious distinction of serving as primary point man for the squad was up for grabs. One of the few takers was the beet-faced psycho, Moses Atticus Tate, anxious to display his ferocity. The morning began with Tate on point, but before long Spec 4 Ronnie Nossef, a book-worm-looking type with thick, Army-issue spectacles, who had been hospitalized for two months with malaria, asked Tate to relinquish the post of pride to him. Regardless of his somewhat fragile appearance, Nossef was imbued with a good share of the give-em-hell fighting spirit that seemed to flourish in the platoon.

Nossef walked point only a few minutes before a staccato screech of automatic carbine fire toppled him over as we were crossing the last level of a terraced hill, which leveled off into the balustrade of bamboo where the sniper was concealed. Nossef lay motionless, his head resting in a growing puddle of maroon-colored blood. Another burst of enemy fire forced down inquisitive heads looming above the terrace wall. Several troopers started peppering the witches' claws grove of gnarled timber from which the Charlie marksman had cut down Nossef.

Sgt. Cuyler, Nossef's fire team leader, turned to the lieutenant and implored, "We've got to pull Nossef out of there, sir, before Charlie zaps him for good!"

The lieutenant agreed and ordered his men to lay down covering fire for the rescue party, consisting of Cuyler and the frenzy-cyed Tate. While the two dashed out to drag their wounded comrade to safety, I hopped up on one knee to add my semi-automatic fire to the steel-jacketed surf pounding the sniper's perch. The lieutenant called a halt to the fusillade as Lt. "Wrong Way" Strong brought up his 3rd Platoon in a beautifully formed but horribly exposed skirmish line along our left flank.

Novak disgustedly shouted to his fellow officer, "Get your men out of that parade ground formation, you idiot! Get their asses down! "

But Strong chose to ignore the 1st Platoon leader. With a chivalric flair that brought derisive laughter from 1st Platoon's onlookers, the pasty-faced knight in the not very shining armor of olive drab waved his black M-16 above his head like a crusader's broadsword and scaled the terrace bank, as if he were Richard the Lion-Hearted storming the walls of a Saracen castle. Then, with all the cockeyed chauvinism he could muster in his high-pitched voice, Strong rousingly commanded, "Follow me men!"

And off they charged. Luckily, there was no enemy remaining to disrupt the flash and flamboyance of this all-powerful onslaught. For weeks afterward, whenever a junior NCO was dispatched with a work detail to burn out the shit barrels underneath the latrine or to police call the company area for cigarette butts, he would inspire his men with the ringing command "Follow me men! "

In the meantime, a Medevac helicopter had been summoned for the point man, who seemed less seriously wounded than we had first feared. He was able to walk, supported by Tate and me, up the incline of a nearby hill on which the Dust-Off chopper was to land. A gaping bullet hole painted Nossef's neck a streaming red, but he seemed little concerned by it.

"Hell, Charlie's gonna have to hit me a lot harder than that before they ship me home in a body bag! " he proclaimed, as if he owed an obligation to the platoon to quiet their fears and restore confidence. "If you heroes can survive a few days out here without me, I'll be back to win the war for you just as soon as I can get this hickie removed from my neck."

We jokingly tried to match his confidence. "By God, Nossef, you just get out here from one R&R from that mosquito bite and now you're takin' off for another one!" ... "Biggest ghost in the company, always digging up one excuse or another to keep your ass out of the boonies." ... "Listen here, Ronnie, don't you play around with those nurses too long just because of that little scratch. I expect to see you humping these hills by next malaria pill day. You're getting combat pay to hump these boondocks, not some Doughnut Dollie in Quinhon." ... "Hey, Ronnie, hands off that red-haired nurse in Ward Five. She's willing, but she's wicked. A whole ward full of guys with the clap can testify to that."

No one seemed more calm and confident than the wounded man himself, who continued to promise, "No sweat, man. I'll be back in tee-tee time. I'm not going to let you pack of glory grubbers grab all the fame and fortune without me."

When we placed him aboard the evacuating helicopter few of us imagined we were seeing Nossef for the last time. Two days later, machine gunner SP/4 Anson, returning to the company after a six-week-long tussle with malaria, informed us that Nossef had died in the hospital. I had, with little suspicion, helped lift my third dead man into a Medevac helicopter.

As Nossef was being evacuated, the rest of the company marched up in straggling files, including the charging chasseurs of Strong's 3rd Platoon, to reunite briefly for a Firefly resupply, complete with the Pony Express and a Brown Derby. Gunslinger Dietrich, fluttering over all the dirt and grime in his command copter as he directed his far-flung companies from a seat in a Huey — rather than from a saddle on a gray charger as had his predecessors in past conflicts — ordered Charlie Company to move toward a great cave garrisoned, according to intelligence reports, by 300 V.C. Some banal mind in Brigade HQ had codified the objective as the "Batcave" in honor of the current craze of TV audiences.

The 1st Platoon, at the rear of the company file, was soon dispatched to track down three V.C. sighted by the scouts of Recondo Platoon. We back-tracked for several hundred meters, then struggled up the hill on which the Charlies had been spotted, as a gunship circled like an angry olive-drab wasp, stinging the hillside with rockets and machine gun fire. All the fire and fury were for nothing, however; the enemy again escaped. Later, as we marched toward another grid coordinate on the map, the rush of artillery arced over our heads as it plowed into a column of Victor Charlies snaking their way through the valley below. The arty had more success in the constant competition for body counts. The Recondos, observing through binoculars, reported seeing at least three gooks fall to the artillery barrage. With darkness fast descending, we achieved our objective for the night and another day of heat, death and frustration ended.

The following day brought more of the same. In conjunction with 2nd Platoon, we finally located the Batcave after scouring a brown and green grid smudge on the map for most of the morning. We found the cavern unable to conceal thirty men, let alone 300. It was concealing no one that day. Later, another "bullshit tip" came down from the hovering Gunslinger which resulted in Sgt. Cuyler's fire team being dispatched to scope out a row of hovels supposedly concealing an arms cache, but concealing only more snipers who popped off a few rounds at Cuyler's men and then scooted.

The rest of the platoon marched on to link up with Captain Silvasy's HQ element and chase a few fleeing Vietnamese with rifle rounds — whether the galloping gooks were guerrillas or just paddy farmers, no one could know for certain until those "farmers" fired rounds in our direction — and to round up three suspects, two wrinkled old men and a boy halfway to adolescence. As evening diluted the day's hot colors to a uniform murky gray, we hiked to a small clearing which we secured as an LZ for Cuyler's returning team. On the way back, sniper bullets sang a sharp melody over our helmeted heads, but we steered a safe course through their scorn. Other contacts with the buzzing hive of snipers were not so inconsequential, however. Two more Strike Force paratroopers died that day in this sniper's paradise. A cherry trooper named Coker, of the 3rd Platoon, was killed when Charlie's bullets found most of that platoon bunched together in a foolish huddle which only a leader of Lt. Strong's caliber would have allowed. The other soldier to fall victim to sniper bullets was a Bravo Company man, a veteran with less than a month remaining in Vietnam. Three men killed in our company, another slain in a sister company, yet a fifth man cut down by his comrade's weapon, and not a single dead Victor Charlie thus far to balance the scales of war.

We fully expected to be the objects of some sniper's murderous attention the following day, but not once were we molested by the frightening slap of rifle rounds cracking in our midst. We longed for the opportunity to reap revenge on our V.C. foes. And now, unhampered by enemy harassment, we carried out that retribution with the all-consuming justice of the torch. With the lieutenant's consent, every hut and hovel along our path was set aflame in a miniature version of Sherman's march through Georgia. Most inhabitants of the hooches torched by our pyromaniacal platoon fled as we approached, but at one miserable dwelling the wailing members of a peasant family had to be forcibly evicted from their home before it could receive its fiery last rites. The ancient matriarch of the clan issued forth an outpouring of grief and hatred as she watched her home being devoured by the rapacious red flames. Her enfeebled old husband looked on blankly with a penetrating sadness fixed in his wearied eyes ... eyes that had probably witnessed many such acts of barbarity, committed by other soldiers who may have worn different uniforms and fought for different causes, but to him were all creatures from the same mold.

We continued on down our destructive trail, some of us less enthusiastic than before, but others yearning for more huts to burn and more peasants to make homeless until our comrades' deaths were satisfactorily repaid.

Nature, long ago conceded by us to have firmly allied itself with the Viet Cong, now struck to inflict further blows on our fading morale. Our route led us through a broad belt of dense undergrowth far worse than anything we had yet encountered. My 2nd Squad was walking point that day, and thus it was up to Rose and me to beat a path through the prickly paradise of thorns and vines. It proved to be almost impossible.

There was no way to find a passage through the green nightmare other than crawling, sometimes on hands and knees, more often flat on stomachs. In six hours, the platoon, with the CO and his mastodon of a first sergeant at its heels, inched 300 agonizing meters. Then nature relented and provided a narrow winding footpath. Later, as we threaded our way through the wilderness to scale a high hill, we could look down on the tiny area of teeth-grinding toil, a Satan's garden. Skirting around the south edge of the green Gehenna was a wide, easily accessible trail, unmarked on our maps and now mocking us cruelly for our unnecessary hours of thorny torture. Our spirits took another bruising blow.

Thoroughly fatigued from our trailblazing exploits, we relinquished point to 1st Squad. Tate, nearly foaming at the mouth by now in his lust for revenge, was given the honor of stalking point. As the sun fled timidly behind a tree-lined horizon, he got his chance for retribution when he encountered a Vietnamese in peasant attire sauntering down the trail toward him. The man yelped in surprise and dashed off in the opposite direction as Tate fired a poorly aimed shot and raced down the trail in pursuit. Tate's rifle barked twice more and the second bullet homed in on its target, striking the gook in the leg as he scampered down a rope into a well. Only the lieutenant's commands to take the man prisoner prevented Tate from ricocheting a magazine of ammo off the clay walls of the well, as he charged up to the wounded man's warren and rammed the muzzle of his automatic rifle down into the dark cylinder.

With all the ferocity he could muster, Tate demanded, "La Di! La Di! you slopeheaded bastard! La Fucking Di!"

The frightened Vietnamese climbed out and, to Tate's surprise, was followed by four companions in Ho Chi Minh sandals and black peasant uniforms. One was a young woman, with tight-lipped pride and fierce-eyed disdain for her American captors. Her male comrades put up a less brave front, holding their hands high, fear twisting their faces and their voices squawking pleas of "Me no V.C.! Me no V.C.!"

The four men were forced to spreadeagle flat on their stomachs, but we allowed the woman to sit. The lieutenant was convinced that they were Viet Cong, citing as evidence the military style close-cropped hair of the men and the fact that they had attempted to flee at our approach. The five were hustled into a summoned helicopter to be taken to Tuy Hoa for interrogation, the men looking frightened and uncertain of their fate, the girl scowling with a somewhat sensual scorn and making me feel like a foreign conqueror with no right nor reason to be invading her land. I had only a vague idea, based upon rumor and speculation, of what went on in the interrogation process at Tuy Hoa, but in my concern for this girl I could visualize electrodes attached to her proud body and her hate for us burning deeper with the electric fire on her coppery flesh.

Next morning we forded a wide, swiftly flowing stream that reflected the jade color of ripening rice to unite with 2nd Platoon and Company HQ. A Firefly resupply chopper buzzed overhead a short time later, as we infiltrated an abandoned hamlet erected around a small yellow stucco Buddhist temple. Minutes after the helicopter had dropped its load and we had begun distributing and trading C rations, three bullets snapped off branches above our heads. The bartering ended abruptly as pound cake, chicken and noodles, and canned peaches were forgotten in the dispersing rush for cover. When no more harassing rounds streaked from the surrounding hedgerows, we reconvened our ration exchange. The sniper had inflicted no damage, but by now the policy of retribution was fixed. A hot, red beast, born of the union of Zippo lighters and dry thatch, was soon crackling in sudden, searing maturity as it fed on the Buddhist shrine.

On September 25 the company moved to a broad mesa, adorned in a yellow-green grass skirt and undulating in the breeze with South Seas sensuality. Welch returned to the platoon the same day and I gladly relinquished command of his Hard Cores. For two days we ran only short recon patrols from the mesa-top position. We had received orders from Brigade to end our scorched earth campaign, but on one of the patrols conducted by 2nd Squad, Welch allowed his pyrotroopers to spark their green C-ration matches against a deserted peasant shack. The CO could see the smoky black exhalation of the fire from atop the mesa, but he was always tolerant of our destructive impulse, as long as we continued to display the proper fighting spirit.

Our next mission marched us toward the pitted strip of concrete called Highway 1. There we were to erect OPs on the hills frowning over the highway to secure the vital route for convoys motoring north. We moved from hill to hill each day right before night had become firmly entrenched over the landscape to prevent Charlie observers from pinpointing our positions for an evening mortar bombardment. The only shots fired during this period were triggered by SP/4 Miksis, while leading a patrol laden with canteens to a well near the highway. With several rounds from his M-16, he chased a fleeing gook who had bolted in fright from the well. Racing after the possible body count, Miksis closed the gap sufficiently to discover that the fugitive was a surprisingly agile old woman, so he gave up the chase.

The days were so quiet that we were lulled into a sense of security which, this time at least, did not prove false. We all realized the danger of being deceived by the volcano's cool cone, while inside bubbled hot lava that could erupt at any time, but these lazy days seemed like gentle charms fallen from that bracelet of terror on which hung the bloody ornaments of Blanco, Nossef, Coker and the others. The continuity of fear seemed broken; we were seduced into the security of tedium. Men fell asleep on guard, neglected to set out the warning beacons of trip flares, let the dusty sighs of the Vietnam countryside settle into unoiled rifle chambers. We turned our backs on war, pretending it was possible to find a safe port in its storm. Luckily, war did not demand an atonement, a sacrifice in death and terror for our disrespect. Not this time. On a dark night three months later, its toleration would end in a bloody fit of fury.

Chapter XVII
An Old Man's Ears

On September 29 a whirling string of UH-1B "slicks" fluttered down on a plowed field astride the highway to return Charlie Company to South Field. The interlude between operations was longer this time but no more restful. The days were spent playing war in mock battles among the sand dunes of Tuy Hoa beach. The nights were given over to the usual beer guzzling, bull-shitting, and balladeering until the beer ran dry, throats grew hoarse, or until the first showers of the approaching monsoon dispersed our revival meetings to the leaky shelter of candlelit pup tents.

The forthcoming wet season promised more problems with the jungle rot I had picked up during the last month. Cuts and scratches festering with filth in the humid climate of Vietnam produced the spreading infection that we called jungle rot. The battalion was full of men bearing its scabby sores seeping yellow pus. A sergeant in Bravo Company had recently died of the toxic rash because he had allowed the rot to go untreated and it had drained its poison into his bloodstream. My arms looked like those of a leper and fungus-green islands of scabs spread in an ulcerous archipelago down my legs and feet. At morning sick call on our first day back, I lined up in a long queue of the ill, at least half of whom were suffering from jungle rot. My arms were medicated with a gooey glop and bulky bandages swathed around them.

Our guitar pickers, Rose and Whitehall, were kept busy evenings with singing and strumming requests from their olive drab audiences. Both had written songs about the war and the battalion. Whitehall's top hit was "Napalm Hill," a guts and glory anthem praising our company's stand under Captain Carpenter at Toumorong...

> There were F-105s flying high above
> A' comin' in low and not to bring love
> A' droppin' napalm our CO called in
> If it be God's will, we'll see daylight again.

Sab liked the song so much that he called Rose, who had the better voice, into his tent to record this "Ballad of Dak To" on a tape recorder, while he sat wiping tears from his eyes and swilling beers in thirty-second chugs.

The only other entertainment was that offered by the whores of Tuy Hoa. Like every other locality in our martial migration through Vietnam, a cluster of tin and plywood shanties, each boasting a bar of tinsel, lawn chairs and aluminum folding tables in front and boom boom rooms in the back, and invariably called "The Strip," had arisen a few steps outside the brigade camp. Once these establishments had started attracting their G.I. clientele, restaurants, laundries and hot tocs (barber shops) would sprout up in their wake to share the commerce. From our view, it seemed that the whole Vietnamese economy would collapse should the United States withdraw from the war. Unemployment figures would skyrocket, as hundreds of thousands of whores, pimps, black marketeers, dope peddlers and other assorted entrepreneurs suddenly found themselves out of work. But in 1966 the legions of prostitutes and parasites had little to fear. The faces would change but there would still be the round eyes and green fatigues of the Americans for years to come.

Bartered sex was left behind with hot meals and shelter when we took the all too familiar stroll to the stretch of sand designated as our battalion helipad to resume Charlie chasing. The fireworks were precipitated early this time as we came under fire even before boarding the slicks. The assailant was not a black-pajama-clad peasant rifleman, but a rusted 55-gallon drum serving as a garbage can. Among the empty beer cans and C-ration cardboard boxes were several hundred rounds of machine gun ammunition, which some idiot had tossed in with the rest of the garbage after the ammo belts had become wet and muddy during the last operation. Someone had tossed a lighted match into the barrel as we were filing by on our way to the helipad, and the discarded ammo quickly started popping like a string of firecrackers, but with a far more vicious bang. Within seconds, the company found itself pinned down by a machine gunning garbage can. I burrowed into the sand less than ten meters away. The comedy of the situation was lost on us as several hundred rounds of ammunition crisscrossed the air above our heads. There was no way to overcome this enemy; we had no choice but to hug the sand until the belligerent trash expended its violent energy. At last the attacker fell silent, and two troopers stormed the pockmarked can to empty its hot contents into the smothering sand. Without realizing it, we had been under the heaviest fire we were to encounter during the forthcoming mission.

Though the garbage can barrage claimed no victim, the company did suffer a casualty before we boarded the CH-47 Chinooks. Minutes after the besieging trash barrel had shot its wad, a single shot cracked from the ranks of 3rd Platoon. Cries for a medic echoed among the waiting chalks of jungle-bound infantrymen, as a battle-shy soldier moaned in pain from a self-inflicted leg wound. He had preferred to shoot himself rather than face the possibility of being shot far more seriously by the enemy. He would not be the only man in the company to seek such an escape out of the enemy-dominated jungle.

A drizzling shower had begun by the time we loaded ourselves aboard the Chinooks and were airborne into the gray, overcast sky. We were to begin and end this mission three weeks later with rain our constant companion. This was the height of the monsoon and the depth of our misery. For twenty days we marched, ate, slept and killed in the oozing mud, our feet never dry and often submerged. Our cosmos was an endless, sodden agony of mud and rain.

The thunder-bladed Shithooks settled on the spurs of a high, bald hill, lowering their tailgates to allow cargoes of thirty infantrymen each to splash out into the increasing downpour. Our new combat cockpit was the fertile rice valley northwest of Tuy An, enclosed by an inner ring of lofty hills — whose lower levels were bordered by hedgerows separating pastures from plowed fields — and an outer crescent of mountains covered by a green cape of dense forest. The 2/502nd's mission was to sweep the encompassing circle of hills to forestall any attempt by V.C. foraging parties to confiscate the valley's rice harvest.

Half sliding down the hillside, like heavily laden skiers negotiating the treacherous course of a muddy brown slalom, we filed over the last hedgerow and rock wall fence to step out onto the watery deck of the paddy-checkered valley. We waded into the sloppy goo and stagnant slush thick with human and animal excrement, our olive drab fatigues turning dark green with the soaking rain and then an oleaginous yellow-brown as we forged through the mud baths of waist-deep rice paddies.

The platoon was halfway across the inundated basin when the head of the single file column of infantrymen came under the concentrated crossfire of two V.C. automatic riflemen firing from two rickety structures in a nearby hamlet, anchored like a palm-masted galleon in a yellow-green sea of rice paddies. We splattered into the adhesive mud, as 3rd Squad, led by the lumbering black bulk of Sgt. Maranville, maneuvered in the mire toward the hidden foe. The rest of the platoon supported the maneuver element from the muddy ramparts of a rice paddy dike, but the V.C. gunmen had fled moments after their burst of fire had split the narrow threads of falling rain. The deserted hamlet was occupied by Maranville's squad, which signaled those treading muddy mush behind the dike to join them in scouring the soggy village. The search turned up two haggard-looking young men, neither of whom looked capable of wielding an automatic rifle. Nonetheless, the dismal duo were tagged as suspects and dragged along, bound by ropes, to a grassy field, where a Huey fluttered in the rain to haul the prisoners to the always busy interrogation center.

According to later scuttlebutt, the hapless pair never returned to their monsoon-swept village. The peasants were parachuted forcibly out of the helicopter without the benefit of a parachute by the chopper's playful crew.

The tromp across the marshy valley consumed most of the afternoon, and the liquid sky was becoming grayer as evening settled in on the platoon, clawing its way up the slick slope of a grassy, multileveled hill. The draperies of darkness had closed on the platoon by the time it plodded its weary way to the flat summit of the hill. Forming a defensive circle, we buried ourselves in leaking ponchos to squat and lie in a mattress of liquid mud as we passed the long wet hours of the night in somnambulistic sentry duty. No one maintained an alert watch; nor did anyone really sleep. The wristwatch was passed back and forth, but never according to the schedule set up. Only when a dozing warrior was stirred from his semi-consciousness by rivulets of rain water streaking down his poncho-hooded face, or when a rush of muddy sludge emptied its brown paste into the folds of his poncho, did the snoozing sentry stir long enough to nudge one of his compatriots and relay the watch.

I spent most of the night sitting atop my rucksack, my damp poncho liner wrapped around me in feeble protection from the icy rain, the poncho's outer armor draped over my huddled body like a moldy tarpaulin over unused furniture in a musty room. There I dozed in fitful minutes-at-a-time sleep, my head bowed on my arms crossed over my knees. Occasionally, while on sentry duty, I would peer through the knotted hood of the poncho, staring with unseeing eyes into the black alliance of rain and night. It was futile attempting to penetrate the catacomb of darkness and the liquid static of the downpour with my frail human senses, but a nagging sense of duty and an ever present dread of creeping communists frequently made me poke my face into the monsoon's wrath to quiet the anxious Cassandras of my fears. Still, reassurance, a fugitive hiding in the suspended wet death of the night, fled. I could not have known if an enemy infiltrator was standing over me with raised rifle aimed at my skull — not until his exploding enmity had crashed into my blind, deafened brain.

The liquid night never relented. As the monsoon-wounded sky dripped its blood, a rain-racked trooper in the platoon observed, "God is taking the biggest piss since creation!"

The ice water from the heavens and the bitter wind nipping like the cold teeth of Arctic hounds chilled us to the bone. As icy beads of rain glided on cold runners down the shuddering ski slope of my bent spine, I rummaged in my rucksack for one of the blue heating tablets used to heat our C-ration cans. Making sure the corners of my poncho were tucked underneath me to conceal my tiny fireplace, I stooped my shivering body over the tablet's bluish flame. The cone of warmth seemed well worth the sacrifice of choking down tomorrow's cold ham and lima beans.

Around midmorning of the new day, Sgt. Tower was dispatched with his squad to reconnoiter the opposite slope of the hill we occupied. The patrol returned a half hour later after a brief flurry of shots, with the scarecrow-skinny, Pfc. Jerry Booth, beaming triumphantly and flaunting his success.

"Hey, hey, Hard Core Squad, where's your body count for the day? This sorry crew in 1st Squad is already one dink up on you for this op. You guys are losin' your claim to fame."

His pride piqued by the pompous cherry trooper, Whitehall fired back, "Who'd ya zap, new meat? Did you waste a ninety-year-old mama-san or a baby water buffalo?"

Booth's victim had been one of two gooks discovered near a hedgerow, probably V.C. scouts. Booth, walking point, had dropped the slower of the fleeing pair with a burst from his M-16, while the more fleet-footed fugitive dove headfirst into a clump of thorn-taloned bushes beneath a swath of rifle fire delivered by Tate. Pummelling his way into the brush line, Tate flushed his prey from nature's concertina wire and wounded him in the arm. Tate bullied his way through the brush in pursuit, but soon lost his body count in the barbed bewilderment. Tate returned to his squad dejected that he had so narrowly missed covering himself with Hard Core glory.

The illustrious warriors of the Hard Core 2nd Squad were naturally envious that the usually unimpressive 1st Squad had drawn the first blood of the new operation. Incensed by their rivals' swaggering, Welch, Whitehall and cherry trooper Pfc. "Butch" Burke conspired to insure that the 2nd Squad's glittering glory would not be dulled by that of a brighter shining competitor.

Once this jungle fatigued cabal had agreed on a course of action, Whitehall goosestepped over to the gloating members of Tate's squad to issue a stirring edict.

"You heroes had better enjoy your little stroke of luck, 'cause you're all gonna have to salute the great and glorious Hard Core Squad when we make our victory march after our next patrol!"

"What kind of victory are you gonna have to celebrate, Whitey? Ya gonna swoon some fair slopehead maiden with a hillbilly serenade? " a smirking Tate asked.

"No, we're gonna swoon a whole fuckin' regiment of Charlies with a M-16 serenade," shot back a pouting Whitehall. "Then you pussies in 1st Squad will have to recognize the fact that the Hard Core Squad has no equal when it comes to zapping Charlie's ass."

"Well, then, Whitey, while you're out wasting half of Uncle Ho's army, how about bringing me back a pair of gook ears?" asked Tate. "My man Booth here pulled himself a couple of gold teeth out of the mouth of that slope he croaked. They make a damn nice souvenir, but I think a Charlie's ear slipped under each side of my helmet's camouflage band would look just real bitchin'."

"I've promised my cousin back home a pair of gook antennas for Christmas, but I'm sure that after the Hard Core Squad gets through kickin' ass there will be enough idle ears laying around that I can pick up a pair for you," Whitehall agreed.

Another rainy and sleepless night followed, during which machine gunners Anson and Hickman speared red tracer bullets into the lights and cooking fires of the valley, which had been declared a free fire zone at night. After a C-rat breakfast, 2nd Squad prepared to move out on patrol, several of its corsairs intent upon returning with a bloody trophy of severed ears. They had taken an oath that the squad would not return without the grisly token of victory. The Hard Core Squad's honor was at stake!

Seven Visigoths followed the weaving trail down from the platoon's hill-top OP, determined to sack Rome. We were soon strolling along the muddy lanes of a hamlet. The first houses were deserted, but eventually we uncovered a gray-goateed old man and his betel nut-chewing wife at the south end of the ville. Welch shouted accusations at the old man, who denied in a voice cracked with age and apprehension, "No V.C. here! No V.C. here!"

Leaving the old couple, we crept on toward the last house in the hamlet, bordered by a high hedge with a few narrow openings wide enough for a single man to pass through. Rose at point placed one foot in the corner inlet and suddenly froze, hunched down, and thrust up an arm to signal us into motionlessness. Waving Welch to his side, Rose pointed out the reason for his sudden stop. There, lounging lazily on the front porch of a yellow stucco house, were three soldiers of the National Liberation Front, their weapons, an M-1 carbine and two bolt-action Mauser rifles, stacked in a gun barrel tepee several yards away. Welch spoke to us in military sign language, ordering the squad to cover him as he crept upon the lolling V.C. from a passage through the hedge to the rear of the front porch, while Rose assaulted the unsuspecting enemy from the gateway in which he squatted.

Welch had stealthily covered half the distance toward the three V.C., when one of them spotted the stalking paratroopers and alerted his comrades. The paratroopers' M-16s belched bullets, but the men who had appeared so slothful a few seconds before suddenly sprouted wings on their feet and vanished into the verdant blindness. Both troopers claimed hits, but we found no red wreckage purpling the muddy ground to validate their claims.

The Charlies had escaped; an easy score had slipped from our black-muzzled clutches, leaving Whitey without an ear to embellish the Hard Core Squad's legend. But all was not lost. The old man with gray cat's whiskers still remained, and his ears, except for the scales of age, were no different from those skull wings carried on the heads of the Viet Cong. Whitehall could still secure his ears, Welch could chalk up a body count, and the squad could maintain its reputation for ferocity.

The squad leader huddled with Whitehall and Burke in murderous plot, while the rest of the patrol crouched at the four corners of the garden. Johansen had joined in the squad's conspiratorial bombast of body counts and souvenir ears upon the hill, but now, concerned that the V.C. might return to recapture their lost weapons and pride, he was interested only in collecting the booty and returning to safety. Rose, Jefferson and I had suffered through the blustering of our Cossack comrades and had added our hesitant contributions to the blood talk of wasted gooks and deserved glory when pressed by the Hard Core condottieri, but we had failed to take their bombast seriously. Not until Whitehall and Burke stomped over to the old man's house and dragged him to the center of the garden. Then I began to wonder, worry and wait, and the humid breaths I sucked in burned as though inhaled from an alien atmosphere.

It is difficult now to analyze my emotions during the moments when an old man's eyes became the mirrors of death and young men I called my comrades talked of murder as if it were but an act of mischief. I find it hard to condemn those men, for I must share in their guilt. I discovered that the war had nearly taken my soul too as I watched the atrocity take place, uttering no protest until it was too late, dreading what was about to happen and yet aware of some dark desire within me that waited with fascination for the blow to fall.

Violent death still brought grief when a friend fell, but the death of a Vietnamese — any Vietnamese, not just the enemy — was looked upon with no more pity than a hunter gives his prey. To so many men in the platoon, the whole gook race, excluding perhaps the kids and the delicate female flowers in white Aou Dai dresses, were little better than vermin. Killing a dink had become different from killing a human being, and even if a bit of remorse remained, war excused and vindicated killing and exonerated the souls of men who murdered but yet refused to consider themselves as murderers. War was working its insane logic on us. We were learning to deny the enemy's humanity, and because it was so difficult to distinguish the enemy from those who merely hated us, it had become easier to kill both.

Thus I crouched down in a corner of that garden in hell, protecting my friends, Whitehall and Burke, as they wrestled the old man to his execution block. I forced myself to stare into the wilderness before me, not wanting to witness the brutal act. But I was unable to restrain the beastly lust for blood that clawed at me to behold my comrades' and my own shame ... to stare in horror and rapture at the monster war had conjured up.

I was still hopeful it would not happen — at least that part of my conscience did so that still confronted the brute of my id, slavering for blood. I still hoped that when the final moment of reckoning arrived, the self-appointed executioners would discard their ghastly ruse; would demonstrate that their lethal bluster was nothing but a bluff carried almost too far.

But it had already gone too far; it was too late now for the executioners to draw back and consider the consequences of their intended act, though doubt and hesitation rose like suffocating, sulfurous fumes. Their laughter faltered; their tough expressions developed cracks of uncertainty. Whitehall pointed his short-barreled grenade launcher at the doomed peasant. Burke's usually jovial black face suddenly turned grim and gaunt. Sweating irresolution locked Whitehall, filled the garden with its tension, and seemed to stop time and the earth's rotation. The old man stood impassively on the cliff's edge of death, a trigger squeeze away from a red-metaled nirvana.

My mind bolted like the recoil of a bombarding howitzer. Whitey wouldn't push the ashen-faced human being over that cliff! My God, he just couldn't. It was wrong, terribly, cruelly wrong. It wouldn't happen ... it couldn't happen! I turned in my morass of sweat and dread to scream out words of protest ... words I should have loosened at the first insane moments. A shot roared its awful voice, drowning out my frantic shout of protest in its louder scream. I would, in effect, still be shouting unheeded words of protest in a score or more of anti-war marches years later. In some part of myself, I am still screaming them out today ... too late, far too late. That unheard scream will probably echo through my soul forever.

The dozen iron pellets of a buckshot round from Whitehall's M-79 crashed into the bowed, black-shirted back of the old man. He crumpled, as if a condor's claw had ripped out his aged spine with one vicious swoop. His back was shattered into a bloody pulp, his severed red vertebrae whipping like the tentacle of an octopus, but the old peasant hung desperately onto the last seconds of life. Standing over their twitching victim, the slayers shuffled uneasily, waiting for this old oak of humanity to drop its last leaf.

Turning to a sullen-faced Whitehall, Burke complained, "Man ... Whitey, you'd better trade that M-79 in for a slingshot. You did a fucked up job of wastin' that old man. Whatdya need, a fuckin' howitzer? "

"Shit, Butch, you know how damn hard these fuckin' gooks die sometimes," said Whitehall. "If you're in so much pain over his suffering, why don't you finish the old fucker off? "

Burke's expression wrinkled into a portrait of reluctance, but his Hard Core creed demanded that he fight off the slightest hint of weakness or remorse. He swallowed his squeamishness and reaffirmed his fraudulent pride with a sword thrust of automatic rifle fire into the stricken figure, who had to be sacrificed on the altar of the Hard Core Squad and its forgery of a legend.

But still the old man, lying in a thickening red gravy at his killers' feet, clung to life. Not until Burke thrust the muzzle of his M-16 against the old man's skull and crashed a leaden fist into his brain did the life that had lingered in agony flee the heap of bullet-ravaged flesh and bones. The peasant was at last dead; 2nd Squad could report back to the lieutenant the attainment of a body count.

The act completed, Whitehall turned away to escape the shame that was corroding his dour exterior. Burke grabbed his arm and reminded him, "Man, you gonna forget why we zapped that old fucker?"

"What's to forget?" asked Whitehall impatiently.

"The ears, man, the fuckin' ears!" answered Burke. "That old gook ain't gonna be hearing a lot of gook gossip anymore and them assholes in 1st Squad are expectin' some Hard Core evidence!"

"Oh yeah, the ears," muttered Whitehall. "The mother fuckin' ears."

Whitehall kneeled down to collect his gory bounty. Brandishing his bayonet, he carved off the ears and tucked them under the elastic camouflage cover band of his steel pot.

As the squad prepared to retire to the platoon OP laden with its spoils of war, rifle shots popped into the banana trees shadowing the scene of our shame. Johansen, his eyes wide with fear, pleaded, "Damn, Sarge, are we going to wait around here for Charlie to give us a medal?"

As bullets chirped overhead, we hastily retraced our steps out of the peasant burg and back up the hill. Upon reaching the platoon, Whitehall proudly displayed his trophies, still dripping blood, to a much impressed Tate, now more anxious than ever to be reassigned to the renowned Hard Core Squad, where a man of his caliber would be appreciated.

It now fell upon 3rd Squad, under the tutelage of Sgt. Maranville, to bring back proof of a slain slope and demonstrate its worthiness to march in the same platoon with the "dink demolishers" of 1st and 2nd Squads. But no unarmed peasants, frozen with fear and about as dangerous as the lotus flowers of their land, offered themselves up in sacrifice to the laurels of 3rd Squad. Thus Maranville had to return with neither gold teeth nor ears, but with only an unexploded 82 mm mortar shell that his men had discovered. Their failure was gracefully tolerated by Welch's valiants, who realized that not everyone was made of the same hero stuff that flowed in their own veins.

The following morning the resupply Huey dropped its load of rations and ammo and picked up Miksis, who was suffering from a bite administered by a huge, hairy, black spider. Welch also returned to the rear area, this time to attend a squad leader's seminar with some star-shouldered strategist and to spread the fame of the Hard Core Squad far and wide.

Welch accomplished his PR mission with flair. He was a fine soldier but an even better publicity agent. He procured more praise for his men and himself than any other comparably-sized unit in the brigade, with the possible exceptions of the Lurps and Recondos. Several editions of the brigade newspaper, The *Diplomat and Warrior*, idolized our exploits, and we even occasionally made it into the *Stars and Stripes*. Welch had manipulated a visit by the brigade CO, General Pearson, who had autographed for each of us a photograph of the grinning stalwarts of the squad. Of course the pieces of legend and adulating articles were all exaggerated and sometimes so embellished as to become almost unrecognizable to the heroes. But none perverted the truth more than the *Diplomat and Warrior* article describing our latest feat of glory....

Three Snipers Fail Test with "Hard Core Squad"

Phu Yen — Three unsuspecting Viet Cong snipers learned about combat the hard way recently and the "Hard Core Squad" drew up the lesson plan.

While guarding the rice harvest northwest of Tuy Hoa, Company "C," 2nd Battalion, 502nd Infantry encountered quite a bit of sniper fire from a nearby village. Repeatedly, a rifle would crack and the troopers would be sent ducking. But because the area was heavily populated, the troopers could not return the fire.

Staff Sergeant Heywood Welch and his "Hard Core Squad" was sent to scout the village. They went in the back way.

Welch split the squad into two elements and deployed them into the village. Set apart from the rest of the village, by about 70 yards, was a hut. Welch started towards it. His point man, Pfc. Wendell Rose, followed close behind. They closed in on the hut and peered through the bushes.

"There was Charlie," Welch recalls. "We saw a Mauser rifle leaning against the wall. He was just sitting there on his porch rubbing his face. Just taking it easy."

Welch and Rose watched the black pajama clad Viet Cong for a few minutes. The distance between them and the unsuspecting enemy was only eight feet. Welch motioned Rose to cover the V.C. while he tried to capture him ... and started stalking the man.

A carbine cracked twice very close by and kicked dirt up around Welch. Immediately, Rose shot the enemy he had been observing and went to Welch's aid. His squad leader did not need it. Welch had silenced a Viet Cong who had appeared suddenly and started shooting at him.

The rest of the "Hard Core Squad" came up from the rear of the village. Welch deployed them around the hut and sent two of his men to search it. As the two paratroopers entered one door, a third V.C., who had been hiding inside, went dashing out another door with a carbine in his hands.

He did not get far. A shotgun shell from Specialist 4 Glen Whitehall's M-79 grenade launcher caught him.

The "Hard Core Squad" collected two carbines, one Mauser, 150 rounds, 15 hand grenades ... and, oh yes, three Viet Cong snipers.

... And, oh yes, one gray-bearded old man. That murdered old peasant undoubtedly would have been proud of his American liberators had he been alive to read of our exploit in making three of his communist persecutors bite the dust.

In addition to the kudos attained by way of this yellow journalism, Welch also managed to spin these events so favorably that he was later awarded a Bronze Star with V for his actions on that day of dishonor.

Decades later, Welch would further gild the lilies he had planted in the *Diplomat and the Warrior*. In his combat memoir, this maestro of falsehood and falsification would attempt to further burnish his own personal glory and that of his Hard Core Squad. For him, the past would forever remain a spinning top.

After a meal of meatballs with beans, beans and franks, ham and lima beans, and other such gourmet treats in C-ration cans, 1st Squad was exiled into the valley at the northern foot of 1st Platoon's Gibraltar to explore and exterminate. Tate led the way. He was savagely determined to prove his merits and win acceptance into the hallowed ranks of SSgt. Welch's Hard Core Squad.

Tate courted violence with vehemence and won betrothal in a stoop-shouldered elder taken into custody by the patrol as it occupied another peasant ville. It was open season on old men. Sgt. Tower turned him over to the guardianship of Tate, and then masked his eyes from the inevitable. His cold blue eyes alight with blood lust, Tate nudged his victim away from the tail of the squad file and shoved him into forced flight. The old man had limped but a few steps when a hatchet blow of fire from Tate's rifle chopped into his back and bathed him in a warm crimson bath.

Later, as the patrol passed back through the village on its return to the platoon, Tate heard the sound of weeping from the hovel which the dead peasant had called home. Slamming his M-16 against his hip, Tate hammered at the hut with a battering ram of bullets. The moans shrilled to a shriek as the echo of the rifleburst shook thatch huts and sensitive men's souls. Pfc.s Landon and Box rushed inside the hooch to find a toothless old woman treading death in a red pond, her legs like a battered puppet's limbs hanging from the torso by the few wires of twitching ganglia. By her side the corpse of her husband hardened with death. Tower was summoned by the troopers, stunned by this cornucopia of blood. His reaction was to nervously order his squad back up the hill, fleeing the scene like a panic-stricken hit-and-run driver. Tate lingered briefly to savor further delights from his madness.

It rained hard that night, but no amount of rain could have washed away the innocent blood shed and the shame incurred. Four people had died in the last two days, the victims of a murderous competition between squads in the sport of body counting. Only one of the four could have been stamped a Viet Cong and he too was unarmed ... the other three, two old men and an old woman. Glory wore the face of madness now.

Troopers mummified themselves in ponchos that night to curl up in the mud and suffer through another soaking. The guard was largely neglected as we hunched in ponchos and risked the fury of the human foe rather than confront the wrath of the rain. No one really cared that night. There was too much mud to care about anything but refuge from its cold, sticky misery.

Early on the morning of October 8 the platoon spun its green thread down from the hill which had been its base for the past three days — our pirates' Tortuga — and from which we had launched the patrols that had soaked us with blood and soiled our honor. We passed by long columns of Vietnamese peasants, smelling of cooked rice and Nuoc Man fish sauce, as they paraded from villages to wade in the rice paddies and gather their harvest. We splashed through flooded paddies, in places the malodorous brown rafts of excrement bobbing at our armpits, and forded a murky stream by wobbling over a splintery foot-wide span of creaking board like a grotesquely clumsy company of acrobats. We walked most of the day in the stinking brown stew, and we stayed wet all of it.

During a brief halt in the trek to choke down cold C-rats, Tate beckoned me, "Hey, Speedy 4, wade your muddy ass over here for a second. I want to show ya a couple of items I picked up in a gook souvenir shop."

"I've seen all the gold teeth and ears I want to for awhile, so no thanks," I grumbled.

Tate flashed a fiendish smile. "Oh these little trophies outshine a whole steel pot full of gold teeth and an entire necklace string of dink ears. Come on and check out Moses Atticus Tate's SPOILS OF WAR!"

I finally labored over to Tate's side to quiet his harping. "All right, Tate, put on your show."

"Oh you're gonna like this," chortled Tate. "I swear on my Smoky Mountain blood, you're gonna shoot your wad when you see this!"

Still chuckling, Tate flourished a greasy hand over his rucksack, as if he were a magician waving a magic wand over a top hat, and reached inside for his rabbit. It was no hare that this sadistic sorcerer pulled from his bag of tricks, but a bloody black mane.

"I guess it's the Cherokee blood in my veins that gives me such an exceptional talent for takin' such a purty scalp," beamed the demon-eyed Tate.

I felt sick. "My God, Tate, couldn't you satisfy whatever crazy blood lust you have by just wasting that old man? You're not a wild Indian; I don't care how much goddamn Cherokee blood you've got. We're soldiers, damnit, not savages. We are supposed to be civilized human beings, even here in all this shit."

Tate made a contemptuous sweeping motion of his blood-and-mud-freckled hand. "Shit, man, do you see any of your fuckin' civilization anywhere in this gook country? The more dink scalps I stuff in my rucksack, the fewer slopeheaded bastards there are to blow the balls off my buddies with their fuckin' Bouncin' Bettys!"

Then Tate pointed out, "Besides, you're all wrong about these gook ringlets. That old man's locks are gettin' just as stiff about now as the rest of his body ... cause that slopehead bitch used to wear her head underneath this here black bundle of fur!"

I desired no more details and started to turn away, when Tate clutched my fatigue sleeve with his bloody claw and said, "Hold onto your balls a second, Specialist. I got another little purty to show ya!"

Before I could escape, this ogre in olive drab cast his second incantation and produced the fruits of his barbaric legerdemain. There in the talon of this Government Issue Beelzebub, wrapped in the plastic used to protect maps, was a slimy red-brown chunk of a human liver.

I refused to hear or see anymore and turned my back on Tate, walking away from his collection of gruesome trophies. I walked away because we were all a team, even down to the last sordid, feral member of it. It was the few of us against the many of them. My comrades-in-arms were all I had; a savage sanctuary from the greater savagery that surrounded us. Because loyalty outweighed conscience, I could not hurl the beast of atrocity from my bent back and straighten up to stand tall and shout NO ... this must stop. By turning away from the scene of our crimes over the past few days, by closing my eyes and conscience, I had confirmed my loyalty and conceded my soul.

As the mauve shadows of evening crept across a sodden world of rice paddies and rugged greenery, the platoon moved through a large village. It was deserted, except for a few frightened people hiding in the underground havens that seemed to outnumber the aboveground structures. We pushed on through the silent muddy boulevards of the village toward the river that had been designated our day's objective.

The head of the platoon column had just emerged from the village onto a broad sandy plain when a crackle of automatic fire sounded from the green hills across the river. After our first reaction had welded us to the ground, we formed a skirmish line, dropped our rucksacks in the sand, and charged in a broken green line toward the river and the unfriendly hills, braying rebel yells and profanities at the enemy. It was almost the charge-into-glory of my fantasies. It was thrilling and exciting; it was like a brief amnesty from the prison of monsoon misery, of dishonor and despair.

Reaching the riverbank, the machine gunners flipped down the bipod legs of their M-60s and searched the hills for the enemy with bullet bloodhounds. Lt. Novak called in a fire mission and within minutes a creeping barrage of HE shells and Willie Peter rounds was scaling the rocky incline ... a mountain climber of smoke and shrapnel. An orchestra of artillery played for several minutes, pounding the mound for harboring our enemies and leaving the darkening hills wreathed in leis of blue-gray cordite smoke.

Another sad night cried upon us, this time its tears mixed with sand to provide us a gritty bed. The yellow heartbeats of flares popped, tripped by the hard rain. They cast their gilded glow against the silver beads of rain like yellow-eyed alchemists turning heaven's tears to golden silk.

With morning the rain stopped and the sky's leaky pipes held for the rest of the day, giving us a chance to dry out poncho liners and to bathe a week's worth of mud and blood from our bodies. The bathing and shaving were soon interrupted, however, as we were forced to splash out of the river in a mad dash for fatigues, steel pots and weapons when a look-out warned of two men approaching from downstream.

The Vietnamese remained out of effective range of our M-16s, but the platoon sniper, SP/4 Ron Holtzman, aligned the crosshairs of his scope-mounted 30 '06 sniper rifle on the two distant figures and squeezed off three rounds from his bolt-action weapon in quick succession. One of Holtzman's targets collapsed into the sand, to be dragged to cover by his comrade. A man's life had probably been snuffed out, but the execution had taken place at such a distance and was so surgically clean — no spurt of blood seen nor screams of pain heard — that the significance of what had taken place could easily have escaped us all. Killing was such an easy, almost effortless sport when it came like this. Holtzman's victim had been faceless; he had been only a target in a free fire zone, almost as easy to slay without cost to the emotions as were the unseen targets of the artillerymen and the fighter-bomber pilots ... those slayers from a sanitized safe distance who killed far more than the men of the infantry, but who did not have to look into the faces of their victims or see the bloody results of their automated violence; who could blame those deaths on the machines of war and not on themselves.

Later, at midday, the platoon leader anointed me patrol leader of a detachment which included 2nd Squad, Hickman's machine gun team, and Moses Atticus Tate, volunteering in hopes of finding further outlets for his sadism. We were assigned the task of searching the village we had marched through the day before. Many of the houses in the hamlet were connected by tunnels, giving the platoon's tunnel rats ample opportunity to display their fearlessness. But there were no arms caches to discover, no cowering Viet Cong in the village-beneath-the-village. All it yielded to us Samurai with automatic rifles were a few aged and sick on whom fear and hatred competed for expression. To Tate's disgust, I made it clear that the hunting season on old men and women was closed.

As we neared the end of the house-to-house search, two young men dashed from opposite ends of a hovel approached by Johansen and me. We both fired at the black-dressed wisps and both missed. Johansen's quarry hurdled a hedgerow and escaped. I chased my quarry down into one of the bomb shelters. Poking the muzzle of my M-16 into the darkness, I discharged a ricocheting burst, as did Hickman, lumbering up beside me with his pig. Then I tossed in a purple smoke grenade, hoping to flush out the foe if he had managed to survive our volleys. Once the purple clouds from the smoke grenade had drifted away to be absorbed in the greater blueness of the sky, we crept cautiously into the bomb cellar to discover the dark umbilical cord of a tunnel by which the suspect had escaped to some other subterranean sanctuary.

As the patrol prepared to return to the platoon, firing broke out west of the village. I placed the men in a defensive cordon and awaited the enemy.

The "enemy" when they appeared were wearing palomino-colored cowboy hats and cherry red bandanas around their necks, the identifying insignia of a local Popular Forces battalion. A few men in my patrol were inclined to blast away at any Vietnamese soldiers, no matter what uniform they wore, but I ordered them to hold their fire and the battle with our South Vietnamese allies was avoided ... for now.

As we prepared for our evening repast of C-ration recipes, several troopers looked hungrily toward a flock of several hundred ducks penned in a corral of bamboo which lay directly under the guns of the platoon's sand dune position. The salivating vision of a duck feast proved irresistible.

With a shout, the brigands stormed the corral and precipitated a riot of quacking ducks and yelling men. Feathers flew, wings flapped, and laughing soldiers toppled and tumbled in a chase through the sand in pursuit of web-footed waves of frightened fowl. Troopers scooped up armfuls of birds, only to lose them in a flapping fury of beating wings and pecking bills. But when the feathers had finally settled, each of the freebooters returned with the neck of a POW duck firmly in each fist.

The raiders hardly had time to lick their chops, however, before the lieutenant ordered the abductors to release their captives. The grunts reluctantly freed their ducks, except for Tate, who swore beyond the lieutenant's hearing, "I'll be damned if I give up these quackin' cocksuckers. They're my fuckin' supper!"

"Ya gonna eat 'em raw, Tate?" asked Joe Jefferson. "'Cause if you try bar-bequeing them birds, you know damn well the aroma is gonna curl around and slap the lieutenant's nostrils to rigid attention."

"Well then, by Jesus, if I can't enjoy me a little duck dinner, then I damn well can get a few eggs out of these critters."

Jefferson asked, "Whatchya gonna do, Tate ... make a nest for 'em in your rucksack?"

"Hell, there sure ain't no need to wait for these ducks to drop their eggs," said Tate. "I'll just give 'em a gentle helping hand. All they need is a midwife like me to start their labor pains."

Tate then took the duck in his left hand, raised it by its neck and bashed it against the ground again and again with enthusiastic fury. The duck's stomach split open, spilling out in slimy pink. Tate angrily tossed the gutted fowl into the bushes and growled, "I'll just be damned. That sorry mother fuckin' duck wasn't even pregnant!"

He then smashed the second duck, pounding it against the ground until two gore-painted eggs — like a madman's Easter eggs — popped out of its ruptured belly. With a gargoyle grin cracking his red freckled face, Tate scooped up the eggs and cracked each shell against his protruding front fangs to allow the embryonic contents to slide in a yellow and albumen blob onto his tongue and down his throat. Smacking his lips, Tate heaved the bloody remains of the duck into the brush and turned to enjoy the nauseated reactions of his comrades.

Chapter XVIII
Raiders

We prepared for another drowsy watch in the sand and darkness. But Lt. Novak, who dreamed the dreams of heroes, saw visions of night raiders and conceived a commando-style descent on a fishing village squatting in gray solitude a klick down the beach where the river married the bay. With night as our mask, the raiding party, with bayonets sharpened and faces smudged with camouflage paint, stalked like olive drab panthers down a beach that the darkness colored cocoa. We walked on stilts of adrenaline; we felt uniquely bold, fearless, elite. Images of every commando and ranger combat movie we had ever seen ran through our minds. We were on a *Top Secret Mission*: we were *Hitting Behind Enemy Lines*. Each of us was John Wayne; we were all heroes.

But the tightening sinews of tension loosened and the air deflated from our ballooning egos as we vandalized house after house in the village, bursting in to discover sleeping peasants who were not the fierce-looking extras hired by our fantasies to play the Southeast Asian successors to the Wermacht soldiers or Samurai sons of Nippon of the movies of our childhood. Mongrels barked and howled, women screamed and small children cried, old men whimpered and babbled like frightened spider monkeys, but there were no Charlies to silence with the sharp gag of our bayonets. The film broke on our commando movie.

We made our poncho-on-the-ground camp a short distance upstream from the fishing hamlet to await daylight. Shortly after the sun had peaked over the horizon, a fishing sampan flaunted its vulnerability before the machine gun sights of SP/4 Anson. His M-60 sent a shark with teeth the diameter of 7.62 millimeters to rip holes in the bamboo ribs of the two-man boat. It was enough to capsize the craft and dunk its crew into the silt-gray waters of the bay.

Anson was jubilant. "By God, I just sank one of Ho Chi Minh's battleships!"

Later that morning, 1st Squad was dispatched downstream to the area where Holtzman's long-range shot had found Vietnamese flesh the day before. The patrol had hardly skirted the nearest mud-gray coil of the serpentine river when a hysteria of screaming small arms fire and whumping M-79 launched grenades announced that Tower's patrol had made contact. The volume of fire quickly increased, but the popping weapons all sang the tune of American guns. The lieutenant hurried the rest of the platoon down the beach to aid Sgt. Tower. By the time we reached 1st Squad, the one-sided battle was over, and a search through boggy fields of sugar cane failed to produce the "enemy."

The patrol had touched off the action when point man Tate sighted two Vietnamese bathing in the river. Together with Sgt. Tower and grenadier Box, he opened fire on the swimmers, who splashed out of the river and dived into the green stalks of a sugar cane field. Then four more "Charlies" were flushed from a hidden cove along the riverbank. Two of the Vietnamese stopped and shouted frantically, "We no V.C.! We no V.C.!" ... but to no avail, as the bullet burp of machine guns and automatic rifles continued. Tower's patrol forded the river in pursuit and on the opposite bank discovered the uniforms, ruck- sacks and red scarves of the same South Vietnamese Ruff-Puff unit my patrol had nearly opened up on a few days before. Luckily for our allies, Lt. Novak was given no body count to report in to the captain, drooling over his handset as the company's kills were announced.

On the morning of October 11 the platoon mounted their olive steeds and galloped through the gray sky on another bullshit trip to another soggy green valley. We failed in our search for the bounty of a hidden arms cache. This was for us a history of failed efforts ... failing to trap the enemy in our ambushes, failing to uncover his arms depots, failing to win glittering victories in battalion-sized search-and-destroy operations, failing to avoid the awful consequences of enemy snipers and booby traps and mines and punji stakes. We waited for the three-day resupply and the return of SSgt. Welch to our battlefront ... our frustration front; our theater of war replete with bamboo spikes, strafing mosquitoes, and a constantly pissing sky. The C-ration refu- eling completed, the platoon ploughed on through the adhesive mud for several klicks, grunts pausing momentarily to bend at the waist and relieve the pressure of rucksack straps biting into shoulders; marching on until a setting sun pop- ulated this mud world with mauve phantoms, whereupon the amoebic creature that was the platoon molded its olive drab coils from the single file form of the march to the horseshoe figure of the ambush. No one walked into our ambush that night ... just like a half a hundred other ambushes I had or would sit through. But three Charlies, who had forgotten that they no longer exclu- sively owned the night, did blunder into the snares of an ambush set by

Weapons and 3rd platoons a klick away, and one of the insurgent soldiers paid for his carelessness with his life.

We stomped on the next day in what seemed aimless, purposeless, endless wanderings to us who knew nothing of the strategic aims of this mission. Near midday, our errant marching was temporarily halted by the rushing, watery obstacle of a monsoon-swollen stream seemingly offering no passable ford. Rose, on point, dropped his pack and LBE and, holding his rifle high, waded into the swirling eddies of the river at a point where it narrowed to a surging jugular flowing the blood of the monsoon. Rose wobbled more than halfway across, the frothing gray water pulling at his waist. He turned to flash back to us a premature grin of success. At that moment, the ashen river swallowed Rose like a great gray whale as he stepped into a current-crazed hole. He bobbed to the surface within seconds, spewing a lead-colored fountain and his hands searching the water for his rifle.

Rose was a good swimmer, but his efforts to retrieve his weapon from the murky depths rapidly exhausted him. When the thrashing trooper finally gave up the search and headed for shore, his body telegraphed an urgent SOS message and then lost power. Rose's ship was sinking.

Having time only to drop my gear and helmet, I splashed into the torrent, my jungle boots pulling me down like cement blocks, and treaded in a wet frenzy to the bobbing exhaustion that was Rose. Struggling frantically, I ultimately pulled him from the current to less agitated waters, where the lieutenant fished the human flotsam from the river into a fishing boat his men had uncovered beached in the shore thickets nearby. I then fought my way out of the current's python-like grip to grasp hold of the side of the boat and be towed to the quiet mud of the bank.

The lieutenant later surprised me by recommending me for the Soldiers Medal for my part in saving our drowning point man. Although I was pleased to receive any medal the military deemed fit to bestow on me ... even now after all the disillusioning events that had so darkened glory's once shining beacon ... I had lost some enthusiasm for those symbols of glory realized. Those things I had seen and suffered, those things I had done and failed to do, all combined to tarnish the medals.

Thwarted on one attempt to bridge the river, the platoon forged on downstream until a likely crossing site was found. Rucksacks and gear were dumped into our expropriated boat, and I was appointed ferry captain to tow the boat across and secure a length of rope to a tree on the opposite bank. Using the rope as a handrail, the rest of the platoon waded across without mishap, although a few of the less sure-footed stumbled and were submerged briefly in a river arguing against our crossing.

We moved a hundred meters upstream from our crossing and there discovered several young peasants driving a herd of cattle across a gentle ford only knee-deep. Chagrin rose. Minutes later the radio crackled with orders directing us back across the river to an LZ for a helilift. All morning long the captain had stressed the importance of the platoon getting across the river. Now our close-quarters combat with the river went for nothing. Disgust reigned.

The pendulous bulk of a Chinook fluttered heavily to the ground to scoop up the platoon, ferry it through the gravy-colored sky to Highway 1, and unload its human freight. The CO was there to greet his incoming platoons, standing like a Minoan king with his Minotaur of a first sergeant by his side. The captain began a new march, executing our role in some grand plan sketched out on a multi-colored topographical map that could not indicate with its geographical symbols the measurements of blistered feet or aching spines; that might show the contour lines of mountains, the wiggly blue lines of streams, the green shades of vegetation, but was incapable of expressing the sweat, the raw running sores of jungle rot, the leeches, the muddy muck that manufactured immersion foot.

The company moved in a long snaking single file of burdened men. Sniper fire snapped through the catalepsy of the 2nd Platoon, forming the rearguard of the company procession, but the sharp pings of rifle fire hardly rippled the weariness numbing the rest of us.

The night was passed in a company ambush, which, sometime during the snore-spangled night, several Charlies strutted right through without raising an alert. We discovered this the following morning when we found a poncho which had dropped off the backpack of a Viet Cong. The company marched on to hump the morning away, ascending a high hill that afternoon to replenish our stocks of C-rats and marry unenthusiastic replacements into our conjugal ranks.

One more rainy night with the company ensued, and then we were once again into the choppers for another quick lift, returning to the scene of the duck debacle. As the six Hueys ferrying the platoon descended toward the riverside landing zone in stomach-fluttering skips, thirty or more black-garbed figures dashed across the beach in sand-flying sprints toward the brush. They were chased by a racket of red tracer M-60 bullets fired by the door gunners on the Hueys. We landed in a whirlpool of sand and assaulted across the dunes. But the Viet Cong escaped and the platoon's sudden spurt of spirit quickly died.

Posting the platoon atop a hill of sand, Novak sent my fire team out on patrol to search a shoreside collection of fishing shanties and fill the platoon's canteens at the well there. We encountered nothing but bitter-looking old peasants and children flashing smiles of brown teeth and holding out paws to beg, "Hey G.I., sop sop ... G.I., you sop sop me," which we responded to by tossing them cans of C-ration fruit cake, silver foil-wrapped disks of chocolate candy, cans of "ham and mother fuckers" (ham and lima beans) — which all G.I.s seemed to hate and which our mortarmen had been known to lob in the direction of the enemy — and packs of C-rat smokes to those urchins demanding "Sa ... leem, Sa ... leem!" After pulling away one horny G.I. trying to barter C-rations with a toothless old woman in exchange for a little boom-boom, we returned to the platoon near dusk in time to witness Anson blow another sampan out of the water with a spew of machine gun tracers.

Lt. Novak now decided to have another go at playing commando. Although his greater responsibility required that he pull a tighter rein on the wild horses of his imagination, the lieutenant was, in essence, a man much like SSgt. Welch. For them, war provided the peak, that supreme challenge, that greatest of all glories. War gave man, softened by civilization, the opportunity to be the truly violent, competitive creature nature intended by taking part in the greatest competition of all ... men employing their wits, daring and determination against other men in a game fraught with peril and played for the highest stakes. War was the natural habitat for the lieutenant and his super squad leader. The sweaty smell of danger worked the pumps of their lifeblood; the adrenaline moments when combat's call orbited the two into a fulfilling flight in which the crack of bullets and the whine of shrapnel provided them their lifegiving oxygen.

I could understand the passions that ruled my lieutenant and my squad leader, for I shared many of them. In describing Novak and Welch, I might seem to be describing myself as well. But there was one important difference. I had been infatuated with an adolescent fantasy of war. The reality I experienced, though it did hold moments of magic for me — but a black magic practiced by sordid sorcerers — was in the final reckoning a dark well of disillusionment and even horror. For Novak and Welch, though, it was the same Vietnam reality, not the fantasy — or perhaps they could not distinguish between the two — that they loved. They needed no justification of a noble cause to fight for, and the barbarity of the war was simply part of the game. They did not question the war and its motives — at least not then. They simply accepted it as the only war offered them and they reveled in it.

But at times even the lieutenant and SSgt. Welch became discouraged by the endless purgatory of rain, mud, and marches to nowhere. It was to play once again the machismo melody that had swelled the egos of the Hard

Core Platoon before the weeks of wet wretchedness had sapped our spirits, to respark the adrenaline flame of combat, that the two plotted a second night raid on the area's riverside villages.

With the onset of darkness, Lt. Novak led his stealthy band of night raiders down the rivershore. The target was a hamlet directly across the mouth of the river from the larger fishing village we had impotently struck on our first night mission five days ago. Novak hoped to catch a sizable number of Viet Cong gun runners who, disguised as innocent fishermen, plied the South China Sea coast with their cargoes of cosmoline-coated death. But again the thrill of victory eluded him; the patrol's only triumph came over a snoring Vietnamese slumbering on his front porch. He fell victim to a bayonet-wielding Welch, eager to increase his bag of zapped gooks and gain some bloody degree of success. The man who had to suffer our frustration was granted no time to identify the flag to which he saluted his loyalty before the razored edge of Welch's bayonet sliced a red line across his throat. His last dreams were ended in a scream that fired ice against my spine. Welch stabbed and slashed maniacally, as the gook shrieked in a gurgling lunacy of gushing purple blood. Thrashing in the epilepsy of violent death, he wrenched free from his captor's steel-edged grip to charge, blinded by his fountaining blood, into the walls of the house. Kicking against the death demons pursuing him, the peasant fell before yet more blows from the savagely stabbing arm of SSgt. Welch. Finally, the screams gave way to a rattling retch, as the victim inhaled his last burning breaths before death came to silence him. The man's crimson life streamed from a score of knife wounds, purpled Welch's fatigues, and burned into the ground. The night air reeked of blood.

We went on to round up several suspects and then set up an NDP near the village. Noticing Welch carve his seventeenth notch into his rifle's stock, I asked him if the tally represented V.C. wasted or all gooks, combatant and non-combatant, he had zapped.

"Look, Mike. This isn't World War II. We're not fighting Germans in gray-green uniforms and hobnailed boots; we're not liberating Frenchmen from the Nazi yoke. This is a goddamn guerrilla war, and in such a war, if the guerrillas have any hope of success, they've got to have the support of the people. They come from the people; they're indistinguishable from the people. You can't separate the two; there's no soldiers and civilians, no combatants and non-combatants. Except for a few corrupt politicians in Saigon and a helluva lot of whores and pimps, everybody in this country has got to be considered our enemy. Charlie's an enemy that's nowhere, but at the same time is everywhere. He's an enemy who is a shadow in the jungle and also the pedicab driver taking you down the street to the whorehouse in Tuy Hoa, the rice farmer innocently planting his rice in the daytime and planting punji pits by night, the shoeshine boy, even the whore giving you a blow job. The enemy is all gooks, all slopes, all dinks. The enemy is anyone who is not an American!"

The next night we struck again, twelve strong this time, raiding the village across the river's mouth from the hamlet we had hit the night before. Lt. Novak's plan was to sail across the river in sampans looted from the hamlet and then conceal his men in the fishing vessels banked on the opposite shore to wait in ambush for the morning arrival of the V.C. gun runners. Only a sliver of the monsoon moon shone as we marched down a beach bewigged with the sharp bamboo follicles of punji stakes. The mission started going wrong from the very beginning, as the wires of Army communications became crossed and artillery illumination flares began popping directly over our heads like shooting stars. Each time a flare slapped back the darkness with its lemon light, we had to embrace the sand and wait for the slow-motion falling stars to burn themselves out. Precious time was thus consumed.

Reaching our sampan armada, the lieutenant discovered that one of the boats was without oars. We therefore had to rig up a tow line to the other two boats. After a great deal of creaking, clanking and cursing by the four-man crews startled the mangy curs of the hamlet into a mongrel chorus of sanctimonious howls, we fierce Norsemen finally set sail in our Viking ships for our raid on the distant coast.

The actual distance to the opposite shore was less than half a mile, but the voyage proved to be hardly less an undertaking for our little fleet than was Columbus' trip to the edge of a flat world. Only a few yards offshore, first one tow line, then the second, snapped. Once these were repaired, we got underway again but made little progress. Pulling, straining, fighting against one another, the two tugs executed a baffling series of maneuvers that had them spinning in circles, crossing each other's lines, ramming into each other like Roman and Carthaginian galleys in a Mediterranean battle. In the middle of all this, a heavy-footed trooper rammed his jungle boot through the flimsy bottom of Novak's boat. While the stricken ship's crew scooped out steel potfuls of water, Welch's boat suddenly appeared out of the darkness and plowed into the side of Novak's scuttled sloop. Into the black water tumbled a trooper. Flailing away like a dying sea monster, the capsized soldier was rescued amid a typhoon of spewing, spitting and splashing by his fellow crewmen.

The sampan squadron continued its passage, but only for a few minutes before misfortune struck again. With a gritty shudder, Welch's boat grounded on a sandbar. Into the water splashed the crew to heave the stranded ship free. But this was only the first of a succession of groundings that wore us out and wore down the night.

At last gaining the opposite shore, Novak's buccaneers deployed two to a sampan to await daylight and the arrival of the gook crews. As we boarded the anchored junks, one grunt slipped from the side of the boat he was to occupy and plunged headfirst into a couple of inches of water and several feet of mud. After pulling him from the glop, we settled down for the two-hour wait until dawn.

As the ocher rays of an ascending sun began to challenge the ebony domination of the night, the first stirrings of an awakening village alerted us to approaching confusion. The disheartening denouement to our commando raid came minutes later, when Burke and Jefferson, in the junk closest to the village, heard the sounds of a man strolling down the trail from the ville humming a peasant ditty. The bushes enclosing the trail parted to reveal an old man in black. He tottered to a spot only a few yards in front of Burke's boat, bent down to scoop a few handfuls of sand away, faced about, and lowered his trousers, wrinkled bare butt centered in the sights of Burke's M-70 grenade launcher. Burke rose up in the boat, took aim, and fired a buckshot round into the old man's ass. He yelped and streaked off the beach, as if the sorcery of ripping hot metal had magically restored him to his youth.

Burke's blast alerted the village and provided the final touch in making a mockery of Novak's night mission. The lieutenant angrily ordered his men out of the boats and into a defensive circle on the beach. When no attack fell on the raiding party, we mounted up and swept through the village, rounding up twenty-three old men and teenage boys to have something to show for the night's mishaps.

The march back to the platoon base was a painful one for our POWs. Several of the disgruntled commandos took out their frustrations on the helpless captives with the hot ends of cigarettes, rifle butts, clenched fists, and bamboo whips. It seemed like a miniature reenactment of the Bataan Death March to me, with the roles of maltreated American POWs and sadistic Asian guards reversed. Joe Jefferson singled out one of the prisoners and proceeded to earn the respect of Torquemada's ghost. Brandishing a long bamboo stave like a tyrannical sea captain's cat-o'-nine-tails, Jefferson methodically lashed the crying captive on the back and head. Pouncing on his prisoner like a panther, Jefferson pummeled him with the butt of his rifle, tripped him, so that he and the old man to whom he was bound by ropes collapsed, and burned the flesh of his yellow-brown arms and neck with a lit cigarette. I was shocked to see such cruelty displayed by Jefferson, a facet of his easy-going, cool-cat personality I would not have suspected. I began to wonder if this war was wrecking all that was human in each of us.

Similar treatment was meted out to others in the cordon of suspects bound to one another like galley slaves. Their wailing became a pitiful concert stinging my ears. I tried to break up the marching inquisition, but Welch restrained me.

"Hell, Mike, they're not hurting them candy ass slopehead bastards. How many of these innocent crybabies here do you think were out on the beach last night planting these shit-smeared punji stakes for us? Let the guys go ahead and have a little fun. Christ, they deserve it after last night's fucked up mess!"

And so these knights of modern warfare continued to display their twisted twentieth century chivalry. Four of the prisoners under later interrogation were tagged Viet Cong "sympathizers." The rest were released, their "hearts and minds" undoubtedly lost to the enemy.

After our corsair strike on the fishing village had flopped, the lieutenant allowed his exhausted buccaneers time to rest. That day and night were largely uneventful for the platoon, although not so for other C Company units.

Three Charlies ditty-bopped into a Weapons Platoon L-shaped ambush and got popped. One of the V.C. dead was a platoon leader, weighted by the maps, flashlight, compass and other accoutrements of combat leadership. The ambushers themselves did not escape the crosscurrent of fire unscathed. Two men were wounded, both of them because of the compassion of the platoon medic. Hearing the moans of a wounded Charlie, the medic, in undiscriminating dedication to his Hippocratic oath, rushed from his position to the aid of the fallen foe hardly before the guns had fallen silent. The platoon leader stepped out onto the trail to order his medic back to his position. At that moment, the wounded gook threw a potato masher, which badly wounded both lieutenant and medic. A volley of rifle fire blew away what little life remained in the bleeding Charlie.

Company headquarters was also involved in an ambush that night, but as recipients of the act. The CO's party blundered into a V.C. ambush that could have annihilated them. But the goddess of war played mistress to Captain Silvasy that night, miraculously bringing his HQ section safely through the storm without a single casualty. His pride ruffled, the captain recaptured his hauteur by calling in a fire mission to batter a nearby village with an artillery ram.

We remained in position for the rest of the day under a bright and warming sun. Our idleness was terminated an hour before sunset, when the order rasped statically on the PRC-25 radio directing the platoon to pass through the village scene of our recent great snafu, cross the river at the north end of that village, and move to an ambush site several hundred meters up the opposite shore. With Rose and me alternating on point, we stumbled through the dark village, seeking a route through the jumble of thatched huts, all pungent with the odors of charcoal and wood fires, cooking rice and fear.

Finally, we reached the rocky sea wall and staggered down to the beach. A wet search by the lieutenant and me failed to locate a ford for the platoon, so we launched an oarless sampan for the crossing. Stripping to fatigue trousers, the swimmers of 2nd Squad floated the creaky vessel loaded with a half dozen troopers into the gray flow of the river ... a quarter of a mile wide at this point. An effort was made to muffle the echoes of our enterprise, for the village blasted the night before lay directly across the river and rumors reported it crawling with V.C. The outline of the village was lost in a dark ridge line rising beyond it and in the obscure, overcast night. With Rose and me towing the boat by lines hooked to the bow of the sampan and others clinging to the sides and pushing, we crossed the river. The boat was unloaded of men and gear in clumsy, confused haste, and the lieutenant somehow formed a defensive ring around his tiny beachhead. But the night's ferrying was far from complete. More than half the platoon still waited on the wrong side of the river.

I waded with Rose, Jefferson and Jim Henk back into the cold water. We were to guide on Sgt. Tower's red-filtered flashlight, but in the black confusion all the flashlights had been boated over in the first ferry. Thus we navigated wide of our mark and had to splash blindly along the shore to locate Tower's men.

Embarking with the second load, we were beset by a rain squall that rapidly developed into a driving downpour, deepening the darkness, compounding the confusion, and intensifying the icy chill of the churning water. Our muscles stiffened with an invasion of ice, as the water below and above surrounded us in a cold captivity. A wretched eternity passed before we finally gained the opposite shore. Men scrambled out of the leaking sampan, leaping from the clutch of confusion into the grasp of chaos. Rucksacks and gear were lost; rifles dropped into the glupping mud. Soldiers, trembling in the deluge, strayed blindly off into the blackness, while the lieutenant harangued his platoon into defensive positions.

One small group remained on the south shore to be towed across to the platoon. Rose, Jefferson and Henk had seen their energy sink into the river, but others volunteered to take their place. The flush of importance I had felt when first appointed to direct the crossing had long since passed into an oblivion of fatigue and cold, rainy hopelessness. But a voice within that spoke the language of pride pushed me back into the black water. When I crawled out of the river dark eons later, crushed by a weariness beyond exhaustion, the world seemed like a great liquid ball, without earth, without solidity. I was shuddering violently from the hours' long immersion in a quarter of a mile of ice water, and there seemed no way I could make it through the final hours of the night stuck in some mud puddle defensive post while the rain continued to torment me.

But the rain had not washed away the lieutenant's compassion. He allowed those who had spent half the night in cold combat with the river to seek refuge in a riverside shack. Sorting out our mud-quilted gear from the debris littering the beach, we ferrymen staggered into the foul-smelling rat roost. The hut was barely intact, its walls splintered and in places caved in by the artillery shelling, but to us it was the marble palace of a Persian Gulf sheik. As we entered, a crumpling explosion bracketed the collapsing shanty. The thought of enduring combat after the wet miseries of the night was almost unbearable. Mercifully, the detonation was not the signal of an enemy attack, but only an M-79 grenade carelessly discharged by a weary Joe Jefferson. No one had the strength left to reprimand him. We collapsed in a huddle, wrapping poncho liners around us and cuddling close to share our body heat. The hard floor, the termites sawing in a concert choir of consumption in the walls against which we had propped our backs, even the foraging rats scurrying across our legs, all passed away under the hypnosis of exhaustion.

Somewhat restored to a human condition, although the weight of continents still dragged at muscles feebly attempting to follow the mental commands to motion, we plodded from the muddy ruins of one ville shortly after sunrise, bound for another hamlet a klick or so down the north shore. The ceaseless bombardment from the monsoon clouds turned the trail into an ocher-brown morass on which troopers, weakened from the night's ordeal and encumbered by heavy loads made heavier by mud and rain, slipped and toppled into, falling to their knees, their asses, or flat on their faces.

We reached the next ville, soaked with rain and robed in mud, looking more like gray-brown horrors emerging from the Black Lagoon than marching soldiers. The platoon formed a skirmish line and advanced through the peasant settlement. Each house was searched, its frightened inhabitants forced to huddle helplessly in one corner while the G.I.s fondled their pauper's property. Underground shelters were scoured by tunnel rats, with smoke grenades thrown into any hole that looked suspicious. Curling plumes of red, violet and yellow smoke rose in a warbonnet on the green skull of the landscape. Ultimately, the individual feathers of smoke mingled in a variegated haze that reflected against the silver wetness of the monsoon. A few suspects were rounded up; young boys barely in their teens and rickety old men. But no real enemy was found nor any of his hidden arms.

Instructed to secure the ville for the rest of Charlie Company, Lt. Novak quartered his men in three of the larger houses. There we tried to dry out, scraped mud from weapons and oiled them, munched on Cs, bananas and ears of dried corn. The company trickled into the village early in the afternoon and a Firefly copter delivered orange sacks of mail, the opiate of a soldier far from home, and a Brown Derby of mashed potatoes, hot chocolate, meatloaf and chocolate cake. A second chopper brought Lt. Col. Dietrich to consult with the CO and show his men he was right there with them in the mud and mire, sharing their dangers — and also our first hot meal in many days. The colonel was there in the crotch of war for all of thirty minutes. Then Gunslinger was snugly aboard his helicopter and up in the sky, where there was no mud and the rain droned a pleasant rhythm on the olive shell of the steel locust. Battalion commanders rarely got wet in this war.

A third helicopter brought veterans, such as DeJesus, returning to action, as well as cherries. As we settled for the night under a palisade of banana trees, throwing our ponchos on a grassy area that glimmered like a great green sponge, a last Huey descended through the drizzling twilight, its rotating blades whipping the rain into a spray to mingle with the streamers of purple smoke from a grenade detonated to mark our position. The chopper brought us two returning old-timers: Pfc. Detwahler, cured of the malaria that had scuttled him in August; and our hawk-beaked machine gunner, SP/4 Hickman, recovered from a fevered tryst with dengue fever.

The replacements and returnees boosted the platoon strength, although it still fell short of the regulation forty-seven men. All the time I was with it, the platoon never mustered more than thirty-five strong in the field. On the average our thin ranks were filled by no more than twenty-five men, and during one mission only sixteen of us jumped from helicopters onto the LZ, our eleven-man paper squads reduced to three or four men in the bush. In this respect, our platoon was not unique. Understrength platoons made up understrength companies to form understrength battalions. And all this while Army clerks waited around in Saigon for a desk to be empty; all this in a huge American force approaching 400,000 and constantly growing with more and more pencil pushers, grease monkeys and other "pogues" "in the rear with the beer," but with precious few grunts.

Battle casualties, R&R and leave, and a host of jungle afflictions from dengue fever to dysentery to jungle rot and immersion foot, all took their toll on the battalion. But malaria led the parade. Though we marked every Monday by swallowing a brick-colored tablet we called the "Horse Pill" and popped smaller booster pills every day, the disease continued to thin our ranks. In my five months with 1st Platoon, twenty of the fifty-five paratroopers who served with the platoon at one time or the other during that period were laid low with the delirium and tremors of malaria, two more than the platoon's total combat casualties. New medicines and treatments had reduced the recuperation period to an average of six weeks, but the disease was still an ordeal. But it was immeasurably more tolerable than a V.C. bullet in the brain and, for some men, malaria offered a way out of the mud, misery and mountains of search-and-destroy operations. They would toss their malaria pills into the brush and could hardly conceal their relief when the symptoms appeared. This deliberate courting of the malarial maiden became serious enough for Brigade HQ to issue orders directing squad leaders to stand by and insure that their men gulped down the malaria pill. When the rate of malaria cases continued at an unacceptable level, company commanders ordered their NCOs to physically check the insides of privates' mouths to insure that the pills had been swallowed.

On the night of October 19 a bereaved Vietnamese mother carried her daughter, no more than eight years old, to the Americans. The girl's back, from the black strings of her hair to her toes, was lacerated with bloody exclamation marks ... the work of artillery shrapnel. She had been swathed in grimy cloth bandages, already heavy with the stench of pus and the squirm of maggots. Our medic was not compassionate by nature. He had been thrilled to assist Morales in zapping the wandering old man on the morning of our LZ firefight and he had delighted in tormenting Viet Cong suspects. But by flickering candlelight, Comiskey employed all his limited skills and limited heart in healing the little girl who had joined the legions of innocents struck down by the war. He worked through half the night, and when he could do no more he collapsed into sporadic sleep beside the straw pallet of his patient. He remained there throughout the night and tenderly carried her to a Dust-Off Medevac at the morning's first light.

It was one of the few times in those mean weeks that I was not ashamed of the American involvement in Vietnam ... not until I remembered that it had been an American artillery shell, fired at her ville because of our captain's embarrassment at blundering into an enemy ambush, that had slashed the fragile beauty of the child.

Another in an endless telegraphing of bullshit tips sent the platoon mushing up another hill in quest of a fantasy cave studded with fantasy arms. One more illusion exploded, we changed course and headed back for the hill commanding the valley's southern sweep. The march was stalled several times as we chased Vietnamese peasants with shouts and shells ... continuing to create many more enemies than we could ever destroy as we rounded up suspects to be deposited in heliborne paddywagons.

Evening crept upon the trampling platoon before it had reached the level summit of the hill where we had homesteaded during the first days of the operation. The Huey taxi service dipped down on a slope of mist to whisk the lieutenant back to South Field, where he was to receive the honors of the brigade's "Officer of the Week."

The morning of October 21 found us once again lifted up into the groggy, gray sky. Once again the helicopter ride, the combat assault; the bladed rain beading men's faces as they sat, three on each side of the chopper, legs suspended out into the air. Once more a lush green checkerboard of rice paddies below us, like glistening tiles of jade on a wet mosaic. Once again a liquid emerald earth swallowing scarlet streaks of machine gun tracers fired from Hueys. And again men dressed in jungle-colored clothes and carrying rifles the color of death, throwing themselves from the open breasts of hovering birds, their rotary wings rippling the green lances of rice into a rolling avocado sea.

The objective was a fortified village lying alongside one of the many rivers in the region. It was a battalion assault, with Charlie Company hitting the village itself, Bravo Company and the Recondos dropped by helicopter into a blocking position on the other side of the river, and Alpha Company covering all other escape exits and acting as a reserve in case the other companies encountered stiff opposition.

It seemed as if I might finally experience my big conventional battle, big at least by the standards of Vietnam warfare. But there was only a flutter of resistance to our onslaught. A handful of snipers greeted us with full metal-jacketed displeasure as Charlie Company splashed into a LZ rice paddy waist deep with the monsoon. Five O' Deuce machine guns and rifles quickly replied with their own racketing insults and rocket-spewing Huey gunships soon added their exploding 2.75 mm invectives. Charlie Company clumsily arranged itself into a skirmish line arcing in the flooded paddies surrounding the ville and advanced to seize its objective. The Victor Charlie snipers did not choose to pursue the argument further and withdrew. My great battle was over before it began.

Once inside the village, the tedious task of searching houses and tunnels commenced. Several suspects were rounded up; as usual, the very young or very old. Our platoon's catch was a withered village doctor discovered hiding under a table in his home. The gray-bearded doctor was escorted to Company HQ, where a Kit Carson — a former V.C. turned scout and interpreter — wearing an honorary Screaming Eagle patch, interrogated him briefly and then released him.

As the old man passed by the platoon file of paratroopers lining the river shore, a single shot cracked the air. Blood sprouted from the arm of the peasant doctor like a blossoming red rose and his medicine bag fell to the sand speckled with a sudden scarlet dew. The old villager grimaced incredulously at the rifle in the hands of SSgt. Welch. Then, as if resigning himself to an inalterable fate, he bent down to grasp his medicine kit with his other hand and continued his plodding pace down the beach and toward destruction.

Another trooper in the file raised his rifle and sent a second bullet spinning toward the man. Blood spurted again, this time from a geysering hole in the peasant's abdomen. A stunned gaze fastened over his face as he crumpled to his knees. His assassin walked forward to thrust the powder-hot barrel of his M-16 to within inches of the kneeling man's forehead. The tiny leaden ram of a bullet crashed through the doctor's skull and exploded in his brain like the white mass of a meteor. Pink brains mixed with red blood in the wet sand.

Johansen, suddenly brave now that the man withered under death's hot bosom, came forward to administer the last rites. Clutching one of the multitude of fire-hardened punji stakes spiking the beach like a miniature phalanx of iron pikes, Johansen drove it deep into the chest of the Vietnamese, as if impaling a vampire's heart on a wooden stake. An eruption of blood painted the stake crimson, while a cocky Johansen remarked to the onlookers, "Hard Core all the way, wouldn't you say? Finishing him off with one of their own little toys meant for one of us!"

Tate decided to add his refinements. Whipping out his bayonet and pointing to the still twitching gook, he said, "I guess Moses Atticus Tate will just have to show all of you amateurish butchers how to properly carve up one of these slopeheads. Otherwise this old man may die of old age before ya finally figger out how to waste him!"

Then he went to work with savage concentration. First he tried to bisect the old man at the waist, but quickly gave that project up as too time consuming and settled for a simple decapitation. Wallowing in a swamp of blood, brains and viscera, Tate first sliced the old man's throat from ear to ear with a brandish of his bayonet. Then he began sawing at the tendons of the neck.

After several minutes, Welch, fearful that the platoon sergeant might appear with his less tolerant attitude towards barbarity, interrupted Tate's slow surgery and instructed him and Johansen to heave the corpse, the head flopping grotesquely by a few yet unsevered neck muscles, into the foliage. Then he kicked sand over the maroon graffiti of mutilation, written with the ink of blood and brains.

I was searching a hooch some distance away and did not personally witness this event, but Pfc. Grogan, one of the new cherries, did and was horrified. I tried to reassure him that such things did not happen often and to explain how they could happen at all — how weeks of fear and frustration, of buddies being blown to hell by phantoms we could neither catch nor kill, had sapped our souls and pushed us over the brink into barbarism. But all my words fell away before the stink of shame surrounding the platoon. I turned away and looked up at the sky. The gray clouds hung like wisps of the old man's beard.

Chapter XIX

Hard Core Test

Another helicopter ride, another hump up another hill, and then welcome news awaiting us at the top ... we were going in early the next morning. Less welcome news followed. We were informed that the labor force of the 1st Platoon was to come under new management. Lt. Novak was to take temporary command of Weapons Platoon while its lieutenant recovered from grenade wounds resulting from his overzealous medic's impetuous rush to heal the wounded, and then he was to be elevated to company XO. He would be missed, for he had become a part of the Hard Core mythology. Novak had given his men a strong self-confidence, wrongly and even barbarously employed at times, but one that had carried us through a harvest of hardship. A friend to his men yet commanding respect and an informal but vital discipline, the lieutenant had demonstrated real initiative in hunting Charlie, tempered by sincere concern for the well-being of his men. Having returned from his hero's coronation at South Field, the lieutenant delivered an emotional farewell speech to a 1st Platoon formation and then he left. The Hard Core Platoon, for better or worse, would not be the same.

The platoon still had SSgt. Welch to pump our veins full with the fuel of a conquering spirit that had made us both nobly strong in the face of adversity and savagely weak before the temptation of atrocity. But for me, at least, the squad leader was losing much of his former glamour. Welch's initiation of the rite of murder and mutilation of the village doctor, following his acquiescence and participation in similar bloody events in the weeks when cruelty replaced combat, deepened my increasingly ambivalent feelings about the man. In one gray and squalid month of falling rain and flowing blood, my mental portrait of SSgt. Welch, a bronzed profile of a Spartan warrior painted in the colors of hero worship, had begun to fade, crack and peel into a grotesque caricature, an olive drab reincarnation of one of Attila's Huns or Tamerlane's Mongols, the red pigment of his victims' blood spreading its stain across the canvas. Welch had once worn the crown of a warrior's kingdom and I had been one of his faithful retainers, a loyal man-at-arms. He had represented to me the perfect soldier: bold, fearless, aggressive, the master of his craft, a virtuoso of battle — everything I had hoped to become in my adolescent fantasies. But the sergeant had let his warrior's crown tumble from his head when he bent his body from the proud posture of a hero to the slink of a slayer. Now he seemed to wear the black executioner's mask, through which burned eyes whose easy blue sparkle had focused to a searing white heat.

Lt. Novak's successor was a lanky second lieutenant named O'Shea, with a head of spikey blond thorns, an acne-cratered face, and a muscleless collection of bones from which the skin seemed to hang in mourning. His introduction to the platoon only sank us deeper into dismay. "Super Soldier" would have found it difficult to win the respect of these men after the glorious image they had constructed of their former platoon leader. O'Shea was not "Super Soldier"; he was not even "Average Soldier," as he would so convincingly prove in the month ahead. Where Lt. Novak had found respect and admiration, Lt. O'Shea would find only derision and contempt.

Minutes after the change of command ceremony, helicopters came in with thundering eloquence to carry the company in aerial acrobatic treetop flights to the battalion TOC. Like bees buzzing down to pollinate flowers, our daredevil chopper pilots swooped so low toward the trees that our dangling legs brushed the leafy topmost branches ... a thrill ride in a deadly amusement park. At battalion TOC, we were herded aboard deuce-and-a-half-ton trucks for the motor convoy to the brigade camp, which was being moved further south along the beach to make room for the expanding jet airstrip. The trip was slow and made slower with the delay caused by the restoration of a bridge across Highway 1 recently blown by Viet Cong sappers. The American engineer officer in charge of repairing the bridge asked for assistance in clearing the area of a throng of gook peddlers trying to sell bottles of Orange Crush and Tiger Piss, bananas and shoots of sugar cane to the engineer troops. Welch formed his squad in a flying wedge formation and charged, scattering the frightened Vietnamese like rice husks thrown into the monsoon wind. We laughed and shouted, felt power coursing our veins, surged with the strength that had wilted under atrocity's baleful glare. Only a pale substitute for victory, it was the only victory we had won in weeks and it felt good.

Once the bridge was reerected, the convoy ground on along the road pitted by the monsoon. As we bounced along, a steely trill of buckshot sang over our tumbling bodies. For the second time, Joe Jefferson's M-79 had spoken without the grenadier's consent, but with his careless coaching. It would not be the last time.

There was no rest for us upon returning to South Field, for the job of sandbagging around all the canvas dwellings of our new campsite faced us — hour after hour, day after day, sandbags, shovels, and sand crystals plastered to sweating backs or sweat-soaked fatigues. I counted sandbags in my sleep ... thirty more needed for Rose's and Whitey's hooch tomorrow; sixty needed to complete Joe Jefferson's and Burke's tent; then 200 for the mail tent and on and on. Vietnam was not combat and glory; it was an infinity of sandbags, a gritty galaxy whose dull stars were gray-green and brown sandbags ... thousands and millions of sandbags. Vietnam's soil was being stolen by the vast erosion of sandbagging; the country's geology could be found tied up in countless burlap bags.

It took four days to stack the sandbag city housing the brigade, and then we expected to be rushed back to our wilderness mistress to swoon under sixty-pound rucksacks in her forested boudoir. But no such summons came to resume the stormy affair and we were given a reprieve for a few more days. Reprieve did not mean rest, however. To Captain Silvasy, the company was like a great broadsword that required constant sharpening to maintain its cutting edge. Thus we spent our days attacking an imaginary enemy in the sand dune battlefields of Tuy Hoa beach, with rifles and machine guns blazing, grenades hurtling, Laws vomiting rockets, and Claymores singing their lethal steel hum.

I had to take charge of 1st Squad while its NCOs were perfecting their craft at squad leader's school at Phan Rang. The most onerous task was attempting to control Mad Moses Tate and stop his terrorist attacks against cherry troopers. I finally had to threaten, with muzzle against reddened brow, to blow the top of his head off before the sorcerer of sadism agreed to end his harassment.

My weariness with command responsibilities was escalating. I had simply wanted to become a foot soldier, not a leader, but for the last two months I had been constantly forced into that role. Welch had promised me buck sergeant, but I wanted that promotion even less than I did the authority and duties I was already saddled with. With three stripes on my sleeve, I would be confirmed in the leadership role that I had consistently tried to dodge.

News of my promotion came from Captain Silvasy, orating bombastically at a presentation-of-awards ceremony at the end of October. I was shocked. Me a sergeant! I felt like the southern slave suddenly given the overseer's whip; the feudal serf suddenly made lord of the manor; the Hindu untouchable allowed to wear the Brahmin's robes. The harassed recruit of seventeen, suffering like all other boots the tongue lashings of fierce D.I.s (drill instructors) in boot camp little more than two years ago, now suddenly become one of those multi-striped demons!

At the same ceremony, I received the Combat Infantryman Badge. I had greatly envied the bearers of that badge during my days as an artilleryman. To me it was the mark of glory attained, the latest of those rainbow goals I sought as a soldier, each marked by the awarding of a badge of recognition. In basic training the most important thing in the world to me was winning an expert marksmanship badge; in jump school I endured three weeks of dawn-to-dusk torture of mind and body by noncom sadists and the terror of jumping five times into 1,250 feet of propeller-churned air to win the winged parachute badge of the paratrooper; in Vietnam I was willing to abandon the relative security of my artillery unit to hump the mountains in sun and storm and face enemy fire to earn the wreathed silver flintlock of the CIB. Now I was anxious not only to face that enemy fire again, but to overcome it through feats of valor and thus win greater medaled honors like the Silver Star. I was even willing to exchange a piece of my flesh for a Purple Heart.

But with the winning of each honor and its metallic representation came eventual disappointment. Ultimately, those medals and badges on my chest became little more than trinkets, the rewards of salivation in the martial Pavlovian reactions of soldiers to stimulants the Army placed before them. Hit an acceptable number of targets and the Army awards you a badge; parachute from an airplane five times and the Army pins another badge on your chest; expose your body to death or mutilation and you win a yet more prestigious award; hit an acceptable number of human targets and your reward is still greater; surrender your body to death or injury and the Army pins on a Purple Heart ... maybe it's pinned to a body bag, but, congratulations, you've passed all the Army stimulus-reaction tests with flying colors. Now bring on a new dog, for the old one is dead and the great experiment of mortal combat must go on.

The platoon continued to sprout new leaves, as old ones parted from its branches and drifted on jet-borne winds back to the "Real World." Cherries arrived to begin their year; veterans left at the end of theirs. Troopers departed with malaria; others returned with healed wounds. Ours was a family constantly reborn with infantrymen fresh from the wombs of basic training camps and AIT (Advanced Infantry Training) to replace either the children of violence cut down in flaming adolescence or the suddenly old young men who had survived the stormy puberty of the foot soldier and had left the family for more peaceful pursuits.

Among the men who left was Rhodes. The Army had at last realized its mistake and assigned the man with the flat tire feet to a rifle security company with the mission of guarding Phan Rang. Rhodes, who had spent most of the last month scrubbing pots and pans at the battalion TOC mess, left us like he had arrived, cocky and certain of his sophistication, and impervious to all who might ridicule his drunken giraffe appearance that did not match his cocky fox manner. We would miss him.

The days passed and there was still no word to gather fresh ammo from the ammo dump, stuff rucksacks full of C-rations, collect maps and chart points of origin coordinates. Soldiers were granted passes into Tuy Hoa, where they found garishly painted whores on whom they worked out their hatred for the gook race and the gook land through the physical act of love. Troopers sat in seedy bars sipping Tiger Piss and fighting off mascaraed cats pawing at their penises as though they were snared mice. Other men turned to other diversions. The fragrance of marijuana drifted like a dreamy fog over the rows of sandbag-encircled pup tents. Pot allowed men to secede from their destructive union with the war; to float free without turmoil or trouble on its transporting clouds. Probably half the troopers in Charlie Company smoked dope periodically during their tours in Vietnam, and possibly as many as half that number became frequent smokers (or "potheads," as opposed to the "juicers" who preferred booze to grass and who in later years would increasingly separate from the "heads" along class, age and rank lines ... young draftees blowing pot while older lifers guzzled booze).

For many, pot became as much a part of their Vietnam experience as were C-rats, M-16s and malaria pills. It was easy to obtain in Tuy Hoa, where troopers often purchased whole rucksacks of grass for a few cases of C-rations. But marijuana was not nearly as pervasive in 1966 as it came to be in later years. Certainly not as many tried it then as did later on. I was one of the non-users, still hung up on the fears that marijuana use was the first irreversible step down into the hell of heroin addiction. Later, when I did try pot during my college days, my student friends were surprised that I had not discovered its easy ecstasies in Vietnam.

They were unaware that I had not been part of the Army which painted peace symbols on their helmets, refused to venture out on suicide patrols, inhaled through the muzzle of an M-16 the fumes of a joint smoldering in its chamber, and snorted the white powder escape of smack. The Army of 1965 and 1966 that I served in was a transitional army, moving from the pre–Vietnam War Army of hard discipline, super masculinity, and a glorious tradition, to the coming-apart Army of 1970 and 1971, plagued with drugs, My Lais, and mutiny from within and the aversion of our own military-hating generation from without.

Ours was the Army of largely working class enlistees who bitched and complained when given an impossible, absurd mission but performed it nonetheless; who could see no reason for fighting for a country and a people they largely despised but were willing to do their duty and get out, and were resentful of the student demonstrations against the war which they often took as a personal affront to their bravery, as indifference to their suffering by middle class kids attending college only to escape military service, as traitorous aid to the cause of the men who were killing their buddies. The soldiers of 1966 were men who could still feel pride in their own valiant deeds and the combat record of their units, but who, under the ignoble circumstances of this strange war, mistook too often bloody atrocities for brave deeds; who might dare smoke a cigarette which made one pleasantly high, but would rarely be tempted to feel the destructively ecstatic rush of heroin flooding the senses in an escape from the awesome uselessness of their Vietnam days and nights. The U.S. Army in Vietnam in 1966 was just beginning to show symptoms of the spiritual sickness to which it would soon seem so close to succumbing.

It was time for the Hard Core Test. This was a trial of manliness and machismo stolen by Welch straight out of the John Wayne hero heritage. Two new inductees into the chosen few of the Hard Core Squad (or Platoon) would face off with clenched fists and proceed to pummel each other in turn ... beginning with a slug to the stomach, then a blow to the chest, and climaxing with a hammer slam to the chin. If a man could stand firmly at attention while the blows were being administered and pull none of his own punches when his turn came, then he was considered worthy of joining the hallowed ranks of the Hard Core Platoon.

The squad leader had coerced many candidates for martial renown into taking the test, including even Lt. Novak. Now the diabolical Tate was waging a relentless war of persecution and derision against Walt Johansen. Tate carried his campaign of instigation to the point of staging a phony Hard Core Test with Joe Jefferson before an audience of beer-swilling grunts. Conducted by Tate's maestro wand of rabble rousing, the drunken choir then sang a requiem of ridicule for Johansen's dead honor. It was more than Johansen could take. A distorted pride still dwelt in his coward's soul. In a desperate attempt to salvage some small strip of honor to shield his mortally wounded reputation against his comrades' contempt, Johansen accepted the challenge and asked that I, one of the few men in the platoon who had not added his voice to the chorus of condemnation directed at him, be his opponent in the joust.

I was taken aback by his invitation to duel. But rather than show real courage by refusing to take part in this travesty, even if it meant losing face with my platoonmates, I picked up Johansen's flung glove. The rowdy crowd was all on my side, making it easier to mislay the true point and purpose of honor as we prepared to do battle in the center of a sandy gladiatorial box, everyone awaiting the blows that would deliver the final cuts in Johansen's emasculation.

I was an unwilling castrator. Though I had no respect for Johansen, I lacked the bully boy bent for pleasure in being the agent of his final disgrace. But by the man's own choice I was to become just that, or risk sullying my own reputation, creating doubts about my own manliness, tarnishing the coin of my courage. I was caught up on the dark and vicious side of something I had thought to be noble and inspiring ... the ideal of courage and a determination to hold up my end of hell. The quiet honor I had admired and searched for, had been warped and distorted by these men, this war, and by my collaboration in its corruption, into something dark and sinister. I had wanted to be a hero, not a bully. But I was trapped. I had accepted too much, had acquiesced when I should have protested, had played their game when I should have left the field or tried to restore the rules. Because I had seen men endure so much and win rightful respect, I had tolerated a few pushing pride beyond compassion, beyond humanity. Once again I found myself caught in the web of a reality I could not have imagined, but one woven with the very threads of my fantasies. I had played quisling to my convictions too long now; I had no other choice but to continue that collaboration.

Johansen elected to strike the first blow. Standing rigidly at attention, I prepared for the first round. Johansen cocked his arm and swung with power. But a second's sigh before his doubled fist plowed into my stomach, he checked his swing, and the anvil slam I had expected became a fluffy feather pillow bouncing against my abdomen. Johansen's conspiratorial expression explained his sudden mercy without the necessity of words. His intention was to play the same put-on just performed by Tate and Jefferson.

But he had chosen the wrong accomplice for his scheme to save his body from punishment while he was rescuing his reputation. No one had been taken in by Tate's farcical performance; no one was going to be fooled by our play-acting pummeling either. Prestige demanded that I play for real this parody of iron-fisted heroes confirming their masculinity in true Western movie style. I swung for Johansen's tightened gut and did not feather the force of the punch. But before my fist could connect, Johansen sucked in his stomach and toppled backwards. Though I had barely made contact, the moans and groans manufactured by the flattened faker were almost convincing.

But Tate was not fooled. "Get your phony candy ass up, you no balls mother fucker, and play it for real, or I'll take the Hard Core Test with you ... and I sure as fuck won't be fakin' it!"

Tate's prompting put iron in Johansen's second blow. My breath fled in panic from a chest pounded by a sledgehammer. Retaliation ruled me now; reluctance had been smashed into a lust for revenge. But the power of my punch was wasted, as the target again ignored the rules of the contest and evaded the blow. Johansen tried to resume the farce with his final swing, the punch falling against my chin with the force of a marshmallow. And again he was down on the ground writhing in pretended pain before I had even completed my roundhouse swing aimed at his jaw.

I glared down at the fraud. "You would have shown a helluva lot more guts if you had just told Tate to shove it when he was instigating all this. You really passed the Hard Core Test with beaucoup balls, Johansen. Get yourself another fall guy the next time you want to rig up a little glory!"

I walked away, as much ashamed of myself as I was disgusted with Johansen, ashamed for lacking the strength to say no to this whole absurdity.

Johansen slowly staggered to his feet to face the assembled contempt of the company. Tate stomped up to deliver double-barreled blows into the outcast's face. Johansen was less nimble before this knuckled salvo and was knocked flat on his back. Nobody offered to help him to his feet. He lay whining in the sand, his shame complete.

Though we were temporarily removed from one war, another one flared within the brigade. Civil war broke out between the 2/502nd Strike Force and its rival battalion, the 2/327th. Beer-boggled hotheads from both battalions fought a series of skirmishes with hand flares on successive nights. Both camps were soon under a siege of red-tailed rocket flares. Like comets, they streaked across a narrow no-man's-land and burst into corollas of ruby flames against the canvas walls of tents and the rings of sandbags. Small fires blazed as the barrage intensified; curses and threats followed the volleys of hand flares across the perimeter; tempers burned as hot as the flames licking at the shelter-half sides of pup tents.

The limited war of flares and fury escalated on the third night. Troopers from Charlie Company slapped palms against the bases of aluminum cylinders to propel green star cluster flares almost point-blank into a beer party of "We Aim to Kill" 2/327th soldiers; illumination rounds sizzled down upon the camp from the coughing mortars of Bravo Company. Like a mob of Parisian paupers storming the Bastille, 2/327th troopers armed themselves with E-tools, bayonets and beer cans, and stormed in drunken fury into Charlie Company's tent ghetto.

A tinny bombardment of crushed and crumpled beer cans crowded the air. Then the company was overrun by a cursing wave of green-fatigued rioters. Officers and NCOs fired their authority against the mob, only to have it hurled back to them on catapults of contempt. Entrenching tools thudded against skulls; the air swarmed with flying beer cans and angry curses. I waded into the wild river of riot trying to mediate a cease-fire, and a sand-filled beer can bounced off the side of my skull and an E-tool blade slammed against my shin. Not even the raging profanity of our first sergeant could douse the fires of riot. Finally, two CS grenades were detonated to spray a choking mist into the rioters, forcing them to stagger, bloody, bruised, gagging on the poisoned air and weeping flames from burning eyes, toward the sweet air beyond the pup tent battleground. The battle, inspired by our body count rivalry and ignited by too much Tiger Piss and twisted pride, was over. Now it was time to count casualties.

Both battalions were placed on tight restrictions and company commanders delivered the expected harangues, scorning us for a lack of discipline and professionalism. But in truth, our leaders were probably not all that displeased with the "Battle of the Battalions," for it demonstrated a fiercely competitive spirit between the units and an explosive pride ... all of which, if properly channeled, could be translated into beaucoup body counts. It was certainly the kind of riot service chiefs a few years later would have welcomed in place of the ominously disruptive racial clashes that exploded on bases and aboard ships.

Charlie Company, the Five O' Deuce company situated closest to the 2/327th's camp, had borne the brunt of the battle and looked it. Pup tents were torn down, shelter-halfs slashed by bayonets or half burned by cometing flares, sandbag parapets toppled. The company shower, made of ammo box lumber and an old oil drum, was a splintered disaster; the movie screen was shredded. Hundreds of beer and soda cans, that hours earlier had served as rockets for rioters, provided a crumpled metal shag to the sandy carpet. Half the company's personnel carried some bloodied mark of the night's disorder, ranging from scratches to fractured skulls, broken noses, and bayonet wounds. The line outside the battalion aid station that morning was far longer than that queuing for breakfast chow. A lingering smog of smoke and tear gas clung to the camp.

Our riot had been a violent burlesque — performed by men caught up in absurd glory games and chauvinistic unit loyalties — of the far more serious civil disorders that would divide our nation along opposite sides of the war's fault lines; that would ultimately divide the military service itself. Although this silly conflict had drawn blood, it was forgotten almost as quickly as it had flamed. We were through fighting among ourselves; it was time to go back to fighting the enemy, to fighting the jungle.

In the meantime, the mad scientists of the sword had been experimenting in their brigade staff laboratories, seeking not the secret of life as had Mary Shelley's driven protagonist, but the secret of a more bountiful death. Their two-month-old martial monster called Operation Seward had chewed up the lives of 239 Vietnamese, eighty-two of them claimed by the 2/502nd. Our leaders desired a monster with a more voracious appetite. Thus they created a new Frankenstein-of-the-body-count and called it Operation Geronimo.

On the same day we were notified of the impending operation, Pfc. Landon, hoochmate of Joe Jefferson, picked up his rifle and blew his left hand off.

Though hardly gung-ho, and though not a Samson of the Hard Core Squad, Landon had never been suspected of cowardice. If he had not suffered in silence, he had certainly not bitched any louder or longer than the rest of us. He had not been a candidate for dishonor or disgrace, like Johansen. Thus, when Landon calmly informed his friend, Butch Burke, that he could not tolerate the thought of returning to more weeks of mud and misery, and then pressed the flash suppressor on the end of the muzzle of his M-16 against the palm of his hand and unflinchingly pulled the trigger, shock and disbelief that the wound could be anything but an accident were the first reactions among his comrades. When we heard the truth, many of us in the platoon wondered if the creature we called cowardice, wrestling within our souls with the ego of pride, might one day win that struggle and convince us that self-preservation meant more than self-respect. Many men in the company wished to escape this country, this war, but not at the cost Landon had paid ... the most precious of which was losing his comrades' respect. For most of us, that was too high a price to pay. Most of us were not willing to pay such a high ransom for release from Vietnam ... not yet, anyway.

Chapter XX

Operation Geronimo

Early on the misty morning of November 6, the battalion boarded helicopters to resume the war with Mr. Charlie. Accompanying each platoon were a half dozen soldiers of the CIDG (Civilian Irregular Defense Groups), looking like Southeast Asian Boy Scouts. From the beginning of the operation our ill-trained, undisciplined Lilliputian allies were objects of disdain. They would do little in the days ahead to improve their image.

The company was deposed from its berths aboard the hovering train of Hueys twenty minutes later, cast into the bitter exile of the mountainous stretch of forest northwest of Tuy Hoa called "The Hub," until it could redeem itself into the good graces of Mars with enemy blood. We failed to shorten our exile that first day as we marched uneventfully down a jungled gorge. The fruits of Geronimo's first day of harvest were solely sweat and aching muscles.

With SSgt. Welch and point man Rose both sick, the new platoon leader had no pathfinder to prevent him from losing the platoon in the emerald endlessness of forested ridges and ravines. Thus we buried the day in a deep grave of perspiration and frustration as Lt. O'Shea guided the platoon column, detached as usual from the company in a checkerboarding sweep, in dizzying circles in quest of a seemingly mythical Hill 388. When the puzzled shavetail lieutenant finally reached what he thought was the long-sought hill, he directed his men up a steep slope to the tree-studded summit. The elephant grass was a green castle wall; our rucksack-weighted bodies, battering rams. Point man after point man was worn out by combat with the concertina of the grass. Upon reaching the top, salty streams of sweat stinging the cuts on our arms, hands and faces, we discovered, by orienting ourselves to terrain features indicated on the map, that we had climbed the wrong hill. But rather than fight through the cutlass-bladed grass again, the lieutenant decided to settle for the rainy infinity of the night and call in a false location report to the CO, hoping the artillery would not select this hill as one of its nightly H&I targets.

While the 1st Platoon was forlornly trampling through a hemorrhaging confusion, the equally incompetently led 3rd Platoon walked unsuspectingly into a camp of NLF regulars at chow time. Dropping their rice bowls, the Viet Cong grabbed AKs to spray a leaden deluge onto the Americans. That metal-tipped torrent soaked the leg of Lt. Strong in a red shower and dampened his RTO with the same scarlet stain. Carrying their two wounded, the platoon beat a hasty retreat and called in the fury of the 2/320th Artillery.

The new day brought more of the same ... more aimless marching through Nature's green bowels; up and down a roller coaster of hills; across the silver rush, like molten mercury, of a half dozen mountain streams; down the dark green colons of ravines. And everywhere, engulfing us, diminishing us, threatening to swallow us into the verdant depths of its sodden soul, was the all-encompassing jungle.

We were a belt of tiny, olive drab asteroids drifting in the solitude of an infinitely green universe. We were trapped in this greenness, which was neither the cool green of temperate springs nor the hot lazy green of summer, but the eternal green of the jungle ... the green without seasons and the cycle of life, death and rebirth, the immortal green that laughed contemptuously at the sun and refused its light, that fixed its gloom over the damp earth and over men's souls.

Back home the trees would be shuddering from the chill of winter's approach, their summer blood having been drained to stain the leaves the color of rust. Soon they would fall in orange and gold tatters, the bright colors of a jester's coat, at the feet of trunks purpling with winter, and the bare trees would stand shivering. But the trees of the tropics, like us, seemed trapped forever in their green armor.

At times the jungle almost vibrated with warnings of the enemy lurking in ambush. The silence of the forest, strangely unbroken by chirping birds and chattering monkeys, seemed to promise the presence of a gathering violence crouching to spring. But the only enemy encountered on this day was a grazing herd of water buffalo, which point man Tate stampeded with a ratcheting shout from his M-16. The night passed just as undisturbed by war's violent visitations. Had Charlie been slinking in the darkness, he would have easily found our position, thanks to our allies. The toy soldiers of the CIDG loosened a clamor as they chopped at trees to clear a sleeping area for their hammocks. Night discipline was obviously an alien concept to them, as the irregulars struck matches and puffed on red glowing cigarettes without taking the elementary precaution of cloaking the burning ends under cupped palms. Nor could we trust them to relieve the strain of guard duty, fearing that they might either fall asleep or betray us to the enemy.

Instances of CIDG treachery were rare; most of the irregulars were recruited from the Montagnards, the original inhabitants of the country, now largely confined to the Central Highlands and despised by the Vietnamese fighting under both flags. Usually their treachery took the more subtle form of noisy indiscipline. But recently a CIDG soldier, jumping first from a helicopter hovering over a LZ, had tossed a grenade back into the chopper before anyone else could leap out. The indigenous soldiers and the American helicopter crew had disintegrated in a popping chain reaction of exploding grenades and helicopter fuel.

Operation Geronimo had thus far failed to live up to its namesake. The 101st sought retribution for a recent blow to its proud martial chin. During Operation Seward, an indifferently defended CP of Bravo Company, 2/327th had been wiped out by the Viet Cong. The company CP had remained fixed in one position for nearly two weeks and had even allowed Vietnamese peasants to approach as closely as they wished, undoubtedly to gather information about the position for the V.C. The defense, which had hardly been improved from the first day's hastily dug spider holes, quickly collapsed under the Viet Cong assault. Ten paratroopers, including the CO, his XO, the first sergeant, and the forward observer team from the 2/320th Artillery, paid for their negligence with their lives. Only three men, all wounded, escaped the massacre. It was the worst single defeat suffered by the 101st during my months with the Screaming Eagles. Operation Geronimo had been conceived in part to reap revenge.

The fourth day of Geronimo brought more monotonous tromping until dusk blurred the forest colors gray and orders crackled through the handset of the PRC-25 radio directing the platoon to a waffle pattern of rice paddies, where we were to take up blocking positions to plug an escape route of a North Vietnamese company locked in combat with Bravo Company a few kilometers distant.

Night had fallen by the time we stretched our thin ranks in three-man posts across the paddies. The moon hung like a great suspended skull, cadaverous in its yellow light. The growls of the beast of battle, now less than a klick away, had risen to a sustained roar. The tantrum of fencing bullets and delirium of artillery shells echoing with gunpowder thunder sang their song down my spine, creating a sensation quite unlike any other. Not even those moments of sizzling nerves and churning blood when the jumpmaster shoved open the aircraft's hatch to confront the wind, and we arose clumsily under the weight of parachute and fear to hook up to the static line cable and await the green flash of the paratrooper's traffic light ... no, not even that could compare with the electric intensity of those cacophonous preludes to battle, when the fluid racing through my veins was no longer blood, but a combustible mixture of terror and euphoria.

As the firefight surged closer, like a rain-swollen river overflowing its banks, an artillery flare popped into a golden glare. Then came a meteor shower of flares and illumination shells. The flares, descending like tiny setting suns, mobilized a shadowed army which leaped up at us in imitative battle. As the night wore on, the waves of the flashflood firefight gradually receded, but the Roman candle starburst of flares continued to paint yellow brush strokes against the night's black canvas.

With morning, the smoldering embers of battle flamed anew as the three line companies of the battalion and the black-bereted Recondo Platoon pressed in on the sides of a dwindling cul-de-sac into which the enemy soldiers of the NVA's 5th Battalion, 95th Regiment, had been pushed. The clatter of gunfire, the steel crunch of detonating grenades, and the thunderclaps of bursting artillery shells hugged the platoon in a metallic storm embrace. Though we made no direct contact with our opponent that morning, the other platoons of the company did find the enemy in straggling ones and twos. They prevented Captain Silvasy's gold-braided heart from breaking by crediting at least a few communist dead to the body count ledger that was largely reflective of the successes of Bravo Company. Second Platoon wasted two North Vietnamese and captured a third, who led them to a sizable arms cache which included two 12.7 mm anti-aircraft guns. Third Platoon also zapped an NVA soldier. But 1st Platoon, trudging half lost in the eye of the storm, sought in vain the battle that was swirling all around.

Later in this day of flickering firefights and pursuit, the platoons joined hands to assault a terraced hill in a long, ragged skirmish line. First Platoon had already climbed it that morning and reported no enemy contact, but Gunslinger, flapping back and forth in his command copter from fifty feet, was so determined to lead a charge up the hill from treetop level that he convinced himself that he detected enemy movement there. Urged on by the battalion commander's heliborne cheerleading, the company struggled to maintain its skirmish line as it staggered wearily up the hill.

After reaching the top and finding it devoid, as before, of the enemy, the company moved ponderously back down in single file formation. As we weaved our way around the spur of an adjoining ridge, machine gunner Terry, who had been dragged out to the field even though only a few days remained until his rotation homeward, noticed a rustling in the bushes to his right. Moving closer to investigate, he discovered an NVA soldier busily engaged in hosing down the vegetation. Terry stood transfixed for several seconds, staring at the similarly immobilized North Vietnamese. Then he fired a hurried burst from his M-60, forcing the enemy soldier into wild flight.

As Terry examined the soldier's abandoned AK-47 assault rifle, he claimed, "Shit, I could have zapped that gook easily if I had wanted to. But I don't want to go home a few days from now thinking I had blown away some poor bastard just trying to take a piss. Hell, he could have been a short-timer just like me!" Nobody bothered to remind Terry that the only short-timers among the enemy were the mortally wounded.

Bravo Company's battle continued through the next day, but the only sight Charlie Company caught of the enemy was a windrow of blood-basted corpses lying among a bamboo abatis obstructing a hillside. As always, I was appalled by the contrast between these obscene poses of real death — faces squashed like some grotesque red fruit, bodies dismembered by a shrapnel axeman, the awful stench, the feasting flies — and the noble, dignified John Wayne deaths of my fantasies ... the deaths of heroes uttering last brave words of inspiration instead of terminal screams of bloody horror, of eyes closing in the last, eternal slumber instead of the sightless stare into the consuming worms.

The body count for the three-day battle of November 9–11, 1966, called the Battle of Phong Cao by the history books, totaled thirty-nine NVA, with thirty-six more captured. The booty in captured arms included fourteen crew-served weapons, three of them mortars, and forty-four individual weapons. The Strike Force had lost five men — four in Bravo Company and one in Recondo — and fifteen paratroopers had been wounded.

And 1st Platoon marched on in befuddling circles, with Terry's volley at a pissing commie the only shots fired. Our Hard Core glory, compensation for drudgery and hardship, faded and ultimately dissolved. Our spirit waned; in its place marched a hollow platoon.

November 13 was a black day. Second Platoon fought a skirmish with Alpha Company for several minutes before an echoing chorus of "Strike Force! Strike Force!" cries halted the firing between friends. The platoon sergeant and a rifleman were wounded by grenade frags. Misfortune continued to trail 2nd Platoon throughout the day. While climbing a steep incline, a soldier offered the muzzle of his rifle to the outstretched hand of a comrade grunting for assistance. The struggling man slipped as he grasped hold of the rifle barrel, jerking hard on the muzzle and causing his straining buddy's impru-dently positioned finger to slam back on the trigger — set off safety and onto full automatic fire. A lightning bolt of eighteen 5.56 mm bullets smashed into the man's head and chest.

Weapons Platoon also marched under an unlucky star that day and another man died. A patrol of six men from the platoon, now under the lead-ership of Lt. Novak, tripped a five-man NVA ambush and was quickly pinned down. The rest of the platoon heard the wild stutter of automatic weapons fire and rushed to the patrol's aid. Brimming a small mound overlooking the ambush site, the platoon silenced the enemy with cascading rifle and machine gun fire. The rescuers then dodged down the unexposed side of the mound to circle cautiously around to the ambushed patrol's position. But one man, Pfc. William Cyr, a cherry trooper with only two weeks in the bush, rashly charged straight toward the patrol. A land mine swallowed the reckless soldier in a ferment of flash and smoke. The nineteen-year-old grunt collapsed like a falling rag doll. Lt. Novak carefully stepped across the murderous mud toward the wreckage that had been a young life. But the lieutenant's bravery did Cyr no good; he was beyond anyone's help.

First Platoon also flirted with misfortune on the 13th. The one substantial incident on an otherwise empty day occurred when ammo bearer Pfc. Grogan lumped his husky frame into a tree fork during one of our infrequent rest halts. Immediately, an expression of alarm, which quickly deepened into one of terror, creased Grogan's face. He stuttered apprehensively, "Lieutenant, I ah, I'm ah, ah.... Shit! I'm sitting on something more than a fuckin' tree!"

The lieutenant's speedy examination uncovered the source of Grogan's discomfort. "Don't get in any kind of a big hurry, Grogan," he cautioned. "You're sitting on a live cluster bomb!"

Grogan's face turned the color of a cold Arctic sky; the sweat of terror beaded his brow. "My God, what'll I do?"

O'Shea cleared away the inquisitive crowd and bent to inspect Grogan's perilous perch. "It hasn't blown yet, so there's no reason it should now. These things are set to go off at a certain altitude above Charlie's head so as to spray him from above. If it didn't detonate when it was supposed to, it probably won't go off at all."

"Damn, sir. I don't need a fuckin' lecture about the thing. I just need fuckin' off of it," gasped Grogan.

"Okay, okay. Just stand up very slowly and very carefully. Just don't nudge it out of its nest," said the usually frantic lieutenant, now surprisingly cool in this crisis.

Grogan swallowed the hard lump of fear in his throat and slowly, carefully, like Atlas lifting the weight of the world on his shoulders, arose and walked away from the mouth of a fulminating volcano.

The heavy, tense seconds collapsed in a half-cry, half-laugh burst of relief. "Oh God ... shit! Thank God! This is one grunt who's gonna take a long, hard look before he plops his tired ass down again! SHIIIT!"

The day following Grogan's torrid affair with the USAF cluster bomb we spent splashing in the cold waters of a corkscrew mountain stream, crossing and recrossing in quest of a gate into the jungle, seeking the contour lines of a craggy elevation shaded by a green parasol of bamboo, teak and Asian evergreen. We looked for a distinct terrain feature in a sea of green indistinctions, a pinpoint within a brown and green grid square on a U.S. Army 1:50,000 inch scale map. Finally, we braked our movement and halted for the fractured remains of the night. Trailing the powdery twilight of monsoon dusk came our reward for the day's severities endured. Two tree-hopping helicopters settled down onto a boggy clearing to pick up our spider monkey allies and flutter kick them back through the wet sky to their village.

November 15 yawned drowsily to life, the tenth day of our latest boondocks promenade. The day's objective was a high scrub-covered plateau, on which the platoon was to reunite with the company. To reach the plain, we had to scale a hill sixty meters high with a treacherously steep and muddy slope. We clawed and crawled upwards a few feet at a time only to fall in mud-coating rolls, like soiled snowballs tumbling in enlarging bounds down the brown slope. Sweat gushed and mixed with mud, making our bodies deltas where black rivers flowed. Troopers became bowling pins as they were upended by others tumbling into them. Eventually, everyone crawled in muddy mantles to the top, where they collapsed in a panting, perspiring heap.

The platoon of mud-men trudged on along a path worming through an elephant grass prairie to rendezvous with company HQ and our sister platoons. Grunts greeted one another with war stories ... a sad gossip of land mines, blood and death. Pfc. Carl Falck of 3rd Platoon had died in the explosion of a booby trap. The first two men, marching point and "slack" in the platoon file, had passed by the trip wire safely, but Falck spotted it and reached out to grasp the thin thread, intending to follow it to its end. The mine exploded in slashing steel fragments into Falck's face. He was destroyed; the man behind him was gravely wounded. Like ravenous wolves attacking a fallen fawn, the steel teeth ripped and maimed the two men ahead of Falck, as well. A marker of stones and twigs was discovered alongside the trail several feet from where the mine had detonated, a warning to other V.C. troops in the area. The discovery came a few minutes too late for Pfc. Falck.

The HQ section also had a war story to tell. Some hours before, the captain had paused in his march to study the map with his first sergeant. Apparently, the rest of the HQ group had dozed off, for no one noticed the approach of a khaki-clad NVA soldier bearing an AK-47 until they heard him muttering, "Me Chieu Hoi! Me Chieu Hoi!" Chieu Hoi was the "open arms" program promising surrendering enemy soldiers all sorts of goodies.

Glancing up, the captain nearly messed his fatigue trousers at the sight of the surrendering North Vietnamese. Had he been so inclined, the NVA grunt could have zapped a captain, a FO lieutenant, a first sergeant, and assorted lesser rank and file.

The company marriage lasted two days before the battalion commander's strategy made the platoons incompatible and forced another separation. We did little during this time; a few recon patrols were sent out, weapons were cleaned, and rations were restocked. Along with ham-and-lima beans and plastic bottles of insect repellent, the Firefly on the C-ration junket delivered stacks of business cards which we were to leave on the bodies of slain enemy soldiers. Each card had on its four corners the eagle's claw battalion crest of the 2/502nd, the divisional Screaming Eagle patch, a winged skull under a parachute, and a pair of crossed M-16s. The salutation, in both Vietnamese and English, read "Compliments of the Strike Force Widow Makers."

The one outstanding event of those two idle days was the fatal shooting and solemn military funeral of Joe Jefferson's air mattress.

Few grunts lugged an air mattress with them into the wilderness. They usually had a life expectancy of one night's inflation, exposed as they were to sharp rocks and spiked vegetation. But our Cajun cat from Louisiana, Joe Jefferson, doggedly insisted on this one concession to comfort. He had amazingly good fortune in preserving the health of his mattress and enjoyed flaunting it before comrades whose beds were made each night in mud or sodden grass. Unfortunately, he was also notoriously careless in handling his grenade launcher, having already accidentally discharged the weapon twice. As we prepared for our first night on the plateau, Jefferson repeated the past by firing a buckshot round from his M-79 "blooper" into his dearly beloved and often deeply envied air mattress, shredding it into green rubber Swiss cheese and breaking his heart.

Jefferson received a tongue lashing from Lt. O'Shea, but his punishment did not end there. That evening the lieutenant had Jefferson scoop out a standard size grave with his entrenching tool. The following morning we buried the shattered remains of Joe Jefferson's air mattress with full military honors. O'Shea demanded that each member of the platoon display the proper solemnity and respect for our fallen comrade, and several of the less grief stricken rapidly found themselves in the front leaning rest position knocking out push-ups for their failure to demonstrate graveside decorum. Holtzman, Whitehall, Burke and I were the pallbearers. The lieutenant needed a man of the cloth to commend the victim's rubber soul to God's mercy. His choice was appropriate ... Moses Atticus Tate, son of a West Virginia fire-and-brimstone Baptist preacher. He produced the little black Bible he always carried in his rucksack alongside his horror museum collection of gook scalps and internal organs, and delivered his pastor pappy's favorite burial sermon.

With the deceased's comrades clustered around the grave, Tate, the man of a dozen psychotic faces, solemnly intoned his service.... "Seed unto seed, dust into dust.... We commend its humble soul to your Holy Grace." He concluded by chanting a teary-eyed requiem and tossed a handful of wild flower petals over the slain air mattress as the pallbearers gently lowered Jefferson's dearly departed companion into the grave. While Jefferson hung his head in remorse, the captain's RTO played "Taps" on his harmonica and the honor guard briskly executed, under the lieutenant's snappy commands, a one-volley salute over the grave. The service completed, O'Shea directed Jefferson to fill in the grave and erect a wooden cross at the head of his air mattress's final resting place, engraved with the bayonet-carved epitaph "Here lies Pfc. Jefferson's faithful and courageous Air Mattress, killed in the line of duty Nov. 16, 1966." The only thing lacking was a casket.

Every man who was the property of C Company, 2/502nd Airborne Infantry would have been content to sit out the rest of the operation planted firmly on his rump and false security on the wide, high plain we were beginning to call the "Big LZ." But soon the familiar receiving line of Hueys gathered us up, wrenched us from our tranquil immobility, and delivered us back into the hard embrace of the hump.

Again we waded through a green sea of futility. We marched through a mountainous Fantasia, whose beauty was obscured by the sweat stinging our eyes. To us, it was only impenetrable jungle that we would nonetheless have to penetrate. We reached a mountain waterfall tumbling over slabs of granite. The platoon moved in a caterpillar crawl past the fall's drifting silver nebula and teetered along a tightrope trail skirting the edge of a high cliff, at the bottom of which a river careened in an angry gray rush. For hours we marched with its roar reverberating against the jungle, but we found neither the enemy nor his arsenal. The platoon leader fractioned his platoon into patrols to better search the boonies. I almost lost my patrol in the galaxy of trees blocking the sunlight. The simian scampering of Holtzman and Jefferson up the tallest trees was required to spot the landmark that would guide our way back to the platoon.

As darkness established supremacy over the abdicating afternoon, the lieutenant left his men clinging precariously to a mud-slick mountain wall while he mounted a stone tabletop to study the terrain with map and compass. Far from our objective, the lieutenant pleaded with the CO for permission to stop for the night. Once it was granted, he pulled his men up the mountain and had them camp on the only slightly less steep reverse slope. There we endured a miserable night, sliding down the muddy slalom in our rainy sleep, crawling in wet weariness back up the incline, and then, still half conscious, slipping down again and again on our boggy backs.

The next day was a reflection of the one before ... the same humping of the boonies, the same planting of the seed of our sweat with the tools of marches, patrols and searches. We fed glumly on the carcass of our inconsequence, spun on marching feet in dizzying circles through the day's dispiriting hours, finally finding ourselves observing from the rocky ridges of another mountain the maroon curtain fall of evening.

The irrepressible quest for the enemy's armory continued as the calendar shrank to November 20, our fifteenth day out. Four platoons continued panning for arms like gold rush prospectors in uniform. With half the day dead and the other half dying, Weapons Platoon found its bonanza and staked a claim. The booty included a haberdashery of black and khaki uniforms, yellowed stacks of insurgent propaganda sheets, an underground pharmacy, and an arsenal of weapons ranging from antiques to the most modern and deadly.

Mission accomplished, the platoons migrated back to the company fold for resupply. A Huey jogged down to a grassy shelf to unload provisions and distribute our only real luxury, the mail. Men returned from R&R and hospitals; other men left with the chills of malaria, the agonies of immersion foot, and the dripping embarrassment of the clap. Then we again rode the same disillusioning carousel ... around and around in the ritual of the march, in the endless routine of our search-and-destroy way of life.

The inquisition of this land was beginning to punish me for my heresy of pride. The rain, mud, and a score of cuts from scimitar grass and stabbing thorns had plotted to scourge my body with jungle rot. Even worse, my feet were cracking like shattered glass, gluing my mud-sodden socks with a goo of blood and pus. Deep, bleeding gashes were etched around toes that felt half severed from my feet. Chunks of my heels, bleached white by constant wetness, crumbled off in bloody flakes. The platoon's obstacle course canter slowed to a walk of the maimed, as several other men and I, all suffering from immersion foot, hobbled along. For the first time, I was beginning to consider requesting evacuation to the rear area. The pride I had nourished in belonging to a constantly shrinking elite of men in the platoon who could boast of never having left an operation before it was completed was crumbling away with my heels and melting under the fires of my pain.

My arrogance, my confidence that I could overcome whatever challenge nature placed before me, was torn away and I was humbled as the lieutenant marched us in a gallop up a razorback ridge festooned with barricades of bamboo logs thrown up by shell storms. The league of cripples was far too lame to keep up the punishing pace and was soon straggling far behind. Again and again I relayed a plea up the platoon file to slow the stampede, but the lieutenant, anxious to demonstrate to the CO that he could actually reach a designated objective at the appointed time, refused. Finally, I could take no more and blasted out a demand for the platoon to halt.

The lieutenant sputtered and stuttered about all the candy-ass pussies in his platoon, but reluctantly agreed to slow his sprint. We eventually staggered to the top, where we refastened our fading star to the dimly perceived constellation of the company. Another cold, rainy night followed, during which we were grateful for the green Army sweaters apportioned to us at our last resupply ... two months after the monsoon's wet chill had begun.

At daybreak the company fired all its old, wet and muddy ammunition in a "Mad Minute" of indiscriminate blasting at the countryside, a preventive fusillade designed to prevent any potential enemy attack. Later, a helicopter fluttered down to dole out a hot meal, like a heliborne welfare soup kitchen. Other choppers whipped earthward to deliver into our unwelcome arms another zoo of CIDG primates. I, however, would not have to tolerate their carnival of indiscipline. The company's senior medic pronounced my feet unfit for further field duty and had me tagged and tucked in among the mess cook's pots and pans heaped aboard the chow chopper for the return trip to Tuy Hoa. I felt guilt at deserting my comrades still stuck in the monsoon mud, but that guilt was soon submerged in a tide of pain flooding up from my pillaged feet.

I returned to the silent rows of pup tents standing mutely like a ghost town on the edge of South Field. It seemed populated by phantoms, the spirits of men still trapped in the jungle. The camp was a cemetery of canvas coffins, sitting empty and open while their living dead occupants stalked the vampire's night of Operation Geronimo in search of blood.

Eventually, I spotted a few troopers caught in the emptiness and ensnared by its silence ... the men of the rear echelon element, the battalion skeleton which always remained behind when the sinew and muscle of the line companies undertook their pilgrimage to the shrines of man's one true universal religion ... war. For those who chose this moment to court refuge from the war, the present overseer of these rear area commandos was, unfortunately, our Slavic dragon, First Sergeant "Sab." This priest of profanity's theory was that the only excusable reasons for a man returning to the rear area sanctum before the conclusion of a campaign were that the soldier was either dead or close enough to qualify. Everyone else — footsore, jungle rotted, drained by diarrhea, or whatever — Sab labeled as ghosts and malingerers, and Sab had an obsessional hatred for ghosts. He played no favorites; anyone in the rear was worse than the fertilizer the gooks used to enrich their rice paddies. Even an exceptional soldier like Rose, whom Sab admired in the bush, became a "malingering cocksucker" in the rear. Just recently, Sab had cried at the ceremony when Rose was awarded the Bronze Star, only to curse him out vehemently the next day for remaining in the rear.

Consequently, after my trip to the aid station, I tried my utmost to keep out of range of Sab's rages and ravings. I succeeded for the first few days, but the first pig ultimately brought me to justice. Hobbled as I was, I nonetheless soon found myself shepherding a lazy gang of gook laborers, burning the maggot mounds in the half-drums of our open air latrines, standing guard, repairing sandbag parapets, and limping in a skirmish line of Police Call trash collectors ... all the while tongue-lashed by our first sergeant.

I ate my second Thanksgiving dinner in country, while my buddies in the boonies stuffed their C-ration-shrunken stomachs with the same turkey feast at a battalion gathering at the TOC base. But the line companies hardly had time to digest their meal before the order went out to saddle up for renewed march. They faced twelve grueling kilometers through a green dimension of hills ... for what purpose and to what end, none of them knew and most were beyond caring. The day of thanksgiving passed.

The bullet-strewn line of communications with the enemy was reopened the next day. Weapons Platoon, which had registered a kill the day before Thanksgiving, scored again by slaying one of a pair of Charlie trailwatchers and capturing the second. First Platoon engaged in combat also, when O'Shea walked his men into a broadside of automatic weapons fire that shattered the nimbus of wearied apathy hanging over the platoon's head. Miraculously, none of the pied pipered children of violence were hit. Not so remarkable was that none among the ambushers' ranks were struck by the paratroopers' return fire.

The band of deposed heroes pushed on; there was always that so-vital objective awaiting them at the dark funeral of the day. The troopers passed by the already swollen corpse of the insurgent killed by Weapons Platoon. Tate dropped momentarily out of the column and rejoined it later toting a dripping head by its black-tussled mane. When the platoon stopped to set up defensive positions for the night, the West Virginia psychopath impaled the head on a sharpened stake and planted his sadist's flagpole before his post.

The relentless merry-go-round continued to spin for the tired legions the following day, as they faced another hump through a region where the mountains spoke suffering and the jungle whispered warning. The men of the Strike Force battalion sighed like those who had nearly lost hope, shouldered their loads, and depended again on their unfailing reserve of fortitude to carry them the nine kilometers they must march through the stormy evening.

But fortitude was not enough to keep some men on their feet. For those feet, like mine, were the victims of a vindictive nature. The trickle of immersion foot casualties streamed to the proportions of a flood. The rear area camp became a convalescence center for podiatric cases. By the end of the month, forty percent of the battalion had forsaken the boonies, though their companies' banners remained drooping in the constellation of trees. As the lengthening roll call of the lame-footed increased, the strength of 1st Platoon dropped to a total of fourteen men. My 2nd Squad was reduced to three: Rose, Holtzman and Jefferson.

Those few who remained in the sticks struggled on in a hellish test of endurance. Twenty-five days after their marching marathon started, 1st Platoon finally reaped a meager harvest for the sowing of so much sweat.

As the platoon fell out from the hump for a few minutes' rest, machine gunner Grogan spotted a pair of insurgent soldiers moving down a ravine below the ridge trail on which the platoon had been humping. Slamming back on the trigger of his M-60 pig, Grogan froze in his firing trance and crashed 147 rounds into and around the two Viet Cong. Amazingly, one of the V.C. still had enough life left to attempt flight. The lieutenant and Jefferson gave chase and were on the verge of overtaking him when Jefferson slipped and tumbled on the crest of a sharply sloped hill, bowling over the lieutenant as he fell. The wounded Viet Cong escaped, but only to some lonely corner of the jungle where his life would surely slowly leak away.

Rose and Holtzman, following limply behind, took the wrong corridor of green and stumbled onto a more lucrative catch than a fatally wounded Charlie scout. Hidden in a dark cleft in the banks of a serpentine stream bed, Rose discovered an 82 mm mortar. The find won for each trooper a fifth of whiskey and for their platoon five cases of beer — the prizes proffered by the CO for such booty (a 60 mm mortar was worth only a pint of spirits and two cases of suds). More important to the lieutenant was that the platoon had won its first success since it had passed under his command. The registering of two kills and the capture of the mortar could not recover for the platoon all its dead and dying prestige, but it seemed like a new beginning. If a new dawn of glory was to come, however, it would not be with Lt. O'Shea leading the platoon. He was soon relieved of his command and given Weapons Platoon to lead and lose. The platoon did not mourn his departure.

Misfortune struck the platoon following its celebration of Rose's and Holtzman's success. While burning the refuse discarded from the spoils of war, a powder bag caught flame and spewed an expectoration of burning rubbish against the side of Weapons Squad leader Hagan, nuzzling close to the fire to dry his rain-soaked fatigues. The sergeant was evacuated, along with a

German shepherd scout dog and his handler, assigned to us for the last two weeks and nearly as useless as the CIDG irregulars. The canine was supposed to sniff out enemy ambushers, but he seemed more interested in his master's rucksack of dog rations than in nosing out the Viet Cong. The dog had been sniffing the ration rucksack when the platoon walked into the ambush the day after Thanksgiving.

The sergeant and the dog flew out together; the dog to his kennel, the sergeant to a Purple Heart. His burns from battle with the trash fire were hardly the honorable wounds of combat, but his Purple Heart was more justly deserved than those often awarded officers. Mockeries of the award included the one pinned on a captain in the battalion for his jungle rot, and the Purple Heart presented to a lieutenant for injuries incurred when he dived into a thorn bush to escape the falling debris of a tree stump blasted by C-4 plastic explosives clearing an acre of jungle for a LZ.

On December 1 the first sergeant diagnosed my condition as "a ghosting cocksucker" and declared my feet healed and ready for renewed combat duty. I was tucked aboard a heliborne taxi with several other half-healed convalescents and flown out to the battalion CP. There, instead of being shuffled out to our companies, we were dispatched to bolster the ranks of the perimeter defenders. I was assigned to a mud-scurvy post garrisoned by two mortarmen from the 4.2 inch mortar platoon attached to Headquarters Company and by Pfc. Reynaldo Ramos from Charlie Company's 2nd Platoon. Johansen was there at the CP too, scrubbing the mess crew's mess, having been awarded permanent KP instead of combat duty, his prize for feigning a malaria attack to escape the platoon's month-long ordeal in the bush.

I spent four days in that slushy wallow, watching the eternally falling rain and trying to stay dry in the muddy nest of my poncho hooch. Both mortarmen were cherries and easy prey to Ramos' wild war stories. Ramos, though surrounded by mud and imprisoned by the falling gray bars of monsoon rain, escaped on the wings of his imagination. He was bitter against the Army for temporarily detouring him off his sure road to success, but optimistic about the life that lay beyond green fatigues and C-rations. Ramos' dream was the Horatio Alger myth with a Brooklyn Italian flavor, and part of that dream was to make enough money to buy the Pentagon and turn it into one giant latrine. Vietnam and its mud were momentary diversions from the princely progression leading to his coronation as King Reynaldo of Brooklyn! But his climb to the top was ended a month later, when a V.C. bullet shattered all his dreams, silly and serious.

Operation Geronimo was drawing to a close. The battalion inflicted one last punishing blow on the afternoon of December 2, when 1st Platoon of Alpha Company ambushed thirty Viet Cong as they were crossing over a cantankerous mountain stream just a few klicks from the mud igloos of battalion TOC. Seventeen Charlies were chopped down. Nine more stragglers from the V.C. platoon were wasted the next day. All told, the campaign had cost the NVA and V.C. 150 KIA, seventy-six captured, and 143 weapons lost, thirty-one of which were crew-served. The 2/502nd Strike Force's contribution to these battlefield statistics totaled eighty-three communist regulars killed, forty-six POWs taken, and sixty-eight weapons captured. Five O' Deuce casualties for Geronimo were six killed and twenty-eight wounded.

My former artillery battalion, the 2/320th, had repulsed during the operation its second enemy infantry attack. A North Vietnamese platoon had tried to overrun Captain Joseph Jenkins' Alpha Battery on the night of November 7. The angry iron hornets of 8,000 steel flechettes from a Beehive round fired point-blank into the attacking North Vietnamese broke the back of the assault. This was the first use of the Beehive round in warfare. The enemy fled, leaving nine of their number dead, including a lieutenant killed by Captain J. Jenkins' .45 pistol. The redleg captain took from his victim's body a 7.65 mm pistol, ironically carved with the battery commander's own initials, JJ, on the stock. One redleg, a chart operator in the battery's FDC tent, joined the nine NVA soldiers in some forgotten Valhalla of the Vietnam dead.

The battalion was extracted from its green monastery of the mad on December 4. Casualties to enemy bullets had been light, but losses to the weapons wielded by nature, mostly malaria and immersion foot, were staggering. The incalculable foe, however, was to add one more name to the list of our dead, a casualty suffered not in the pestilence of the armed jungle, but in the false security of our rear area camp.

As the exhausted warriors of the battalion filtered into their pup tent shantytowns, which they had not seen for thirty punishing days, a trash barrel, similar to the one that had pinned our company to the sandy turf two months ago, exploded on the boundary line between Charlie and Bravo companies. A man from Bravo Company crumbled over his sandbag-stockaded tent, half his head blown off by a 60 mm mortar shell. It had been buried in the trash barrel by a V.C. agent who had infiltrated one of the gook labor squads hired by the brigade to do some of the dirty duty of KP and shit barrel burning. Charlie knew many ways of killing; he was never confined to the orthodox slaughter of infantry assaults and mortar shellings. The Viet Cong were magicians of death, murderous sorcerers who could conceal death in the folds of security and even in the flowers of innocence.

It was a bad beginning to a hoped for period of rest. And those fantasies of restful recuperation soon exploded like the head of the man from Bravo Company. The 101st had haunted the hills of Phu Yen Province for nearly eight months during its twin hitches there in 1966, and one battalion, the 2/327th, had passed the first eleven months of the year stomping the green forests and wading the rice paddies of the province. But the 1st Brigade was the mobile fire brigade of the American Army in Vietnam, ready at the clanging of the bell at Pentagon East at Tan Son Nhut to board airborne C-130 fire engines and race anywhere in country to douse the flames of insurgency with M-16 and M-60 fire hoses. Thus, upon returning from a month's misery of jungle humping, we once again had to slap away the harping beggars of rest and prepare to sky-sail toward the next adventure in the 1st Brigade's odyssey, stalled, like Odysseus on Circe's island, for nearly five months in the sands of Tuy Hoa beach and its green hinterlands beyond.

Chapter XXI

Kontum

We were to re-erect our carnival of combat amid the Central Highlands again. The provincial capital of Kontum, some forty miles southeast of the brigade's victory in the mountains around Dak To, would become our new hive from which we would buzz in helicopter swarms to inject our sting. The North Vietnamese were reportedly gathering strength for an assault on Kontum and the Screaming Eagles had been summoned to the rescue.

After a battalion beer bust on the night of December 5, we nursed hangovers all the following day, my twentieth birthday, by tearing down the brigade's circus city of tents and sandbags ... seemingly more sandbags than there were stars in the firmament. Late that evening we were herded into trucks and driven to the black airstrip at South Field. After the Army's ritual hurry-up-and-wait delay, we were crammed aboard C-130 flying freight trains. The flight was short. Vietnam is a small country by air, though it seemed vast by way of jungle boots. Landing with engines feathered on the short airstrip outside Kontum, we were motored to a temporary camp in a square of yellow ARVN barracks.

At last we were granted a few days' rest, with little harassment and only a few work details to tolerate. There was time to reflect on who we once were and who we had become, and time for those who, like Grogan, had killed their first man in combat and who now had to confront a barrage of emotions erupting within ... emotions of self-loathing and self-pride, of remorse and relief, of comradeship and communion with their victims, of prestige won with comrades-in-arms and respect lost with the arbiters of their souls.

Other men were going home. Maranville, Anson, Miksis and Bresnahan followed Terry to Phan Rang and a seat on the Freedom Bird before Christmas. The Army's Operation Santa Claus was endeavoring to rotate home early all men with DEROS dates prior to January 15, 1967, so they could spend Christmas with their families instead of with the war. I had received no orders; my stocking held only the date of January 8, 1967, inside. Resigned to another

Christmas in this compassionless land, I was thinking strongly about extending two more months to slip under the ninety-day limit required for an early out. I began to feel less affinity to those short-timers with calendars on which they colored out their last ninety days in Vietnam on the naked anatomy of a pin-up, the breasts reserved for the last two days prior to rotation and the final day of liberation centered between the nude woman's legs. As the days drew closer to my DEROS date, I felt progressively less a short-timer. I was not yet ready to go home. The old desire for glory which had made me extend the first time had been gravely wounded by the weapons wielded by fear, frustration and dishonor. But the urge remained to be a part of something bigger than my insignificant self, to play my tiny part in the history unfolding (even if I was beginning to recognize it as an ugly chapter in our history). Most intensely, the indefinable bonds of loyalty and comradeship which locked my fate to that of the men of Charlie Company, pushed me toward a prolongation of my sad romance with this war.

The sword of leadership in the platoon had now passed to the more competent hands of Lieutenant Larry D. Earls, an amiable, rotund man who had risen from the ranks (a "mustang"). Though without the flair and flash of Lt. Novak, the chain-smoking Earls symbolized the confidence and competence greatly needed by the platoon. If the men could no longer be the honored and envied celebrities of the company, they at least would not be the goats, the laughing stock of the Strike Force, as they were becoming under the fumbling leadership of Lt. O'Shea.

The new platoon leader took command as our brief respite from field ops was ending. New operational orders put us onto the red dust crusted beds of cattle trucks. A convoy carrying our battalion of infantry and a battery of the 2/320th Artillery rolled out of the barracks square in Kontum and along a narrow dirt road, churning up a thick fog of ocher-colored dust. After hours of butt-bruising riding, the thorny branches of overhanging bamboo slapping our helmeted heads, the convoy lurched to a halt at the foot of a stunted airstrip. It was overlooked by the jumble of barracks, bunkers, watchtowers, trenches and mortar pits, with palisades of shell casings and canisters, which made up the Special Forces compound of Polei Kleing.

The company was sprinkled around the camp in widely spaced OPs of three men each. We were brigade reserve, to be committed to the field once the other battalions had made significant contact with the foe. There, almost in the lap of Charlie, the captain contrived training exercises for us to keep the company in fighting trim.

Even less welcome than the training were the parade and ceremony for General Westmoreland, who had come to honor us. Though such occasions of unit pride and prestige had once stirred my soul, I now preferred a can of C-ration beans-and-franks and an afternoon nap under the shade of my poncho liner to any honor the commanding general could bestow on us. Westmoreland presented the 2/502nd with a Distinguished Unit Citation in recognition of the battalion's narrow victory at An Ninh in September 1965, and a campaign streamer citing our bloody achievements in Operation Geronimo to add to the battalion flag, already a multicolored standard bearing the pennants of World War II glories.

The general's alms was possibly timed as an intoxicant to our spirits as we leaped into battle. The following morning, minutes before the sun yawned over the horizon in its orange awakening, we departed the airstrip of Polei Kleing in our helicopter shuttle service to throb in staircase procession toward the peaks of the Central Highlands.

The whirling iron sleighs, bearing men into battle, skied on blue sky-slopes through an awesomeness of mile-high mountains adorned in great green capes of teak and bamboo. The first wave fluttered down to become lost in the burgeoning greenness. Helicopter after helicopter was swallowed up in the immensity, this realm of propagating nature that spread in leafy indifference to microscopic men and their puny pogroms against one another. Jet-feathered hawks struck with talons of 20 mm cannon fire and dropped eggs of high explosive and flaming napalm. The long guns of the artillery punched at the mountains' contempt with white phosphorous fists. But the man-made storms were little more than gray and orange dabs on an immense canvas of green grandeur; nothing more than blossoming crimson and silver-petaled wildflowers on the majestic mountain slopes.

Down into the catatonic vastness churned the Hueys to labor litters of armed men from their open wombs. The warrant officer piloting the helicopter carrying my squad hovered more than eight feet above the slender strip of elephant grass bordering a mountain stream. I waited for the pilot to settle the Huey down to the usual hovering height for a combat assault of two to four feet, but he refused to go lower. Thus I had to hurl myself and the sixty pounds hanging from me out of the chopper's open hatch and toward the pitiless ground. Eight very rapid feet later, I crashed into the stream's fringe of sharp stones and prickly bushes. I landed on my hands and knees, but the weight of my rucksack reared high on my back and somersaulted me onto my head. Fanning the cuts on my palms and rubbing my bruised knees, I looked up to see my squadmates flinging themselves from the helicopter. One by bruising one, the men collided with the earth in a thudding bombardment of falling bodies. The battle shy Huey pilot was fleeing for aerial refuge before the last body had hit the ground.

Bruised but unbroken, we formed up with the company to begin Operation Pickett. Charlie, as usual, refused to appear where and when staff planning had presupposed. For five bone-weary days we searched in vain for him. Each day was a sweaty copy of the day before ... hard humping up the spines of mountains and through a forest of trees as high as 200 feet. Some trees boasted a circumference at their bases that the outstretched arms of three men could not ring.

We stalked an ambiguous enemy in the enduring evening of the forest, domed by a double and even triple canopy that blotted out the sun. The mountains teemed with life, but not the human form that we hunted. Giant birds, like winged dinosaurs of prehistoric ages, soared overhead, their huge wings flapping a locomotive rush over the forest peaks. Chattering circuses of spider monkeys shattered the seriousness of our purpose. Elephant tracks widened narrow mountain paths. Seven-step snakes — so called because if a man were bitten, their venom could kill him after he took seven steps — slithered through the grass, and emerald-colored bamboo vipers coiled in reptilian twists through the branches of bamboo. One was roped around a low hanging branch I reached out to grasp for a handhold while thrashing up a slippery incline. I braked my hand with horrified recognition just inches from the snake's triangular head.

Most prolific were the parasitic legions of insects. Carnivorous ants streamed in marshaled columns from their mounds to attack us as we lay prone at night. We squirted insect repellent around our poncho beds, but this failed to stem the fury of the vicious inch-long aggressors. When the phalanx of angry ants did not prey on me in my sleep, lumberjack legions of forest termites picked up the pennon of harassment. Hosts of the chomping insects sawed the twigs under my body, ringing my ears with their chain saw buzz.

Worst of all were the leeches. At each halt in our march we were forced to pluck the bloating parasites from our bodies with squirts of insect repellent and a hefty tug. Usually they fastened themselves to our legs around the tops of our jungle boots, but I also had to pry some from my groin, stomach and armpits. One trooper discovered a leech entrenched on the head of his penis. Another tipped up his canteen, which he had just filled from a leech-infested pool, to feel the slimy squirm of a leech lodge on the back of his tongue. He immediately threw up the leech and his C-ration lunch.

Charlie remained the only inhibited creature in the jungle, too bullet-shy to show his face. But his presence was noted by the sharpened bamboo fangs of punji stakes paralleling every jungle turnpike. The hunt went on, the machete-brandishing point man and slack man having to function more as bulldozing trailblazers than alert vanguards. On we grunted over saw-toothed heights, scooting down the slopes on the tattered seats of our fatigue trousers, humping under a shower of floating propaganda leaflets dropped by a Psy-War plane urging the communist falcons to trim their talons and desert to General Nguyen Cao Ky's beneficence.

At last Gunslinger came to the conclusion that Charlie was not to be found on the Five O' Deuce's present chessboard. The companies were ordered to congregate on landing zones for a heliborne shift to another location. Closing in on the company LZ, the platoon, not yet having found renewed glory under Lt. Earls' leadership but at least never wandering in the groping blindness that had characterized O'Shea's command, settled wearily on an overlooking hillock crested with a decaying carpet of fallen foliage.

Amid the yellowing ruins of vegetation on that mound, we uncovered a small thatched hut. Inside were twine-wrapped bales of cannabis. The marijuana was handed over to Company HQ encamped down by the LZ, but not before several troopers had executed a little sleight of hand to requisition sizable plugs of the pot. Our seizure of the marijuana must have aroused the indignation of the harvester, for seconds later three rapid fire shots rang out from somewhere in the forested crescent, splintering the tree under which 2nd Squad had taken up lodging for the night. Grogan and Burghardt indiscriminately sputtered off a reply of machine gun bursts into the mountainous arc. It was wasted ammunition. Lt. Earls quieted the M-60 with a cease-fire order, and we prepared to pass an apprehensive night, wondering when the sniper would decide to streak a few more rounds toward us.

The morning brought us more labor. The bulk of the company plodded down from their ridge top positions to clear a landing zone out of a narrow patch of level ground, lying like a bullfighter's arena at the center of a forest-tiered stadium ring of mountains. It was hot, hard work, but eventually a LZ was hacked out. We then formed up in five-man chalks to await the rotary ballet of helicopters. As the first chopper appeared and bent the treetops, several shots rang out, their shriek echoing over the thumping howl of the chopper. The sniper's challenge was met by the rocket attacks of two escorting gunships. They roared up over the ridge mass to release their rockets into the opposite heights and followed their impact with a jet stream of machine gun bullets chipping furiously away at the mountainside. The sniper was silenced.

Whipped by helicopter winds, the soldiers were sucked into hovering Hueys to be lifted up into a sky stunned by the sun. The air was so thin in these heights that the groaning helicopters had to bite at the sky with all the power of their rotary teeth to lift off. The number of soldiers carried in each chopper had been reduced from the usual six to five, but still the helicopters had to make several leaps before they could clear by inches the trees barring their ascent at the exit end of the LZ. Ultimately, the last clawing chopper grasped hold of the sky and tiptoed across the treetops toward a new landing zone.

We were winged to another jungle mine to prospect for a bloody ore. With 1st Platoon serving as a guidon, the company waded along the curves of a chocolate brown canal. Later, the tramping cordon of infantrymen passed through an NVA ghost camp, where the only spoils of war taken were three orange-nosed, silver-finned 82 mm mortar shells.

Those mortar rounds were to be our only reminders that the war was against a human enemy in addition to the rocky arrogance of mountains, the impenetrable jungle void, the blood gluttony of leeches, and the saber teeth of army ants. This new hunting ground proved to be as barren of the NVA as the first. Up rocky heights, down ravines, through a limitless jungle ... tres-passing for days on the enemy's domain, always wondering if Charlie would surface or remain hidden.

The platoon paused in its unyielding pursuit of the spectral foe late on the afternoon of December 21 to hack out an LZ from a bamboo-sheathed mountain. We were to receive a Firefly resupply and send back a half dozen troopers to help construct a new tent city for the brigade. Fighting off hordes of incensed army ants whose dirt condominiums we had razed, we cleared a one-helicopter LZ. Lt. Earls tossed a violet-colored smoke grenade to mark our location. Eventually the circling Firefly spotted our LZ, a tiny shaven square on a vast green beard, and descended to unburden itself of a three-day ration supply and take on the new load of three rearward bound foot soldiers. The helicopter had to commit every bit of its strength to become airborne again. A second copter, bearing Holtzman, Jefferson and a cherry grunt, had an even more difficult time.

The bird attempted several sputtering high jumps over the sky-barricading trees. Each time it was forced to shudder back to the LZ after the grasping rotary wings of the helicopter failed to pull the craft over the green towers blocking it from the freedom of the sky. Finally, the chopper pilot roared his engines to their highest pitch and wobbled skyward in a final assault on the forest barrier. Every sweat-swathed man sucked in his breath and held it as the helicopter fought with the slender air and the bamboo pillars holding up the sky.

Fluttering weakly, like a wounded butterfly, the chopper bounced upward, then fell again, pitching and yawing like a rolling ship in a stormy sea, listing and lurching from side to side. Foot by engine-shrieking foot, the bucking iron bronco edged toward the treetops, brushing the green bonnets of the first trees. Then, with a final burst of power, it bounded the last few feet between green incarceration and blue freedom.

Just when it appeared the helicopter had successfully vaulted the jungle palisade, the Huey's power faltered and it plummeted into the spreading palm of a pillorying tree. Crashing through the splintering branches, the helicopter disappeared behind the tree line. My heart sank to my weary feet, as I waited for the crunching thunder of the crash.

On the other side of the trees, grunts and helicopter crewmen were tumbling like broken-stringed puppets. Jefferson was tossed half out of the convulsive copter, but Holtzman and the cherry trooper somehow managed to cling to the wildly rocking chopper and pull the dangling soldier back aboard at the same time. Then, just as the stuttering helicopter seemed about to weld explosively with the ground, the clawing blades at last gripped the lean mountain air in a firm grasp, and the bird shuddered safely on to the battalion TOC.

And so the trek continued into a landscape lush with nature but devoid of the enemy. Our jousting in the LBJ-Ho Chi Minh tournament had won us no knightly laurels. Christmas was but a few days away, and a government, which had dispatched more than a third of a million of its young men to aid the Saigon regime's corruption and the National Liberation Front's brutal revolution in the destruction of this country, decided to give peace a few days out of a year otherwise leased exclusively to war.

Our government-granted licenses to pillage and kill in the name of "the containment of communism" were to be suspended for twenty-four hours so we could practice peace on earth and good will toward men, before resuming our mission of providing from the muzzle of an M-16 an eternal peace for men toward whom we were to show only a will of steel. Christmas 1966 had little meaning for most of us. All it could be was an opportunity to drown guilt in the suds of beer and to escape through the forced cheerfulness of our comrades' company the foggy reasons-why, the uncertain for-what-ends, the hopeless how-much-longers. There would be no Christmas joy, only an inebriated joyless joy. For me, the one thing that would be sacred about Christmas in Kontum was the comradeship of my platoonmates ... men whom I had known only five months, but with whom I had shared a lifetime's experience and who were, consequently, the closest friends I would ever have.

Thus on the morning of the 23rd, the company was reunited to fell the yellow beard of bamboo on a mountain's craggy chin so that helicopters could whisk us from war to the artificial peace of Christmas. Back "in the rear with the beer," there were formations, police calls and weapons inspections. Christmas cheer. And while we were cleaning our weapons, John Steinbeck, author of dust bowl and Depression literature, walked among us, perhaps searching for material for a book about another kind of depression, in which a nation's sense of mission and its soldiers' sense of purpose had gone awry.

The battalion guzzled its Christmas Eve spirits that night in an empty warehouse. There were pyramids built of cases of beer and gaudily wrapped packages from do-gooders, well-wishers, and support-the-boys-in-Vietnam superpatriots. Many men got drunk; war stories polluted the air. The company troubadours sang homesick favorites such as "Five Hundred Miles (Away From Home)," which we retitled "Five Thousand Miles (Away From Home)," and "Blowin' in the Wind." Some men sat singly or in contemplative knots, sipping at warming cans of beer, remembering other Christmases in other places, before innocence had succumbed to knowledge and hatred had hatched from high hopes.

For me, it was not a happy night, but still somehow profound. It was hard to find Christmas peace and love in Kontum, but there was a kind of love that night in our booze-rowdy camp. Not a tender love, it was hard and was expressed profanely. But it was there. Men do not share what we had shared and survive it without bonds forming. Ours was a special kind of closeness that could come about only in war. It existed where war did and nowhere else. When we would leave the war behind us, we would also leave that comradeship, and no reunion could ever regain it. Because of the special circumstances and passions invoked by war, we would never again feel as close to other human beings as we did to our comrades that night.

Thus we passed Christmas Eve gulping beer and weaving war stories into the early hours of the morning. Our half-hearted attempts at singing Christmas carols were interrupted when we had to rush off to extricate Joe Jefferson from a platoon of angered ARVNs. Jefferson and a buddy had stormed drunkenly into a Kontum bar to accuse its ARVN clientele of cowardice and of being unworthy of even inhaling the fishhead farts of their Viet Cong cousins. The arrival of American MPs and South Vietnamese "White Mice" (national policemen) broke up the drunken debate.

Afterwards, I sat with my hoochmate, Ron Holtzman, in boozy philosophizing on the rights and wrongs of the war. By then most of the Christmas celebrators had passed out. A few troopers were still awake, huddled in circles of nostalgia, the acrid-sweet mist of marijuana smoke drifting over the liquored camp.

Holtzman asked, "If you're so uncertain as to why you're here humping Indian country, why the hell are you thinking about extending again?"

"Well, I suppose to get that early out for one thing," I replied.

"Do you mean that after surviving eighteen months in this green rectum with your ass intact, that you're willing to tempt fate further, just for three extra months as a civilian?" asked a dubious Holtzman. "Mike, you've got a whole lifetime of civilian duty ahead of you. Don't take a chance of blowing it for a few extra months away from the U.S. Armpit!"

"All right ... I guess it's more than just the early out business that's holding me here," I admitted. "For some reason, I'm just not ready to go home yet. I suppose I'm just not satisfied or fulfilled or ... or something, yet."

Holtzman shook his head. "Not yet fulfilled with what, man? Blood and death. Mud and mountains and leeches and ... and mother fuckin' C-rats. You're really hard to understand, Mike. Here you are wallowing in guilt, not at all sure anymore that we're LBJ's cavalry-to-the-rescue, and yet you say you haven't seen enough of it ... that you're not sick and tired of it and ready to go home. Man, I really don't understand you at all."

"Hell, you're right, Ron," I said. "I must be a schizo or something. I'm not sure anymore that what we're doing is right. Shit, I find it really hard to believe that wasting peasants and napalming villages is going to stop the spread of communism.

"But it's more than whether the cause is right or not. You see, I went straight from Combat Action Comic Books, where most kids begin and end their fascination with war, and went right on to *Crecy's Fifteen Decisive Battles of the World*. And then I graduated from book-bound battlefields to this real battlefield without ever realizing that glory is just a fancy, phony word to cover up the smell of shit and death ... which is so damn awfully real.

"But I guess I'm still mesmerized by those military history books ... my holy books. My brain tells me glory isn't real — at least not real in this hellhole — but my heart just can't accept that. So I guess I'll go on looking for it here. I keep hoping I'll stumble onto it somewhere out there in the bush. I know damn sure I'm not going to find it or anything else that matters to me back home."

Holtzman shook his head again and said, "I would have thought that the 'Nam would cure anybody of a glory hang-up. Glory's just a word they use like an enema to loosen your ass when it's all puckered up tight from fear and horror. It's nothing but candy they hand out to encourage you to waste other human beings just as terrified and confused as you. And after you've taken their candy, you're going to have an awfully sour taste in your mouth when you've realized just what you had to do to earn it. Morales wanted glory too. Was that what you call that stuff he was puking up on that LZ? Was that red pool his head was laying in what you call glory? "

Before I could reply, a beer-bloated Whitehall awoke in the hooch next door and interjected grumpily, "Why don't all you fuckin' hawks and doves go fly away into your nests and let us Don't-Give-a-Good-God-Damn Dodo Birds get some sleep!"

"Wow! Smoke our asses will ya, Whitey!" Holtzman exclaimed. "Roll back on your face and blow some zees, you rum-dumb hillbilly, and let us intellectuals figure out the Birdman's motives for sending us all here."

"Hell! It don't take no fuckin' intellectuals to figger out why they unloaded us on the 'Nam!" grumbled Whitehall. "They were gonna ship us down to hell, but the mother fuckin' devil put up the No Vacancy sign, cause even he didn't want our mangy asses. So they really gave us the royal shaft and deposited our butts in an even worse place ... this mother fuckin', balls bustin' Vietnam. And that, my philosopher friends, is the one and only reason ... there was just no room left in hell!"

Christmas morning brought the brigade commander playing Santa Claus, stuffing the stockings of his soldiers with Silver Stars, Bronze Stars and Purple Hearts. A battalion of red-eyed grunts was planted in parade ground formation to honor the latest batch of instant heroes. Medals were pinned to chests by a hand-pumping, bantam rooster hosting a brigadier general's lonesome star.

I was among the group receiving a bloodhound's bone for the spilt blood of the enemy fox. An Army Commendation Medal with V for Valor was pinned to my shirt by the general. The glow of pride I had once expected was now but a faint flickering of ego's flame. This medal was one of the golden goals of glory I had set for myself upon volunteering for the infantry. But now the flood of self-esteem I once would have felt was little more than a trickle ... for I had grown, or at least had learned. I had caught sad glimpses of the inglorious truth.

Others received their indemnities: their bribery for tolerating and inflict-ing pain. Lt. Novak and Sgt. DeJesus received the Silver Star; SP/4 Herman was awarded a Bronze Star. None of them could have desired those scraps of colored cloth and inscribed metal more than I had in my glory-thirsting naivete, or could have felt now such an aching hollowness inside, as I did, where pride should have swelled.

After Christmas dinner at the mess tent, the battalion gathered to be entertained by the "First Lady of Vietnam," comedienne Martha Raye, who would serve a far longer tour in Vietnam than anyone among her G.I. audi-ences — a total of almost four and a half years during the period 1965–1973.

We were then given passes into Kontum, 2nd Squad following the tall-talking Whitehall, who promised to lead us to the fairest pulchritude in the Central Highlands. The "Number One Baby-sans" proved to be exactly as I had cynically pictured them in my mind — rouge-painted jackals. Leaving a grinning Whitehall as the prey for these hyena harlots, who rapidly fell to hair-pulling, fingernail-slashing combat over their one victim, we left to seek amusement elsewhere.

Jefferson was soon enticed away by the soulful strains of his idol, James Brown, pulsating from a booga-looing bar that catered to the brigade's soul brothers. Holtzman and I drifted disconsolately from one tawdry bar to another, looking among the female gargoyles for some woman who stirred more lust than revulsion, passing by chocolate-skinned, loin-clothed Montagnards, laughing at a crinkled old woman who suddenly and with total indifference pulled down her peasant trousers to stoop and poop beside a busy street.

Holtzman and I returned to the brigade base, as dismayingly chaste as we were before we left. I was still looking for another Helen, the Quinhon bar girl I had gone dinkee dau (crazy) over, in every Vietnamese face. But there were no Helens in Kontum.

Jefferson returned a few minutes before the curfew hour of 1800, berserkly drunk and determined to terminate the company commander and his first sergeant. He armed himself with an entrenching tool and headed for the orderly room tent. Three of us wrestled him to the ground and then, after a moment's reflection, wondered why we had stopped him.

Chapter XXII

Punji Stake

Our Christmas return to Kontum was accompanied by a flurry of rumors about a battalion jump. I had always hoped for the chance to combine the two most exciting experiences, combat and parachuting, into the ultimate thrill of a combat jump. The thought bombarded images in my mind of the night drop zone battlefield of Normandy, lit by exploding klieg lights of bursting shells as the paratroopers of the 82nd and 101st floated earthward under canopies of silk and nylon toward the erupting hedgerows.

Again the ancient shaman in my soul, not yet buried and forgotten, resurrected himself ... his wounds unhealed, gaping and still streaming blood, but strong enough to again work his witchcraft. Once more the battered glory-urge within asserted itself and whispered into the inner ear of my soul that there still remained pigments with which to paint my image into a corner of a fresh masterwork of war — one that could hang proudly in a Louvre of Mars' masterpieces with Marengo, Chancellorsville and Sedan.

But my jump into glory's slipstream was not to be. No paratrooper was to win the small bronze star mounted on the parachutist badge — symbolizing a combat jump — until the 2nd Battalion of the 503rd Airborne Infantry from the 173rd Airborne Brigade parachuted into War Zone C on Washington's Birthday 1967, during Operation Junction City — the first American combat jump since the 187th Airborne Regimental Combat Team had jumped at Suckchon and Munsan, Korea, in 1950 and 1951, and, except for a few jumps by Special Forces teams, the only combat jump of the Vietnam War.

There was to be no combat jump for us, but training jumps were scheduled for the first time in more than a year. On the 27th, after a day of refresher pre-jump training, mostly practicing PLFs to ensure that troopers landed on the five points of contact — balls of feet, calf, thigh, buttock and push-up muscle, and not on their heads — the 2/327th peppered the sky over a DZ of dried paddies with popcorning canopies of parachutes trailing the slipstreams of C-130s. A battalion of paratroopers ornamented the sapphire sky with white and olive-colored umbrellas drifting slowly to earth, where, 1,250 feet later, they folded in a parasol's collapse of nylon.

The last sticks of parachutists jumped as a strong wind suddenly whipped across the drop zone. Men hooked to parachute risers and suspension lines were dragged across the dikes of the paddy DZ, a mean wind puffing hard against the schooner sails of chutes. A dozen paratroopers, those fragile masts of men rigged to the nylon sails, cracked on the shoals of the drop zone sea. Broken bones abounded before troopers could free themselves from the wind-driven chutes by flipping the canopy release snaps on the harness connectors.

The Five O' Deuce's turn was to come next, sometime early the next month. It would be my first leap in fourteen months into the prop blast ecstasy of the paratrooper, and I was awaiting the moment when I would fasten my chin strap and ready myself for the jumpmaster's commands to "Stand up!" "Hook up!" "Check equipment!" "Sound off for equipment check!" "Stand in the door!" and "Go!" Churning inside me was the mixture of rapture and dread that always enriched my senses before a parachute jump. I little suspected that I would not be present to make that jump.

The day following Christmas was spent in patrolling around Kontum's forested suburbs. The sole result of this patrol was to offer more bodies up to the malaria bite of the mosquito. Machine gunner Grogan, under pressure from his father, a much decorated Marine Corps colonel, to shine in battle, was helpless in combat against the mosquitoes and he followed Foxx and Tate to the convalescent center at Cam Ranh Bay. Tate had already caused a flap or two at the hospital. Upon arrival he had pulled a .45 pistol on a soldier and threatened to blow him away because he was an REMF. Later he tried to impress the nurses by asking if they wanted to see his ears. When they indicated they had better things to do than dig out his ear wax or blow in his ear, Tate said, "No, I mean these," and opened a brown plastic C-ration condiment bag to display his collection of gook ears. This time his handiwork was not ignored and passed off as the fruit of an overzealous fighting spirit. He was judged unfit to be returned to society, even to the hard core society of the bush, and was institutionalized.

Rose too fell victim to the mosquito hit teams. He had just returned from R&R in Tokyo and had rejoined us in the bush with the John Donne quote "I am the man, I was there, I suffered" written on the camouflage cover of his helmet, when he came down with the familiar symptoms. Rose was the last man to take an easy way out of the jungle and leave his comrades "pointless." Consequently, he ignored the first symptoms and persevered until the fever raged so hot he had to admit that the mosquitoes had beaten him. Rose was later told that had he gone one more day without treatment, he would have died. The company was without its "Hard Core Pointer" for six weeks.

The platoon returned to Kontum on the afternoon of the 27th. There I signed another set of extension papers, postponing my final farewell to Vietnam by another two months. I was really unsure of my motivations this time. Perhaps I felt adrift, lost, without purpose or direction. There had been no aim to my life as a civilian or as a garrison soldier, and now that my pursuit of glory was ending in disillusionment, I felt like a crewless derelict floating aimlessly with the ocean tides. That ocean was the war, and though its waves seemed to take me nowhere, I was at least familiar with it, and the possibility of dropping anchor in my home port upon my return to the States held no real attraction for me. I no longer knew for certain what I sought in Vietnam, but whatever it was, there seemed less likelihood of finding it back home. And so I stayed.

The familiar alarm sounded again, alerting the men of the battalion that another heliborne wagon train was about to depart for Indian country. Ammo magazines were charged with fresh ammo; canteens were filled from the OD-colored Lister Bags hung from A-frames; C-rats, water purification tablets, plastic bottles of insect repellent, and blue heating tablets were passed out. Fragmentation, white phosphorous and smoke grenades, Claymore mines, trip flares, hand signal flares, and 66 mm LAWs were distributed. Maps, flashlights and compasses were readied by those who were to lead; RTOs checked the batteries and calibrations of their radios. Like red savages warpainting themselves for battle with the intruding white man, the company performed the familiar ritual of preparation. Then began the long wait for the order to move out; it was to be a night helicopter assault.

When the word was sounded most of the men were sitting with eyes fixed on the outdoor movie screen, though their minds belonged to the jungle night that awaited. Hueys, their headlights and flashing red and green running lights transforming them into giant fireflies, swallowed us whole and fluttered obesely into a night sky hot with apprehension. Thirty dark, tense minutes later, the swarm of iron insects snapped back open their glowing white eyes as they began their descent to the rippling grass of the LZ, marked by the vermilion glow of flashlights in the hands of the Pathfinder advance guard. The landing was unopposed, but confusion still ran unreined in the dark green tides of elephant grass. Finally the company gathered itself together in the darkness and set up defensive posts overlooking the LZ. The thunder and lightning of the helicopter combat assault had passed like a sudden tropical storm. The night returned to the insect murmur of the jungle.

The first day of the new mission was discouragingly reminiscent of those before Christmas. Charlie continued his elusiveness, although his signature was written all over these mountains in the booby trap calligraphy of punji stakes and bamboo spear traps. The company rammed its way through dense brush at the foot of a mountain that frowned upon us with a cynicism which we spent the rest of the day overcoming. The vine-cocked bamboo lances of the enemy were everywhere along this treacherous devil's spine, but we survived the climb without casualty.

The following day we made our first contact. The man on point saw three enemy soldiers dart their heads out from behind a screen of trees. Squeezing the trigger of his M-16, the point man heard the ping of the firing pin striking a dud round. He pulled back on the bolt to eject the bad round and finally popped off a single bullet at the fleeing Charlies. One of them turned briefly in his flight to hurl a couple of rounds back at his pursuers. As the North Vietnamese escaped, we picked ourselves up off the ground and moved cautiously forward in a skirmish line.

A cry, like the flutter of a harp, sounded as Holtzman stumbled over the vine trip wire of one of the bamboo crossbows. A booby trap javelin sliced into his leg below the kneecap. The bamboo pike had penetrated two inches, but pride and loyalty to his comrades made Holtzman assure the lieutenant that he was able to march on. By nightfall, after long humping and high mountains, his leg was swollen in blue knots and was as stiff as wood.

Other men were wounded that day. In Weapons Platoon a private, failing in his campaign to contract malaria, chose a harder escape from the bush by squeezing off an M-16 round into his foot. Third Platoon also suffered a casualty. After struggling to the top of a hill, the word was passed down the platoon file to move off the trail and take a break. One exhausted soldier backed wearily off the trail a few steps to let the weight of his rucksack drag his body to the ground. The sharpened point of a punji stake, concealed by tall strands of grass, lay planted, waiting for the careless move of some unwary grunt to fulfill its mission. The tired trooper suddenly became grotesquely animated, screaming and squirming violently as he impaled himself on the bamboo halberd, its shit-smeared point thrusting deeply up into his rectum.

December 30, flowering to life with the great yellow blossom of the morning sun, spoke no omen that this was to be my last day in the bush. The day began like all the other days; another mountain ridge to climb, more jungle to hack our way through. I was walking point that morning. The path was thickly sown with an abatis of punji stakes. The dung-covered tips of sharpened, fire-hardened bamboo glared cruelly at multiple angles calculated to snare human limbs and tear them apart. The ridge was like a great porcupine, its sharp quills erected against the approach of its enemy. As point man, most of my attention was devoted to clearing a narrow route through the waves of this booby trap sea for the tiptoeing line of grunts behind me.

I was carefully smashing down the angled punji stakes when carbine bullets snapped the tips of the trees above my head. Enemy fire was coming from a mountain mass staring over the ridge on which we marched. A Huey gunship patrolling above charged the NVA riflemen at treetop level, burping a leaden vomit of machine gun fire and hiccupping an exploding chain of 40 mm grenades along the unfriendly slope. I ducked instinctively and turned my head to determine what course of action Lt. Earls would take in the face of the percolating fire. As I did so, I also thrust my left leg forward in a blind step directly into a pit bearing the uncompromising bamboo blade of a punji stake, a foot-and-a-half of which stuck menacingly out of its berth of earth and grass. A white-hot flash of pain exploded through my senses. The poisoned prong slashed deeply into the meat of my lower leg.

The first eruption of pain passed as I reached down to wrench free the stake buried in my leg and to angrily hurl the bloody-tipped blade down the mountainside, disgusted with my self-mutilating clumsiness. I turned to those men behind me, who were scurrying for cover as the gunship and enemy marksmen continued their duel.

"Joe, Ron!" I called. "One of you guys is gonna have to take over point. I just tripped into a punji stake!"

Limping over to a flat, gray rock, I slumped down and stared at the scarlet stream gushing from my leg. Suddenly the hammers of pain pounded through my body again. Dizziness grabbed me as the trees uprooted themselves, the mountains crumbled into dust, and the heavy sky collapsed inward in a blue avalanche. Everything was pulled into a great whirling twister of pain. I weaved from side to side, barely maintaining a wobbly seat on the rock slab as I fought a battle of the will to cling to consciousness — a battle I seemed to be losing for several seconds. The temptation to submit, to swim into the limbo of unconsciousness, was great, but I fought back and eventually the spinning scene of bamboo and brush slowed. The medic applied a dressing to the seeping tear in my leg, but blood continued to trickle from the wound and dyed my green fatigue trousers a deep purple.

Lt. Earls inspected the wound. "Did you get pinned on it jumping for cover?"

"No sir," I replied, rigid with pain. "I just walked right into it like a dumb-ass dud cherry."

"Hell, them fuckin' sniper rounds panicked us all into the briar patch," consoled the lieutenant. "I backed my ass into one of them shit sticks and one of the new guys stepped on another. Just scratches though. A couple of

Doc's penicillin shots and a few band-aids will fix us up fine. But I'm afraid you really ripped yourself open on that bamboo bastard."

Numbness was returning now to submerge the pain. I stated with forced optimism, "I'll be back out here humping these hills again in a couple days, sir."

The lieutenant doubted that. "That's no little pinprick you've got there, Sergeant." Then he cautioned me. "Be sure to remember though, in case some brigade brass hats want to know, you stuck yourself when you jumped for cover. You know how Brigade's been smokin' our asses about all these so called 'avoidable' punji stake casualties. It don't look good on those Brigade bureaucrats' balance sheets when so much of our high tech army is gettin' blown away by booby traps and pinned on punjis."

"I'll remember, sir," I assured him. "I've got no desire to tell everybody in the brigade how cherry clumsy I am."

Showing a concerned look, Lt. Earls asked, "Do you think you can limp a couple more klicks down the trail? HQ's got a possible LZ there, and we'd have a bitch of a time even wenching you out of this shithole."

Trying hard to show the lieutenant and my bush buddies that I was man enough to endure all, I answered, "I'm sure I can make it. Nobody ever made a finer crutch than the M-16."

I gritted my teeth to barricade in the moans that might indicate to my comrades that I lacked balls. For even now, pillaged by pain, what mattered most was the respect of my platoonmates. A great many kilometers had passed under my tromping feet, but this was the longest hump Vietnam ever demanded of me. A raging fire seemed to consume my leg with each step; the gash seemed to tear wider and extend further up my leg. I tried to shift most of my weight to the uninjured leg, leaning heavily on my rifle-cane, but the pain hardly lessened. Finally, Henk, Jefferson and Burgess took pity on me and I tossed away a measure of pride by allowing them to act as human crutches for me. The march seemed endless, but the end finally came and I fell to the ground to rest, one trouser leg purple with oozing blood, the rest of my uniform dark green from fountaining sweat.

Linking up with company HQ, the captain and Lt. Earls discussed the possibility of wenching me out of the jungle by Medevac cableship. They decided against this and agreed instead to direct the incoming helicopter onto a one-skid landing on the side of the mountain. The Dust-Off chopper fluttered in a hover with one skid two feet above the falling slope. A sergeant from Company HQ ran ahead to direct the helicopter in, while I stumbled over the ground and painfully tried to climb over the log ledges of a fence, constructed to prevent cattle from wandering down the steep slopes as they were being herded down the trail by Vietnamese drovers.

My wound ripping wider as I strained to scale the log fence, I finally had to resubmit to pain's pleasure and strip away another patch of pride by begging for help. The sergeant ran back to pull me over the logs. I hobbled over to the Medevac ship, its pilot struggling to hold his craft in the difficult position in this thin mountain air astride the descending slope.

At last reaching the helicopter, I prepared to drag myself up into the open abdomen of the bird. But the medic aboard motioned me away, and shouted and hand signaled above the surf breakers of the rotary wings for me to drop my hand grenades — a precaution the Medevac crews always took following the destruction of one of their copters by the accidental explosion of a wounded man's grenades. With the pulsating pain shouting louder than the flying medic, I failed to understand him. For several agonizing moments I faltered there, desperately trying to make sense of the medic's objections to allowing me aboard. Then my escort translated the medic's gesticulations and rapidly unhooked the grenades attached to my ammo pouches. Freed of my frags, I was finally lifted up into the helicopter.

More than pain possessed me as the helicopter headed for Kontum. On one level I assured myself that I would soon rejoin my friends in the platoon and my enemies in the jungle. But something deeper tugged at my senses — a realization that the bonds that had held me to my misdirected fascination with this war were at last severed — at least in a physical sense; that the closeness of a comradeship conceived in adversity and forged in battle was ended. And somehow a feeling of sadness overwhelmed me. Through all the pain and blood, and the relief that came from realizing that my self-imposed exile into the bamboo boonies was over, I still felt sad and already strangely nostalgic. I felt a sense of loss for those things the war brought and demanded. Even many years later, reality often seemed more a night defensive position, a Firefly resupply, and a platoon file of men in green uniforms and steel pots, than did my current environment — a peaceful, civilian world that seemed an illusion, trivial and irrelevant.

Landing at the brigade clearing station for casualties, I was carried on a stretcher by two T-shirted medics to one of the operating tents. A brigade surgeon cleaned the poison and filth out of my wound and administered the first of many needle jabs to my ass. He notified me that I would be evacuated the next morning to the 17th Field Hospital at Pleiku, where my leg would be stitched back together. I was then lugged to a ward tent, where I struggled for sleep to drug the rockets of pain shooting through my leg. Sergeant DeJesus, recovering from dengue fever, passed by my cot to compare my wound to his four and agreed to transport my half-hearted assurances to my buddies remaining in the field that I would soon be back there with them.

Early the next morning, after awakening to throbbing pain and swallowing a breakfast of powdered eggs and B-ration bacon, I was helped to a helicopter which was to carry me and two other casualties to the Pleiku hospital. It was my last helicopter ride in Vietnam.

Touching down at the Quonset hut complex of the 17th Field Evacuation Hospital, I was hustled on a wheelchair by a white-jacketed orderly to the receiving desk, where I submitted the usual answers to the usual questions which held this hospital and the whole U.S. Army together with paperwork girders. Then I was inspected by a resident surgeon; he used me as a teaching aid in his lecture to a circle of newcomers on the effects and treatment of punji stake wounds. I was later wheeled into a pea-green-walled operating room, where a medical team prepared to further clean the gash of its water buffalo dung infection.

After a spinal tap, the surgeon started to remove the infection. Several times during the operation, I lifted my head to observe him scraping, cutting and cleansing the bloody gorge in my leg. Between the tap and several shots of morphine, there were no sharp jolts of pain, only a constant pressure seeming to bear the weight of a hemisphere down upon my maimed limb. The operation completed, the wound was left unstitched so that the torn muscles might heal properly. I was rolled to a ward, where a score of hospital beds were occupied by the moderate to severely wounded, and deposited into a bed made empty just a few hours before by the death of a gravely wounded grunt from the 25th Infantry Division.

I observed the coming of my second New Year in Vietnam from my bed in the casualty ward. The lights, usually flipped off in this ward at 2100, were left burning until after midnight so that we who were able to or so desired could witness the birth of 1967 and hear the thunderclap of the 25th Infantry Division's big guns as they blasted a New Year's greeting to Charlie.

The Five O' Deuce was still out in the sticks, observing the end of a year that had seen the battalion deployed far from its base camp for all but the first two of its fifty-two weeks. During those eleven-and-a-half months, the 2/502nd had slain over 800 enemy soldiers by body count and captured 178, along with 345 weapons. For that bounty the Strike Force had paid with the lives of ninety-eight of its riflemen. In the nearly seven years that the O' Deuce humped the bush of the 'Nam, only 1967, during which 119 Strike Force troopers were killed in action, took a higher toll than the year we had just passed through. All told, 422 men who wore the light blue-on-dark blue oval cloth background on which the paratrooper's badge was pinned — the insignia of the Strike Force battalion — were killed in Vietnam from July 29, 1965, to January 19, 1972, and another 2, 500 were wounded.

Though pain was a persistent companion, my suffering was somehow drugged and made more tolerable by the greater agony of many of my ward-mates. A wounded soldier nearby bore hundreds of stitches all over his torso from the shrapnel slashes of a B-40 rocket explosion at his 1st Cavalry Division firebase at LZ Bird, which had narrowly repulsed a massive NVA attack on December 27. The worst hurt in my ward was a black soldier from the 25th Infantry, lying in the bed directly across the aisle from me. Both of the man's legs lay wrapped in thick dressings, like two mummified pharaohs. The dressings had to be changed frequently, and when they were I could see the raw, red meat of limbs shattered by the explosion of a land mine. He was in constant, hellish pain, screaming profanely at the medics for injections. I can still remember the lines scored by pain in his dark face and his sobbing pleas for relief that came infrequently because the doctor feared the soldier might become hooked on morphine. I can still see the medics attempting to calm him and can still hear his cries. The chestnut-haired nurse, lost in baggy fatigues but still an attractive sight to men starved for round-eyed softness, would hold the wounded soldier and gently demand that he stop crying and cursing and try to fight the pain like a man. Finally she would give in to his pleas and administer the morphine, smothering screaming nerves with its numbing pillow, and allowing the soldier a few precious hours of sleep before the smoldering nerves burst again into flames. The man was still bawling like a baby when I left the hospital two days later.

Few casualties remained very long at the Pleiku evacuation hospital, except for those too severely wounded to be moved. Thus, on January 3, I and several of my wardmates were carried by Army ambulances to the airstrip for transfer aboard a C-130 to the hospital in Quinhon. The night before, this airfield had been hit by a mortar and rocket bombardment. We had experienced some apprehension at the 17th Evac, when two stray shells detonated on the hospital grounds, showering the corrugated steel sides of our Quonset hut ward with shrapnel and dirt. The lights were turned off in a hospital blackout for several anxious minutes as 105 and 155 mm howitzers began their kettle drum reply, but no more enemy shells fell and we were allowed to resume our suffering undisturbed. It was the war's farewell to me; the last time its deathly breath blew even remotely close; the final time I would hear the steel shouts of its thundering voice.

Landing at Quinhon, where unrequited love had struck me silly more than a year ago, I was shuttled by hospital bus to the 5th Field Hospital. There I was dumped into a ward with my fellow wounded, many of them casualties from the fight at LZ Bird. Compared to the privation that was the grunt's lot in life, I now sat — or rather lay — in the lap of luxury. I had lost my groundpounder's legacy: the heat, insects, mountains, prickly Wait-a-Minute bushes, and the always looming specter of a cunning, killing enemy. In its place I now had a soft bed, ice cream, a raven-tressed nurse to drool over, and "The Beverly Hillbillies," "Gunsmoke" and "Batman" on the ward's television set. The only "Combat" I had to endure now was that blaring from the TV.

My leg was finally sewed together with sixteen large, staple-like, metal stitches the following morning. My wound patched up, resembling a swollen red zipper along my leg, I was wheeled back to my ward.

That day and the next, Charlie Company casualties poured into the hospital, carrying with them tales of near disaster befalling the company. I caught bits and pieces from the incoming wounded, stories of men killed and wounded, of ambush and falling mortar shells, and heard the roll call of the dead. I realized that I had escaped by a single day being a participant in a whirlwind that had swept up my company. I was both relieved by that knowledge, glad that I had not had to witness the death and maiming of many of my comrades, and guilt-stricken because I had not been fighting beside them when the heavy shit came down.

The final scrap of sad news came to me later, after I had been flown to a hospital in Japan. Scanning the small-print morgue of the weekly casualty lists published in the *Stars and Stripes*, which included a heartrending number of names that had once been on Charlie Company's personnel roster, my eyes fell upon the names of Lt. Larry D. Earls and Pfc. Reynaldo Ramos. How and when they died were not stated; the casualty columns furnished no details of the final moments of a man's life. It was not until March, while I was serving my final months in the Army at Fort Campbell, that I received a letter from James Henk giving me the full story of the sanguinary series of disasters that overtook my company, beginning but one day after my Medevac departure from the field.

Chapter XXIII

New Year's Truce

Henk wrote me from his new assignment with a security guard company in Saigon. Along with Joe Jefferson, he had been transferred to the "Saigon Commandos" shortly after the bloody debacle of the first days of 1967 — the worst for the company since the napalm roast on Carpenter's Hill in June 1966. Henk had received training at Phan Rang in early December on a new electronic device called alternately the "Smell O' Meter" and the "Charlie Sniffer," which was supposed to be capable of smelling out the enemy's location through the use of its high-tech nose. Both he and Jefferson had also been considered for assignment to a spit-and-polish honor guard company detailed for the pomp and ceremony attendant upon Westmoreland's Saigon headquarters. But both men ended up standing guard in front of a Saigon hotel serving as a BOQ (Bachelor Officers' Quarters) for MACV personnel during the day and buying Saigon teas for the bargirls on Tu Do Street at night.

According to Henk's account, the tragic chain of events involving Charlie Company began on December 31. The three-day New Year's cease-fire had gone into effect at 0700 that morning. Each platoon was to move to a LZ for resupply. Then defensive positions were to be set up for the duration of the holiday truce and from which only defensive patrols were to be run.

At 1330 hours, a Firefly skimmed across the treetops to unload at the LZ shared by 3rd and Weapons platoons and to take aboard two short-timers awaiting rotation. Just as the resupply chopper thrust its tail skyward and pointed its nose toward the forest in hovering preparation for the leap high above the jungle canopy, two mortar shells sliced through the air and erupted in dirty geysers on either side of the helicopter. The short-timer's superstition — that often the men who had but a few days remaining until rotation were the ones who got zapped — now seemed weighted with truth for the two frightened grunts aboard the Huey. But the chopper pilot gunned the engine and steered away from the LZ before the next pair of mortar rounds impacted in ruby flashes. The chatter of an automatic weapon followed the mortar detonations. Lt. Strong, recently recovered from his leg wound suffered during Operation Geronimo, yelled into his handset for a gunship attack on the surrounding heights. Presently, Hueys arrived and released their fury on the enemy hills, and the clatter of small arms fire died away. It could have been far worse, and soon would be, for the platoon had taken only two casualties: one grunt had caught an assful of mortar fragments; another was struck by AK fire.

Hit much worse was 2nd Platoon, which, like 1st Platoon, had been ordered to saddle up and move ASAP to the scene of the LZ flare-up by the shortest route possible. That route led the platoon into a squad-sized NVA ambush, which guillotined the point man with the chopping blade of an automatic rifle and flailed the flesh of two troopers gaiting down the trail behind him. The ambushers then fled before their targets could recover to retaliate. Carrying the corpse of their point man in a poncho shroud, 2nd Platoon continued on to link up with the rest of the company.

Time was consumed extracting the body and the wounded, numbering five in all, including the third serious punji stake injury in as many days — a man from Weapons Platoon who had punctured the sole of his foot on one of the devilish devices. By then darkness was approaching and Captain Silvasy was reluctant to launch a counter-attack on the hill mass from which most of the hostile fire had come. He therefore decided to postpone the assault and requested an air strike to punish the gooks. Two prop-driven Skyraiders and the brigade's 105 mm artillery bracketed the enemy-held hill with bombs and shells.

After a cold, rainy New Year's Eve atop an adjacent mound of earth and trees, the company attacked the unfriendly hill the next morning. They met no resistance and uncovered only a small hooch, alongside of which was a freshly dug grave containing the corpse of a NVA soldier killed in yesterday's firefight.

Captain Silvasy decided to spent the rest of the day and night on the hill. Early that afternoon, 1st Platoon was sent out to patrol around its base. They discovered that the North Vietnamese were still prowling the area when, for some reason, several of the enemy began hollering at an L-19 spotter plane tittering overhead. Perhaps they hoped by this crude tactic to draw the platoon into an ambush. If so, 1st Platoon refused to go for the bait. Earls chose, instead, to return to the company bivouac to inform the captain of the enemy's presence. The company commander had been warned, but tragically failed to take proper heed, neither instructing his men to prepare better defensive positions nor sending out listening posts.

Charlie Company, a weary band of armed men reduced to only seventy in number from its authorized 164 by the inevitable attrition and erosion of warfare, began its own "La Noche Triste" on the night of January 1, 1967. "The Sad Night" was particularly cold and a bitter wind howled fiercely. The wind continued its cold complaint through the dark hours until 0200; then its ululating cry struck several startlingly thunderous notes — the crump of exploding grenades. With demoralizing suddenness, the perimeter was whipped by a new wind, a lashing iron gale of automatic weapons fire and bursting hand grenades. A flash-fire seared the company's defensive circle of three and four-man posts — not from outside the perimeter, but from within. The North Vietnamese had infiltrated undetected between the American positions, occupied by men deafened by the wind and blinded by the night. For ten minutes of exploding hell, the NVA sappers tormented the terrified paratroopers with as many as forty grenades, and then slipped as easily through the gaps between the grunts' positions as they had entered.

Like Cortez's conquistadors during their own sad night more than four centuries before, Charlie Company had been sorely hurt. Six grunts were dead, three from Weapons Platoon and three from 3rd Platoon. The six slain troopers had been in two posts, and nearly everyone at both positions had been asleep. It probably would have mattered little if the guards had been awake, for the wind and darkness had made it virtually impossible to detect the stalking enemy, slithering up to both positions and rolling a dozen grenades into the sleeping faces of the G.I.s, snuggled together in their poncho hoochos.

There was only two survivors at the two positions, one of whom was Pfc. Carl Konopa. He miraculously escaped the grenade shower untouched. Possibly, the shrapnel-slashed bodies of his comrades absorbed the steel intended for him. Konopa was only seventeen, a once gung-ho grunt who had lied about his age to overcome the eighteen-year-old minimum age requirement for Vietnam service. But his enthusiasm had died along with his buddies, and he was soon pleading his lack of years to escape the hell he had once anticipated. Konopa's pleas had withered before the fire-snorting profanity of the first sergeant, who probably felt that puberty was a good age to begin fighting a war. Three months later, Konopa would indeed escape his self-attained hell ... he would go home, but in a box. He would still be just seventeen when the helicopter carrying him to a new mission molded with the ground.

The second survivor was an explosives demolition specialist detached from the 326th Engineers. Twenty-four years and one war later, those terrifying minutes on Grenade Hill returned to him with a vengeance during his voluntary deployment to the Persian Gulf. The soldier had suffered not a scratch during that first night of 1967 in the Central Highlands, but in 1991 Operation Pickett finally made him a casualty when he collapsed into the emotional turmoil of PTSD in the sands of Saudi Arabia, just before Desert Storm commenced.

Besides the six dead soldiers, nine more were wounded. The body of a NVA sapper was discovered at daylight; he was probably the attackers' only casualty. Six men dead, nine wounded, and no one had seen in the course of the bloodbath a single North Vietnamese infiltrator.

The dead and wounded were evacuated by helicopter shortly after sunrise, and several replacements, unbloodied "new meat," were received into the company's depleted ranks to replace partially the night's losses. It must have been a grim introduction to the bamboo battlefield for the cherries.

The platoons separated and then moved out, with everyone shaken and scared, afraid it was not yet over, that further tragedy, more death was fated for the company. All that day the broken-spirited body of men marched under an atmosphere of dread.

Every guard was alert that night ... tensely, nervously alert. They would not be caught napping again by the murderous grenadiers. Fingers were wrapped tightly around triggers; hearts thumped an anxious beat; frightened minds concocted creeping images of killers from the swaying shadows of trees. The situation was ripe for accident and tragedy. It came.

Around midnight, Lt. Earls, rolling uncomfortably on the sharp stones under his poncho bed, rose to seek softer ground. Several feet away one of the RTOs was awake on radio watch. The man had lost a couple of close buddies in the early morning massacre; he did not intend to suffer the same fate. Suddenly he heard a rustling noise among the bushes a few steps away. The image of a grenade-bearing gook flashed across his mind and ruled his reflexes.

The RTO's finger jerked back on the trigger of his M-16. Yellow arrowheads flashed from his screeching weapon. The radioman burst free from the bars of terror imprisoning him with the reassuring roar of his rifle. His sleeping comrades awakened to the certain horror of another nightmare materialized into death-dealing reality. But after shaking the terror loose from their imaginations, the men of the platoon were content to discount the burst of fire as the understandably nervous reaction of a tense young trooper whose only assailant had been the shadow of a wind-tossed tree.

At daybreak, the body of Lt. Earls was discovered, slumped a few feet from the RTO's post. He was riddled with six bullet holes, one of which had crashed into the center of his forehead and must have killed him instantly.

Two days later, Reynaldo Ramos' dreams were ended in mid-flight by a sniper's bullet. Operation Pickett ended on January 14, after the Five O' Deuce had lost sixteen KIA (ten of whom were from Charlie Company) and thirty-five WIA, while wasting only thirteen NVA/VC (the brigade in total had zapped eighty-one). A week later, the 1st Brigade finally returned to its base camp at Phan Rang, after fifty-three weeks in the field, the longest stretch any major unit served away from its base area during the war.

While catastrophe stalked the company, I lay in the Quinhon hospital, watching the tube, getting needled in the bare behind by penicillin-filled hypos, and hoping that I would remain in Quinhon long enough to heal and hobble downtown to see Helen again. That hope was dashed on January 6, when I was informed that I was to be transferred by an Air Force Medical Evacuation aircraft to Japan, where I was to be hospitalized for the duration of my convalescence.

On the 8th of January, 1967 — ironically the date I was originally scheduled for DEROS before I had signed up for an additional two months' extension — I left Vietnam, its lessons and its losses, its counterfeit promises and strange rewards, its demands and disillusionments. Strapped to a stretcher aboard an Air Force plane, I was airborne in just a few minutes. The last picture of this land that had held me, owned me, and stamped me with its permanent mark, was of the shanties surrounding the airfield, the flattened beer can buildings, the green background of rice paddies and unconquerable mountains rising beyond.

Staring into that sweeping green, I saw other things. I saw the smutty, laughing faces of brown-eyed kids grappling in a cloud of dust for C-ration candy thrown into their midst by passing G.I.s. Over that image appeared the faces of other children, bravely holding back tears as their blood flowed in red rivers from shrapnel slashes ... then the lost look from ashen faces and unblinking eyes, from which the tears had long since been drained, as they stood in shock over the napalm-burned bodies of their parents.

I saw, too, as if from the fluttering high view of a helicopter, the breathtaking beauty of this land of forested mountains and rice paddy checkerboards. Then other images clashed with, defeated and destroyed this one of beauty ... images of the physical and emotional pain inflicted on those who lived, fought and often died here in Vietnam, with its alternating heat and rain, its slithering and stinging population of reptiles and insects, its leech-lush mangrove swamps and dung-rafted rice paddies, its mountains with bamboo quills stabbing at the sky, its dagger-like thorns, rapier stalks of elephant grass, and concertina strands of Wait-a-Minute vines.

I heard the ripple of friends' laughter; the incantation of their spoken dreams; their recitation of letters from loved ones; the grumbling of the suffering soldier; the excited shouts and frenzied commands in the dementia of battle ... and the cries of pain from the wounded, the yelp of sudden death, the stone silence of instant obliteration.

I smelled the jasmine fragrance of delicate female flowers in brilliant Ao Dais and conical sunhats, the sweet harshness of French-cologned Saigon street-walkers in their cosmetic camouflage and slit skirts; the musty odor permeating the thatched hut peasant villages, the sting of stale urine on small children and the stink of dung-fertilized rice paddies, the thick smell of cooking pots of fish and rice, and the smog of burning opium; the strident perfume of exploded cordite and gunpowder drifting in smoky white whips across a star pattern of howitzers, the pungence of smoke grenades and burning peasant huts ... and, more powerful than all, the sick-stomach stench of rotting bodies, shrouded in blood for a funeral attended by flies and maggots.

An album of faces flipped through my mind. I saw the warm, honey-colored face of Helen, her lips lacquered the sweet red of candied apples ... the blood-framed face of a dying Morales; the impish face of Whitehall, warbling a sentimental ballad in one image ... severing the ears from a murdered old man in another; the pasty grimace of DeJesus' face, set in a sculpture of pain ... the look of stark terror on the face of Grogan when he sat on the cluster bomb; the golden velvetness of a Thai prostitute named Pin, weeping over a life already compromised and corrupted at sixteen ... the waxen, swelling face of some nameless peasant boy of sixteen or seventeen who had sacrificed the rest of his years on earth to the cause of the National Liberation Front.

I had seen, and now viewed once again, superimposed over the last clouded image of Vietnam, an intimate face of life as I had never witnessed it before and would probably never do so again ... and the sudden expression of violent death. My 490 days in Vietnam, 153 of them with the Strike Force, had ended. Vietnam disappeared into the fog of clouds and slip-stream. It was gone; it was done.

Epilogue

My flight carried me first to the Air Force hospital at Clark Air Force Base in the Philippines and then to Tachikawa Air Force Base in Japan. From there I was shuttled by helicopter to the 7th Field Hospital at Johnson Air Force Base and admitted to a ward of two-bed rooms.

What luxury my wound had wrought! From a row of pup tents or a hard rack on the jungle floor to a semi-private room on a real bed with real sheets, with my meals served royally in bed.

After nearly three weeks in the hospital, I was handed a sloppily fitting set of Army dress greens and bused with other healed veterans to the processing and embarkation point at Camp Zama. Quartered there until the last days of the month, I passed my time browsing in the post library, swigging down cheap drinks at the NCO's club, and buying the martial ornaments with which to decorate my uniform. Fully adorned with the tinsel and glitter of the combat veteran, spit-shined jump boots and polished brass, I was handed my reassignment orders and placed aboard a jet transport bound for Travis Air Force Base. After a ten-hour oceanic leap aboard a C-141, I landed in California. I caught a hop aboard the aerial tortoise of a C-118 cargo plane to Tinker Air Force Base outside Oklahoma City. From there, it was commercial jet to Wichita and on by bus to Plainville, Kansas. I was home.

My thirty-day leave was anything but happy, as I sang my own variation of the Post-Vietnam Blues. My Vietnam experience was like a great, disenchanting sea into which my emotional raft was slowly sinking. I spent the whole leave feeling incredibly sorry for myself. Depression clung to me like an evil aura, like a malignantly thickening second skin. I was beginning to wonder if I was not dinkee-dau, the Vietnamese word for crazy.

My early discharge was not to be; I had missed the ninety-day cut-off mark by a few weeks when I returned stateside. After my leave, I flew to my new assignment: Fort Campbell, Kentucky, from where my "great adventure" had begun nineteen months ago. I was assigned as a fire team leader to Charlie

Company, 3/187th Airborne Infantry Battalion of the 101st's still stateside-stationed 3rd Brigade.

Almost immediately, I was sent to the boonies of North Carolina's Smoky Mountains to play war for two weeks, only two months after I had played the deadly game for real. I later executed my fifteenth and sixteenth jumps from low flying C-130s, after several refresher leaps from the post jump school's thirty-four-foot tower, the terror of the paratrooper trainee. But mostly, like any good short-timer, I devoted my time to ghosting, marking off the dwindling days on my short-timer's calendar, celebrating each passing day that brought me closer to my ETS (Expiration of Time in Service) by guzzling drinks at the post's NCO and EM clubs.

I met a Clarksville, Tennessee, girl named Rena Katherine, eighteen years old and touching me with warmth and innocence, her hair like a soft brown cascade, her timid smile communicating more to me than all the conversations of my life. I fell in love with her and married her two months after my discharge. It seemed that I had left war and loneliness behind me. But I would find that I was unable to break the bonds by which Vietnam continued to psychically shackle me and escape the indefinable loneliness which all men who have experienced war must share.

Although my Vietnam odyssey was over — at least in a physical sense — it continued for many of my former comrades and for the 101st. After a brief rest in the new wooden barracks at Phan Rang and a five-day sweep in surrounding Ninh Thuan Province, which netted the brigade seven kills in Operation Farragut III, the brigade moved on southwest on February 1 to carry out Operations Gatling I and II near Bao Loc and Phan Thiet, where we had conducted a thirsty search for the enemy in the barren days of April 1966. The Gatling ops were no more fruitful than Austin II had been and only seven Charlies were bagged. Then it was halfway back up the coast toward Phan Rang for Operations Farragut IV and V in the Song Mao area in late February and early March. The area was as dry and desolate as it had been a year ago and soon practically the whole battalion was suffering from vomiting and stomach cramps caused by tainted water brought to the grunts in gasoline cans.

The human hunting was little better in this region, but the wildlife offered some action. DeJesus, newly promoted to staff sergeant, killed with a machete a fourteen-foot-long boa constrictor, and another 1st Platoon grunt bagged a nine-foot king cobra. But the biggest kill was made by Welch, now a platoon sergeant, who on March 5 enlarged his legend, with the help of a burst from Burgess' M-16, by shooting a 450-pound tiger who had ideas of chowing down on Rose as he was crossing a stream at the point of the platoon file.

On March 28, DeJesus, wearing his snakeskin belt, and Welch, carrying his tigerskin rug, moved north with the brigade beyond Phan Rang and Cam Ranh Bay to the area around Khanh Duong in Khanh Hoa Province. Operation Summerall rang up no big body count but did mark the end of almost two years of 1st Brigade operations carried out almost exclusively in the II Corps Tactical Zone — the one exception being Operation Checkmate in December 1965, conducted around Ben Cat in III Corps. On May 6, the brigade boarded LSTs for the first time since the first deployment to Tuy Hoa in January 1966 and sailed from Nhatrang bound north for Quang Ngai Province in "Eye" Corps. There the 101st was to join the 196th Light Infantry Brigade and the 3rd Brigade of the 25th Infantry Division to make up Task Force Oregon, the first Army divisional-sized unit to deploy in I Corps to help the Marines contend with the NVA in the most heavily fought over tactical zone in the country.

Landing near Duc Pho, the Strike Force spent the first few days in I Corps building Carentan Base Camp. Evidence that the area was mined lay in the twisted hulk of a helicopter, on which nine soldiers had died when the chopper had settled down on disaster. Rose, scouting the area, found a boot of one of the victims, the decomposed remains of his foot still inside. But the hunk of junk that was once a helicopter was not warning enough to save a Strike Force trooper.

A mine detonated as everyone took a break from digging in to wolf down Cs. The wind was throwing up so much sand that Rose and Welch had decided to drop down in their holes to chow down. A buddy of theirs, called "Tiger" because of the tattoo growling from his arm, had walked toward their hole to shoot the shit during the lunch break. Tiger got to within ten meters of Rose and Welch when he stepped on a 105 mm mine fused with a 155 mm charge. The booby-trapped artillery shell reduced Tiger to a red spray and wounded five more troopers, but Rose and Welch were saved from injury by their decision to gobble their C-rats underground.

I Corps was far rougher territory than the relatively secure areas the 101st had campaigned in during the preceding months. Action came fast and was often furious. Operation Malheur I brought the battalion's biggest battle since Toumorong in June 1966. This occurred on May 18, when Bravo Company ran into deep shit on the steep slopes of Hill 424. Alpha and Charlie companies moved to Bravo's rescue from south and north respectively, but the battle went on through the rainy night and into the morning before the 1st NVA Division broke contact and withdrew. During this action, Grogan finally fulfilled his Marine father's expectations by going battle berserk as he tried to win the war single-handedly. He won a well-deserved Distinguished Service Cross for his valor that day, but then sullied his heroics by denigrating his comrades' efforts and accusing Rose, whom he envied for his prowess and reputation, of cowardice, even though the "Hard Core Pointer" had taken out at least two enemy bunkers during the combat.

Hill 424 cost the Strike Force twelve KIA, ten of them from Bravo Company, and thirty-eight WIA, but the O'Deuce had accounted for forty-five NVA slain. By the time Malheur I ended on June 4, the 2/502nd had accumulated a body count of 152 (out of a brigade total of 399). Total Strike Force casualties were thirteen KIA and sixty-five WIA.

Malheur II followed hard on the heels of Malheur I, and though it began with a tragically common, friendly fire disaster when U.S. artillery rounds struck B Company, killing three grunts and wounding twenty-one, the operation ultimately was successful. Malheur II ended on July 28 after fifty-one days in the field, one day before the second anniversary of the brigade's landing at Cam Ranh Bay. The body count register totaled 470.

First Platoon accounted for its share of those bodies. One night, gooks, high on dope and not giving a damn, demonstrating more balls than brains, used flashlights to illuminate Charlie Company's positions in an assault on the company NDP. Rose and his platoonmates zeroed in on the beams of light and wasted a half dozen or more. That strange encounter was the essence of combat, but during another skirmish the war again flashed its perversity and cursed Rose with enough ghosts for a lifetime. He tossed grenades into a bunker he thought was occupied by enemy soldiers, but instead held only women and children.

Rose DEROSed on June 22. The night before he caught the Freedom Bird out of Nhatrang, he found release from a year's worth of triumph, terror and tragedy by joining twenty-five other rotating paratroopers in an all-out drunken brawl with a bar full of REMFs. The MPs who broke it up knew better than to press charges against the haggard, hard-faced, twenty-year-old grunts.

DeJesus absorbed more iron during Malheur II, taking his fifth wound on July 14 and spending the next two months in the hospital before rotating home. He would make the Army his home and career and retire, like Welch, as a mustang major. Holtzman, who had tried so hard to talk me out of a second extension, ironically decided to extend to get out of the boonies and into a helicopter as a door gunner. However, his plans were changed by a punji stake wound that ended his tour. Meadows, who had been wounded in the leg in September 1966 and who hated the war and the Army with such passion, confounded everyone by extending and paid for that decision with his life on September 27, 1967.

Most of the men with whom I served survived their tours. Rose survived too, of course, almost miraculously without a scratch. But for several weeks he suffered a bureaucratic death, which his grieving family had to endure before the Army's record keepers discovered that it was Jim Rose from another unit, and not Wendell Rose, who had died. Johansen continued to slither to places of safety and thus survived as well, but not before Rose, enraged by yet another cowardly act by Johansen, went after him with an entrenching tool and delivered a few lumps to the man who had managed to avoid all those that the war and the bush had inflicted on all the other, braver men of the platoon.

Rose, post-war, would endure many hard years — failed marriages, fraught memories, and an over fondness for strong drink. But a good woman, God and gospel music finally provided the solace that liquor could never really bestow. Even the loss of Shirley, his last wife, to cancer did not reorient him away from the light and back toward the shadows. Johansen, on the other hand, remained a captive to his craven soul. The man, who nimbly avoided every hazard in Vietnam except for Rose's E-tool, expertly employed his talents for fraud and deceit to obtain a 100 percent disability from the VA for PTSD.

Jim Henk, after his tour in Saigon, eventually returned to Chicago, where he exchanged olive drab for blue and remained in uniform as a Second City cop for thirty years.

Of course, several men of Charlie Company survived the war without physical damage, but returned with psychic and spiritual wounds far deeper and much more disabling than those we all carried home in our baggage from the bush. Eighteen years after my return, I started to receive phone calls from a 2nd Platoon veteran. After long years of drug and alcohol dependency and futile psychological counseling, he had started calling up fellow veterans of Charlie Company to seek their help in filling in great gaps in his memory of 'Nam and to try to reconnect and make sense of shattered pieces of his time in the bush. He told me wild, totally unsubstantiated stories about Captain Silvasy having to threaten Sab with a court-martial in order to restrain the first sergeant from blowing him away when he refused to open fire on a group of fleeing villagers; and about Ramos, with whom I had spent the last days of Operation Geronimo during convalescence from immersion foot, being wasted not by gook snipers but by his own comrades, who resented his ghosting and gutlessness in the boonies. The veteran had spent his first night in the bush hiding from the monsoon rain in an abandoned peasant hooch. Upon waking, huge, hairy spiders were crawling over him and his tour was a horror from that moment on, ending with his wigging out and being pulled permanently from the field. Whether his stories had substance or were just part of the shattered mirror reflecting his Vietnam nightmare, I have no way of knowing.

While Vietnam destroyed many of my comrades physically or emotionally, it boosted the fortunes or careers of several Charlie Company leaders. Captain Carpenter, of Napalm Hill fame, was promoted to major general in 1986 and received command of the 10th Mountain Division. Captain Silvasy, who some had thought deserved a court-martial for allowing his company to let down its guard with disastrous consequences during the 1967 New Year's truce, survived a serious wound from the explosion of a Chinese Claymore mine that decapitated the man standing next to him and went on to command the 2nd Brigade of the 82nd Airborne Division in its assault on the island of Grenada in October 1983. Lieutenant Novak continued his military career. He returned to Vietnam as a company commander in the 173rd Airborne Brigade, where he was reunited with now Lieutenant Welch, in 1968–69. He retired from the Army as a colonel and died in 2010.

"Sab" was made battalion sergeant-major and later retired a veteran of three wars and bearer of the DSC, a Silver Star, four Bronze Stars with V, and four Purple Hearts. And Welch, the bravest and baddest soldier I ever knew, who commanded the respect and affection of every man he led or befriended, but who could also nonchalantly rewrite the rules of engagement according to his own deadly whim, went on to greater glory. His Army career, which started as an alternative to going to jail for falsely soliciting contributions for the Red Cross, ended sixteen years later after his promotion from the ranks in the summer of 1967. Welch had returned to the U.S. in August 1967, married, and a year and a half later returned to Vietnam, where he was assigned to the 173rd Airborne Brigade. While serving as a company commander with the brigade, he narrowly escaped being fragged by a disgruntled "shake-and-bake" sergeant. After his retirement as a major, Welch still required the highs provided by travel and adventure and thus commenced a second career in the Merchant Marine.

One by one, the men with whom I had served rotated homeward or died, until the company wore a completely different face. The old men went home, but the brigade banner remained to be carried by new men as the 101st continued operations in Quang Ngai and further north in the Chu Lai area of Quang Tin Province. Operations Hood River, Benton, Crook, and Wheeler followed the Malheur campaigns, and by the end of November 1967 the 1st Brigade in its first six operations in I Corps had chalked up a body count of 2,405 NVA/VC.

The 2nd and 3rd brigades of the 101st were airlifted to Vietnam before Christmas 1967. The U.S. toll of 5,008 killed in action in 1966 was nearly doubled in 1967 and nearly tripled in 1968, the year of the Tet Offensive. During the country-wide conflagration of Tet, in which the enemy violated another truce on an incalculably more massive scale than he had against Charlie Company during New Year's 1967, a platoon from the 101st landed on the roof of the U.S. Embassy in Saigon to help retake it from a V.C. sapper squad that had penetrated the grounds in the most dramatic incident of the offensive. There would be many battles — the A Shau Valley, Hamburger Hill, Firebase Ripcord — and many years of combat ahead for the 101st, most of it spent in I Corps. The Screaming Eagle of the 101st, its feathers singed by six and a half years of combat and over 20,000 casualties (3,000 of which were suffered by the approximately 5,000 men who served in the Strike Force), would not fly homeward to its Fort Campbell aerie until January 1972.

One more comrade needs to be accounted for: Donny, the friend who had accompanied me in my flights of fantasy during a childhood devoted to the worship of war. This comrade from days when the combat was imagined became a comrade only once when the combat was real. This occurred when his helicopter battalion, to which he was assigned as a mechanic, ferried the 2/502nd in my first battalion night helicopter assault in September 1966. Somewhere in the waves of Hueys flying me and my buddies into a dark LZ, Donny rode as a door gunner, but we did not encounter one another.

His first tour was completed without harm or particular hazard. He then signed up for a second year to take advantage of the cheap booze, sex and thrills offered by Vietnam. But the second tour carried a heavier price tag. The war became less of a lark when he caught glimpses of its impact on the homefront during his thirty-day leave between tours. The war had already claimed his cousin, and two of his high school pals came home paraplegics. While cruising the streets of Wichita, Donny witnessed his first anti-war demonstration and the passions the protesters provoked. A Green Beret dashed up to a girl carrying the yellow starred, red and blue banner of the Viet Cong and proceeded to knock her down and kick her in the face with his combat boot. A week later, Wichita erupted in a race riot and Donny watched National Guard troops deploy into an urban battleground that he had foolishly thought was a city at peace. Soon afterward, he left for Cu Chi and a war he was more familiar with than the one tearing apart his community and country.

Back in the 'Nam, Donny's helicopter outfit supported the Big Red One for some time, then went north in November 1967 to fly the 173rd Airborne into the hell of Hill 875 near Dak To. During the battle, his aviation battalion had sixteen of its choppers blown out of the air. While spending a night on perimeter guard, Donny himself caught some shrapnel in the back from the explosion of a recoilless rifle round.

The war began to grind Donny down. He dealt with its demands by downing a quart of liquor a day. When he was not flying in or repairing choppers or drowning his reality in alcohol, Donny was visiting the fifteen-year-old girl he had purchased for $50 a month from the refugee camp outside his base at Tuy Hoa. The girl was named Kim Wah and she called Donny "Loom," which means "Laughing Buddha." After Kim Wah presented Donny with a son, he married her in a Buddhist ceremony. But his little family disappeared, along with America's faith in the war effort, on the first day of the Tet Offensive, January 30, 1968. When a Viet Cong force overran Kim Wah's refugee village, the U.S. military responded by dropping napalm. Kim Wah and Donny's son were among the many refugees who burned to death along with the Viet Cong. Donny started screaming and didn't stop until he had become "Maximum Casualty" and was shipped to Okinawa as a battle fatigue casualty.

Following "rehabilitation," Donny, now calling himself "Max," was returned to Vietnam, assigned this time to the 13th Combat Aviation Battalion in Can Tho in the Mekong Delta. There, Max experienced more horrors of war in the paddies and in the war at home. When white lifers in his battalion raised the Confederate flag and started celebrating in the NCO club upon hearing the news of Martin Luther King's assassination in Memphis, Tennessee, on April 4, black soldiers gathered around transistors to listen to Radio Hanoi play tapes of battle sounds from the rioting ghettos of America. A few days later a frag blew up the NCO club.

Shortly afterward, Max was permitted to shuttle his way north to Tuy Hoa to reclaim his possessions that had never followed him to Okinawa and the Delta. There he encountered one of the refugee girls who had worked as a hoochmaid for his company in Tuy Hoa. She was lying in an irrigation ditch soaking her white phosphorous–burned arm in the scummy water. The lower part of her arm was black and gangrene was advancing into the upper arm. Though the hoochmaid had paid nearly $200 in MPC for two shots of penicillin to arrest the infection, she was still in constant agony more than two months later. Max took her to an American hospital, but following Tet, Vietnamese civilians were routinely turned away because of an inundation of U.S. casualties. Max then paid a Vietnamese doctor $55 to amputate her arm. With little anesthesia to numb the pain, Max held the hoochmaid's head in his arms as the doctor sawed through the bone. The maid bravely held back her screams, but finally passed out when the surgeon cauterized the amputation with a white-hot iron.

Max returned to Can Tho and to the bottle, and not long afterward, in a drunken rage, punched a major. Ninety days later, he was discharged as unfit for further military service due to character and mental disorders. He spent the next two years in a drunken fog in the San Francisco area and culminated his career as a wino and vagabond by blowing up two government vehicles and doing an eight-month stretch in jail. Four months later, wandering around in a state of liquor-induced amnesia, he was picked up by the police and confined to a mental hospital. Donny-Max found salvation by immersing himself in the anti-war movement and particularly by joining the Vietnam Veterans Against the War, about the same time that I was enlisting in the same army of veterans who had seen too much of the war and had collectively said "Enough." Our journeys were long; we both traveled a hard road away from the dazzling light that war somehow illuminated out of the darkest deceits.

With the advantages of distance and hindsight, when I looked back on the things that I and hundreds of thousands of soldiers on both sides had done, the scenes I had witnessed, the suffering I had helped bring to Vietnam and its people, I finally realized with certainty that the war was wrong, that there was no justification, no phrases high sounding enough to right our nation's wrong in blundering into a conflict without a certain purpose and with no real sense of how to wage the war; that napalm, bombs and bullets could not give birth to democracy in Vietnam. I spoke out against the war, marched in anti-war demonstrations, and campaigned for the peace candidacies of Senator McCarthy in 1968 and Senator McGovern in 1972. I found myself marching again, but this time bearing banners pleading for peace rather than an M-16 dispensing death.

In April 1971, I fought my most important battle in the war-against-the-war. It was a battle unlike any I had waged in Vietnam ... a battle for peace in Southeast Asia, and not as a grunt with the Five O' Deuce, but as a Vietnam Veteran Against the War.

Operation Dewey Canyon III took place in Washington, D.C., April 19–23, 1971. (The first two Dewey Canyon operations had taken place in I Corps at and over the Laotian border in 1969 and early in 1971 in support of the ARVN thrust into Laos to cut the Ho Chi Minh Trail.)

It had been four years between operations for me; four years since I had last donned Army fatigues and jungle boots to stalk the jungles of Kontum Province in Operation Pickett. The contrasts between Pickett and Dewey

Canyon III were overwhelming. The area of operations for Dewey Canyon III was the Capitol Building and the parks and boulevards of the nation's capital, rather than the Central Highlands of Vietnam. The enemy were no longer the Viet Cong and the North Vietnamese, but national leaders, institutions and misconceptions which prolonged the ugly conflict. We fought not with weapons of destruction, but with pleas for peace, lobbying efforts directed toward congressmen, and the marching, chanting and singing solidarity of soldiers for peace. Our objectives were not the destruction of villes nor the counting of bodies, but the winning of the hearts and minds of the American people. We were determined to impress upon an unresponsive government our remorse for the suffering the war had forced us to inflict on the Vietnamese people and our resolve to end a conflict which had uselessly taken our brothers' lives and crippled many within our ranks, both physically and emotionally.

Ours was an unprecedented demonstration; a protest against a war by some 2,000 men who had fought that war. We were veterans of the 101st Airborne Division, the Americal Division, the 1st Cavalry Division, the 1st, 4th, 9th and 25th Infantry divisions, the 1st and 3rd Marine divisions, the 26th and 27th Marine regiments, the 1st Brigade of the 5th Mechanized Division, the 3rd Brigade of the 82nd Airborne Division, the 173rd Airborne Brigade, the 199th Light Infantry Brigade, the 11th Armored Cavalry Regiment, the 5th Special Forces Group, and dozens of aviation, combat support and logistical units, as well as U.S. Air Force and Navy outfits. Dressed in jungle fatigues and wearing combat ribbons, we were a statement to our blundering national leaders that our generation would no longer be dutiful cannon fodder for their military adventures.

Among us were men weary with years of peace demonstrations and ready to strike back at the establishment with the same violence that the government had forced us to dispense upon the Vietnamese, but the predominant feeling was that such a display of violence would be self-defeating and detrimental to our purpose of waging peace. But this did not mean that we lacked the commitment to our cause necessary to undertake civil disobedience if it came to that. We were willing to accept a bust passively and the possibility of confinement in jail for our dissent to a war which had already demanded of us far greater sacrifices. To us, we who had lost comrades in Vietnam, and who ourselves had been wounded and even lost limbs in an unjustifiable war, facing the possibility of arrest was an insignificant sacrifice to help end the horror.

We refuted violence when it seemed tempting after we were refused entrance to Arlington National Cemetery to place wreaths at the gravesides of our brothers killed in 'Nam ... we, who would have been welcomed there had we returned from Vietnam in a body bag. We were informed that we were not allowed inside because we represented a political organization. Yet earlier that same morning a deputation from the pro-war Daughters of the American Revolution had been admitted.

Violence, which our military training had taught us, was rejected twice more: once, when the same government which had dispatched us to occupy a foreign land now refused to allow us to encamp on the public grounds of the Washington Mall, and again, when the doors of the Supreme Court were barred against our admittance for our questioning of the war's constitutional legality. We were told that we were obstructing the course of justice when we questioned the justice of the Vietnam War.

In all three of these instances we remained committed to our goals. We returned to Arlington, where, after further protest and negotiation, we were finally admitted. We voted to stay overnight on the Mall, waiting for a police assault that never came after the government backed down and decided that the televised image of Washington cops cracking the heads of crippled vets would make poor P. R. We returned to the Supreme Court, where 110 of us were busted and briefly jailed, but then released with the charges dropped when it was pointed out that our only crime had been to demand justice, not to obstruct it.

The veterans achieved victory in their three major confrontations with the government. But the victories won by Dewey Canyon III would be measured by the impact its combatants in medal-decorated jungle fatigues had on the American public. And the final victory could come only when the last American soldier was home and the killing was ended. That victory would not come for almost two more years — January 27, 1973 — and even then it was only partial. Though all American soldiers had finally come home — except for the more than 2,500 MIAs — and a paper peace existed, the killing went on.

In 2006, forty years after my sojourn in the savage wilds of Indochina, I attended a battalion reunion of the O'Deuce in Atlanta, Georgia. Eight of the men with whom I served in the 1st Platoon, including Rose and Henk, were present. So also was Welch. We had written each other often in my first years after Vietnam, but after I turned against the war and joined VVAW, Welch expelled me from his Hard Core Hall of Heroes. He, of course, was the lodestar of the reunion and he strived mightily to promote the mythology of the Hard Core Squad. We never exchanged a word.

Johansen was in attendance as well. He bemoaned my narrative depiction of him as a coward. Then, staying in character, he threatened to slug me in the jaw as he rapidly exited the room we were in — thus avoiding the possibility of even the fraudulent punches we had exchanged in the Hard Core Test in the sands of Tuy Hoa beach four decades before.

In general, however, this gathering of eagles was more a companionable relinking of talons than a clawing at old resentments. Old grudges, rivalries and political differences were held in abeyance in an atmosphere thick with war stories and camaraderie. Wounds of the flesh and of the soul had, in all the intervening years, healed or at least scarred over. The men of the platoon had got on with their lives, no matter how rough and ragged the individual journeys may have been. Under the heels of time, even the gravest in the warrior's list of sins — disloyalty — had been ground down to a pardonable venality. Under the grace of memory and shared sacrifice, even Johansen's betrayal of the soldier's code of courage and conduct in the field, and, yes, even my later apostasy from loyalty by questioning the worthiness of our cause and the methods of its execution, could be and were absolved.

I would return three times to the land that had freed me from my ignorance, if not my adoration of war. In 1991, as a middle-aged man, I visited the sites around Tuy Hoa and Quinhon where so many of my fellow teenage warriors had surrendered their youth. While a half a million American servicemen and women were rolling to an easy victory in the desert sands of Kuwait, I accompanied eight other veterans of America's last major conflict before the Persian Gulf War, back to old battlefields and still vivid memories. Five of us were combat veterans, four had been wounded, and two permanently disabled by our war. We each sought, and to varying degrees found, our own separate peace with our own personal war. For me, the trip was like the last station of the cross; the completion of a pilgrimage that had begun on America's streets under protest signs as I shouted out against my war, that had moved on to hushed reverence before the granite reflection of the names of my fallen comrades on the Wall in Washington, and now ended here, the source and origin of my piety and my pain.

While a new generation of Americans in uniform was winning in the desert America's shortest and sweetest war, it was easy for us there in the jungle to recall America's longest, and in many ways, most agonizing war. For Vietnam, after twenty-four years, still seemed exactly the same; the same peasants, the same craters clogging Highway 1, the same sights, sounds and smells; everything as before, except for the sight of slaughter, the sound of battle, the smell of death.

Ten years later, when I returned with my wife, Rena, increasing development and prosperity had begun to change Vietnam. Generations turn and time tumbles away from the past. By the time I came back for my third post-war visit four years later, motorbikes had claimed mastery over bicycles on the streets of Saigon, Highway 1 was paved smooth as an interstate, and I felt no longer like a returning veteran of a long-ago conflict, but just like another tourist.

The image of U.S. helicopters evacuating the last desperate dregs of a war and an era from the rooftop of the American embassy in Saigon on April 29, 1975, had brought to mind my own helicopter extraction from the Vietnam battlefield eight years before with the punji stake wound in my leg. Those intervening years should have worked their healing magic to close the wounds and fade the scars' red memories. But I remained a casualty.

The gash in my body had healed in a few months, but it required a far longer river of time to wash away the wounds Vietnam inflicted on my spirit and soul. While the war continued — for twice as long after I left it as America's involvement in World War II — the wounds were still open and bleeding. Maybe now, I thought, as I watched the televised image of North Vietnamese tanks rumbling down Tu Do Street, the war's endlessness finally ended, those wounds will begin to close. Somehow, I had doubted it.

Vietnam clung to my emotional side, a haunting presence that was more than just a memory. My Vietnamese months were omnipresent — usurping reality and exiling the rest of my life to empty absurdity. My life before and since its embrace with war floated through a misty inconsequence, broken only by the sharp, stark clarity of my seventeen months in Vietnam.

I remained a hostage to the ghost of a small Southeast Asian country that took many forms but always whispered the same words. It spoke to me from the mutilated grayness of an old peasant murdered by my squad for the crime of being Vietnamese; from the ashes that were once a young mother clinging to her baby in the molten embrace of napalm; from the wounded eyes of children orphaned by war's deadly drama; from the splattered blood and broken dreams of men with whom war had forged a closeness beyond comradeship; from the emerald tiles of rice paddies and bamboo-bearded mountains ravished by B-52 bombs, 105 mm artillery shells and Agent Orange defoliants. It related to me a pain, a remorse, a bitterness beyond articulation. It told me that I had been lied to, that I had been used by the lie, and that I had made a liar out of myself by so many times turning my face away from the disillusioning truth.

That apparition, so heavy with the bones of countless bodies, had forced upon me an awareness of the fragility of both my body and soul; had made me stare in terror into the vulnerability of my life, of all life; had drained the youthful arrogance of assumed immortality from my veins. Death, which we had kept at a distance in the bush because it was always so close, now hovered and hid in every peaceful corner. Vietnam had made death as intimate and imminent as life.

I had journeyed to Vietnam under the sails of an obsession, a glory lust that compelled me to trace the boundaries of my manhood in the exploding terrain of combat. Weaned on a diet of war's glory, fed intravenously on patriotism, I set foot on Vietnam's soil certain that I had taken the first step down my personal path of destiny. But I found that Vietnam and its war existed in a starless universe light-years away from those innocent days when toy guns were extensions of my arms and the rat-tat-tat of submachine guns, stamped from the metal of my imagination, echoed through the summers of my youth. I found that I had to trade pieces of my soul for the Judas silver of combat decorations and medals for valor; that I must barter away my integrity to satiate my passion for glory.

The homecoming had provided the final disillusionment. Where once I had foreseen parades and praise, I found instead indifference. I felt like an escapee from a Southeast Asian leper colony. My leg wound became the least of my Vietnam-inflicted scars, for a delayed action cluster bomb had been dropped into my soul and had exploded through my psyche with the slashing splinters of bitterness and the shrapnel of remorse in the months after my return. The scars were hardly less deep and painful on April 30, 1975 — the day the war ended. They were scars shared by tens of thousands of Vietnam veterans, who went there determined to demonstrate a personal and national courage and virility, but, like America's battered conscience and moral purpose, returned from their awful maturing experience of Vietnam as victims of their own myths.

Military History of Micheal Clodfelter

Micheal Clodfelter enlisted in the U.S. Army on June 9, 1964, at the age of seventeen, just a few weeks after high school graduation. He graduated from basic recruit training in August and subsequently completed training as an artillery surveyor at Fort Sill, Oklahoma, and earned his Parachutist Badge by completing Jump School at Fort Benning, Georgia, on November 13.

Clodfelter was assigned to the 2/320th Airborne Artillery Battalion of the 101st Airborne Division at Fort Campbell, Kentucky, originally as a cannoneer with Bravo Battery, and later as an artillery surveyor with Headquarters Battery. His artillery battalion sailed with the rest of the 1st Brigade of the 101st from Oakland Army Terminal on July 8, 1965, destined for the Republic of Vietnam.

Landing at Cam Ranh Bay in South Vietnam on July 29, Clodfelter served for more than a year with the 2/320th in Vietnam, taking part in operations Highland, Gibraltar, Sayonara, Van Buren, Harrison, Fillmore, Austin II, Austin VI, and Beauregard in the Central Highlands and along the central coast.

Before his first tour was completed, Clodfelter voluntarily extended for an additional six months in Vietnam and requested transfer to an infantry battalion. On August 9, 1966, he was assigned to Charlie Company, 2/502nd Airborne Infantry. During the next five months, he took part in operations John Paul Jones, Seward, Geronimo, and Pickett in Phu Yen and Kontum Provinces of the II Corps Tactical Zone. In the course of those operations, Clodfelter was wounded twice and promoted to Sergeant E-5, serving as both a fire team leader and a squad leader.

Clodfelter's second wound, a punji stake injury to his left leg on December 30, 1966, resulted in his medical evacuation from Vietnam on January 8, 1967. After hospitalization in Japan, he returned to the United States on February 1. During his seventeen months in Vietnam, Clodfelter earned the Soldier's Medal, the Army Commendation Medal with V device (for valor), the Purple Heart, the Combat Infantryman's Badge, the Vietnam Service Medal with three stars, the Vietnam Campaign Medal, the National Defense Service Medal, and a Presidential Unit Citation.

Clodfelter served the final months of his active duty with Charlie Company, 3/187th Airborne Infantry, 101st Airborne Division at Fort Campbell. He was separated from active duty on June 8, 1967, and received his honorable discharge following three years on inactive reserve.

Index